READING RESEARCH

Advances in Theory and Practice

Volume 3

READING RESEARCH

Advances in Theory and Practice

Volume 3

G. E. MACKINNON
Department of Psychology
University of Waterloo
Waterloo, Ontario, Canada

T. GARY WALLER
Department of Psychology
University of Waterloo
Waterloo, Ontario, Canada

ACADEMIC PRESS 1981
A Subsidiary of Harcourt Brace Jovanovich, Publishers
New York   London   Toronto   Sydney   San Francisco

ACADEMIC PRESS, INC.
111 Fifth Avenue, New York, New York 10003

United Kingdom Edition published by
ACADEMIC PRESS, INC. (LONDON) LTD.
24/28 Oval Road, London NW1 7DX

ISBN 0–12–572303–2

PRINTED IN THE UNITED STATES OF AMERICA

81 82 83 84   9 8 7 6 5 4 3 2 1

CONTENTS

SEGMENTAL ANALYSIS ABILITY: DEVELOPMENT AND RELATION TO READING ABILITY
Rebecca Treiman and Jonathan Baron

A COGNITIVE–DEVELOPMENTAL THEORY OF READING ACQUISITION
George Marsh, Morton Friedman, Veronica Welch, and Peter Desberg

IDENTIFYING AND REMEDIATING FAILURES IN READING COMPREHENSION: TOWARD AN INSTRUCTIONAL APPROACH FOR POOR COMPREHENDERS
Ellen Bouchard Ryan

LIST OF CONTRIBUTORS

Numbers in parentheses indicate the pages on which the authors' contributions begin.

JONATHAN BARON (159), *Department of Psychology, University of Pennsylvania, Philadelphia, Pennsylvania 19104*

RODERICK W. BARRON (119), *Department of Psychology, University of Guelph, Guelph, Ontario, Canada N1G 2W1*

A. J. CAMPBELL* (39), *Psychology Department, Queen's University at Kingston, Kingston, Canada K7L 3N6*

PETER DESBERG (199), *Department of Psychology, California State University, Domingues Hills, Carson, California 90747*

MORTON FRIEDMAN (199), *Department of Psychology, University of California, Los Angeles, Los Angeles, California 90024*

MAUREEN W. LOVETT (1), *Division of Neurology, Department of Paediatrics, The Hospital for Sick Children, Toronto, Ontario, Canada M5G 1X8*

GEORGE MARSH (199), *Department of Psychology, California State University, Domingues Hills, Carson, California 90747*

D. J. K. MEWHORT (39), *Psychology Department, Queen's University at Kingston, Kingston, Canada K7L 3N6*

ELLEN BOUCHARD RYAN (223), *Department of Psychology, University of Notre Dame, Notre Dame, Indiana 46556*

REBECCA TREIMAN† (159), *Department of Psychology, University of Pennsylvania, Philadelphia, Pennsylvania 19104*

VERONICA WELCH (199), *Department of Psychology, University of California, Los Angeles, Los Angeles, California 90024*

* Present address: Behavioural Studies Group, Bell-Northern Research Ltd., Ottawa, Canada.

† Present address: Department of Psychology, Indiana University, Bloomington, Indiana 47405.

PREFACE

In the last decade or so the quantity of research on reading has increased rapidly. The people concerned with such research represent diverse orientations, backgrounds, and interests, i.e., psychologists, linguists, neurologists, classroom teachers, and those concerned with the assessment and remediation of reading difficulty. The extensive research that is being published on reading, and that this variety of people is trying to follow, appears in an ever-increasing and bewildering array of scholarly publications. It has become difficult for the researcher, the student, and the consumer of research on reading to keep abreast of developments in the field. In essence, both the reading community and reading research are fragmented into diverse subgroups. Communication and interaction among these subgroups are seriously lacking.

With this background in mind, this serial publication, "Reading Research: Advances in Theory and Practice," has been created. Its major purpose is to provide a publication outlet for systematic and substantive reviews and syntheses, both empirical and theoretical, and for integrative reports of programmatic research. The expectation is that such contributions will appeal to a broad, multifaceted, interdisciplinary audience, will help professionals keep abreast of growing knowledge in the various areas of reading research, will help serious students of reading come to terms with the diverse and complex field, and will help researchers by providing fresh viewpoints on areas close to their own.

The Editors have attempted to organize each volume in the publication around a particular theme or topic. The first volume was concerned with reading readiness. In Volume 2, the focus was on learning to read. The third volume continues with this topic; specifically, the authors were asked in preparing their chapters to speak to the question, "What does a child learn when he learns to read, and how can the learning be facilitated?" Within this general framework the contributors to Volume 3 consider current theory and research on word identification and comprehension, and explore the implications of this work for the teaching of reading.

The book begins·with a critical review of current theories of reading by M. Lovett. The chapter examines many of the unresolved issues illustrated by existing models, and focuses on the particularly difficult problem of how readers at varying levels of skill deal with meaning.

Lovett takes issue with a commonly held view that what the reader acquires when he begins to learn to read are special skills that become relatively useless once he attains fluency. Evidence is presented that children bring rather sophisticated discourse processing skills to their first encounters with text. Lovett argues that long before decoding becomes fully accurate or automatic, beginning readers develop informational priorities during reading that are similar to those of the skilled adult. What appears to develop in the acquisition of fluent reading is an increasing ability to decode automatically and an increasing capacity to deal with higher order units of text.

In Chapter 2, D. J. K. Mewhort and A. J. Campbell offer an information processing analysis of some of the mechanisms that underlie the word identification skills of the mature reader. These authors take as axiomatic that reading depends on the reader's use of prior knowledge at every stage in the process of reading. They argue that to account for word identification requires a system in which prior knowledge is used in the analysis of current input. The model they then propose describes how the mature reader's knowledge of the statistical structure of letter use— not only letter frequency relationships but more importantly the complicated and rich rules of English orthography—contributes information in the process of identifying single words. What a child learns when he learns to read, they suggest, may depend critically upon the kind of written language to which the child is exposed, and the opportunity he is thereby afforded to acquire knowledge of orthographic rules.

In the third chapter R. Barron reviews current research on the development of word recognition skills. The chapter focuses on what children know about printed words, how this knowledge is expressed in reading-related tasks, and how it changes with increasing age and experience. Barron examines the research on the development of several related facets of word recognition: the ability to use orthographic structure in recognizing words; the ability to attend to or otherwise employ different units of information in printed text (e.g., spelling patterns, syllables, and morphemic units); the role of purely graphic information in the development of word recognition; and the use of visual and phonological information in obtaining access to the meaning of words. Barron argues that while access to meaning may be facilitated initially by attention to the purely visual aspects of print, beginning readers do not rely exclusively on either visual or phonological information, and can employ both kinds of information in garnering the meaning of printed words. Barron suggests that instruction in phonics may force children to attend to orthographic structure and thereby may provide an important opportunity for children to begin acquiring knowledge of the orthographic rules underlying the written language.

What children know about spoken words and the relation of this knowledge to reading is addressed by R. Treiman and J. Baron in Chapter 4. Treiman and Baron examine children's ability to segment spoken words into their constituent phonemic or syllabic parts. They contend that such an ability requires the knowledge that words consist of smaller units, units that can be disassembled and rearranged to form yet other words. Novice readers appear to lack this knowledge, and yet such knowledge may be critical if children are to grasp completely the alphabetic principle upon which our written language is based. Treiman and Baron consider the development of word segmentation abilities in the broader context of perceptual development. They present evidence suggesting that young children tend to represent the sounds of words or syllables "integrally," as indivisible wholes, and not "separably," in terms of segments. What changes with development, they argue, is the way one represents spoken words. Moreover, Treiman and Baron find that the ability to segment words into parts is related most highly to a particular aspect of ability in reading—namely, the ability to use spelling–sound rules. How to account for this relationship and the importance it may have for educators are issues that are then pursued by these authors.

G. Marsh, M. Friedman, V. Welch, and P. Desberg, in the fifth chapter, consider reading acquisition in the broader context of cognitive development. These authors examine the abilities of readers at varying levels of experience and skill to read aloud unknown and novel words. They contend that what readers do when they attempt to read aloud unknown and novel words can reveal their knowledge of the orthographic structure of written language. Marsh *et al.* find that the strategies used in reading such words aloud change in a regular way with readers' experience and skill. They argue further that the knowledge of orthographic structure a child is able to acquire and the strategies he can employ productively with this knowledge are both related to his general progress in cognitive growth. The educational implications of these notions, particularly for the instruction of poor reading children, are then discussed.

In the final chapter E. Ryan proposes a framework for analyzing individual differences among children in the strategies they employ for dealing with units of text larger than single words (e.g., sentences and paragraphs), and for teaching comprehension skills to poor readers. Like the other authors in this volume, Ryan views the extraction of meaning during reading as a constructive interaction between the written text and the reader's prior knowledge. Moreover, readers are seen by Ryan to differ in their ability to exercise strategic control over the reading process as a function of their varying levels of experience and skill. Experienced skilled readers, Ryan argues, know how to employ selectively their prior knowledge in garnering meaning from text, and thus exert considerable executive control over what they do when they read. Less experienced and less skilled readers are seen to be deficient in strategic control. Training, therefore, in productive comprehension strategies should be a major focus of remedial programs for poor readers. To this end, Ryan discusses how the procedures recently developed to investigate meta-cognition and the techniques of cognitive behavior modification might be employed to great advantage in instructional programs.

The Editors would like to thank Marion Tapley for her assistance in the preparation of this volume. We would also like to thank the editorial consultants for this volume, F. A. Allard and G. Underwood, for their advice and enthusiastic support.

G. E. MacKinnon
T. Gary Waller

READING RESEARCH

Advances in Theory and Practice

Volume 3

READING SKILL AND ITS DEVELOPMENT: THEORETICAL AND EMPIRICAL CONSIDERATIONS

MAUREEN W. LOVETT

Division of Neurology
Department of Paediatrics
The Hospital for Sick Children
Toronto, Ontario, Canada

And so to completely analyze what we do when we read would almost be the acme of a psychologist's achievements, for it would be to describe very many of the most intricate workings of the human mind, as well as to reveal the tangled story of the most remarkable specific performance that civilization has learned in all its history.

EDMUND BURKE HUEY (1908)

For much of this century, the act of reading has intrigued students of human cognition. Reading research has a long history dating back to Cattell's (1885) early work on letter and word perception, Huey's (1908) discussion of imagery in reading, and Buswell's (1920) investigation of the eye–voice span. Despite this history, advances in our understanding of the reading process have been a long time coming, and many of the questions Huey posed in 1908 remain essentially unanswered.

Since the mid-1960s, new life has entered this field with the advent

1

of cognitive psychology and with extensive developments in the area of psycholinguistics. Indeed, most notable contributions to the study of reading in recent years owe a substantial theoretical debt to sources such as Chomsky (1970), Miller (1965, 1969, 1972), Neisser (1967), Norman (1968, 1969), and Sperling (1970). This article includes an overview of current theorizing with an emphasis on the unresolved issues illustrated by existing models. Particular attention will be focused on what appears to be the most difficult and the most basic question of all—how the skilled reader deals with meaning. Final sections of the article will deal with the status of developmental theories of reading and with the special conceptual and methodological problems they pose.

I. SKILLED READING: CURRENT THEORETICAL APPROACHES

The problem of understanding skilled reading at first glance appears one of understanding how unitary processes and operations—of which in isolation we already know a little—interact to enable a rapid and continuous extraction of meaning from text. Early model builders designed flow charts with as many components as there were processes thought important to reading; Sperling's (1970) model included six long-term memory stores alone! These models were generally assembled on the principle of serial processing; each input is traced, in fixed sequence, through many levels of processing until it ascends to the upper echelons of cognitive activity and semantic interpretation.

Contending that "much of what is written about reading is either too vague to be tested or too banal to bother" (p. 331), Gough (1972) has provided an updated and comprehensive model in this tradition. Like other information processing theorists, he attempts to delineate a sequence of perceptual and cognitive processes which when serially combined constitute the act of reading; Gough's model describes what transpires in 1 second of skilled reading. Denying the existence of a perceptual unit larger than the letter, Gough assumed that letters in the reader's icon emerge serially, at the rate of one every 10 to 20 milliseconds, into a character register. They are subsequently decoded or mapped onto a string of systematic phonemes (described as "abstract entities related to the sounds of the language . . . only by means of a complex system of phonological rules" (p. 337). It is this phonemic translation that allows the originally visual input access to an internal lexicon, primary memory, syntactic and semantic integration, and finally comprehension. Organization according to spelling patterns, pronounceability, syntactic features, and meaning is available only at higher, hence later, levels of processing; higher order organizational systems do not filter down to affect the initial analysis and encoding of information.

Gough's model was built on the assumption that lexical entries include a representation of systematic phonemes as well as syntactic and semantic feature sets; the retrieval mechanisms permitting access to the lexicon were rather vaguely attributed to the process of normal language acquisition. Gough made no pretense of understanding the semantic memory and comprehension requirements of skilled reading: the model's semantic interpreter was labeled "Merlin" and its depository the "PWSGWTAU"—or the "Place Where Sentences Go When They Are Understood"!

There are several problems with this model. The most serious concerns its linearity: higher order processes are isolated from lower order ones, and hence cognition is effectively isolated from perception. This stance is contrary to current definitions of perception and cognition which suggest that most complex acts of information processing are accomplished through the *interaction* of higher and lower order processes and that perception itself is an active, cognitively influenced operation (Neisser, 1967, 1976). Kolers (1972) dismissed linear models as a class for what he called their failure to do justice to "the remarkable interactions between 'data' and 'program' that are found" (p. 201). Certainly, there is considerable evidence of such interactions affecting visual search, memory storage and retrieval, and even eye movement patterns. Wanat (1971) reported eye movement data which indicate that visual fixation varies with intrasentence linguistic constraints. Evidence from earlier studies (Morton, 1964; Tulving & Gold, 1963) suggested that the amount of information needed to identify an item varies inversely with the amount of contextual information available. Schvaneveldt and Meyer (1973) described a lexical decision task wherein subjects judged pairs of associated words an average of 85 milliseconds faster than pairs of unassociated words. In each case, an allegedly lower order process was affected by higher order structure, contrary to the predictions of linear theory.

In reaction to the rigid reductionism of many linear models, one popular theory has described reading as a "psycholinguistic guessing game" (Goodman, 1967, p. 127)! Theorists of this persuasion, including Goodman (1967, 1973), Kolers (1970, 1972), and Smith (1971, 1973), have argued that word recognition is more than a serial integration of letters, just as fluent reading is more than a serial integration of words. This approach draws extensively upon the analysis-by-synthesis principle first proposed by Halle and Stevens (1964, 1967) to explain oral language comprehension and further articulated in Neisser's (1967) theory of cognition. Two basic assumptions are made: (a) that all lower order functions in skilled reading are influenced by higher order ones, and (b) that reading is essentially "externally guided thinking" (Neisser, 1967, p. 136). The skilled reader is characterized as an active processor of textual information—one who is able to deal directly with the overall structure and semantic content of word sequences, circumventing laborious stages of letter-by-letter, and even word-by-word, perception. This feat is allegedly accomplished through a strategy of selectively sampling the text, forming predictions about its structure and content, and testing these predictions against the data of further sampling. The success of the reader's strategy will depend upon the natural redundancy of the language he samples (i.e., the cues afforded by its orthographic, syntactic, and semantic structure) and upon his own knowledge of linguistic constraints (Goodman, 1973). As Smith and Holmes (1973) have explained,

> What distinguishes the skilled reader from the novice . . . is not (as is frequently supposed) the amount of visual information that he can pack into a single fixation, but the amount of nonvisual information with which he can leaven the featural input and make it go the farthest. (p. 63)

An analysis-by-synthesis model of reading has definite appeal. It ventures into the semantic realm as few other theories have dared. It capitalizes upon the basic principles of cognitive psychology and is compatible with current models of language comprehension. Finally, it places reading under the power of the reader, allowing it to change form according to the reader's informational needs; this flexibility stands in sharp contrast to the specific, exclusive processing paths of linear models and to the passive type of perceptual processing they imply.

Despite their potential for organizing complex data into a compelling theoretical package, these models as a class remain inadequate, primarily for their failure to generate testable hypotheses [see Venezky, Massaro, & Weber's (1976) criteria for model evaluation]. There is considerable variability in the extent to which sampling theorists have been willing to operationalize the model. Kolers (1970) claimed that the linguistically sophisticated reader *sees* the concepts the words represent and not just the words themselves; this statement, similar to Smith's (1971, 1973) claim that only units of meaning enter the reader's short- and long-term memory systems, was pronounced somewhat dogmatically. There was little serious attempt to reconcile these proposals with what is known of the parameters of our perceptual and memory systems. The implication was that partial processing (i.e., sampling) allows the skilled reader to circumvent any such limitations; Kolers and Smith, however, failed to specify exactly how sampling proceeds, and there is as yet no convincing evidence that reading is, in fact, a partial processing operation.

Hochberg (1970) was more concrete, at least, in his discussion of sampling mechanisms. He suggested that the sampling, predictive, and reconstructive processes of reading rely on selective eye movements and the mechanisms of peripheral vision. Mackworth and Morandi (1967) reached a similar conclusion, that is, that "the peripheral retina . . . quickly screens off the predictable features and leaves the fovea free to process . . . unpredictable and unusual stimuli" (p. 551). There is some marginal evidence for these claims. Hochberg, Levin, and Frail (1966) found that masking interword spaces in the peripheral field resulted in selective impairment of the performance of good readers; poor readers' performances were considerably less impaired. Nodine and Lang (1971) and Nodine and Steuerle (1973) examined the visual scanning patterns of young readers and nonreaders. In a letter matching task, readers required fewer fixations, less fixation time, and fewer cross comparisons per letter than nonreaders, findings which were interpreted as evidence of eye movement planning and of the reader's more effective use of the peripheral field. These data do support the view that early input processes such as eye movements are never divorced from higher level, more cognitive influences; however, wholesale extrapolation of these findings in support of the type of semantically influenced "peripheral search guidance" that Hochberg proposed seems unwarranted.

It is clear that eye movements are guided by overall textual structure and by the reader's task. Wanat's (1971) data suggested that the greater the degree of intrasentence linguistic constraint, the fewer the number of fixations and the briefer the amount of fixation time needed by the skilled reader. When confronted with less predictable text, e.g., a passive sentence in which the agent remains unspecified, the adult reader will require longer and more frequent regressive fixations than when reading a similar sentence in which the agent is explicitly mentioned.

The issue of what and how much information can be processed in peripheral vision, however, is far from clear. Rayner (1975) designed a procedure to estimate the reader's perceptual span and the type of visual information available within its perimeter. His data indicated that while gross characteristics such as word shape and initial and final letters are detectable 7 to 12 character spaces from the fixation point, recognition of a word's meaning is restricted to a much smaller area, specifically 1 to 6 character spaces. Although Rayner's findings do suggest that the skilled reader processes peripheral information, the confines of semantic peripheral processing appear quite limited and certainly inadequate for the extensive mechanism Hochberg proposed.

The concept of reading as a hypothesis-testing operation has been revived and redefined with the promise of some specificity in Rumelhart's

(1977) recent "interactive" model. Contending that reading can be described only in terms of a system of highly interactive, parallel processing units, completely bidirectional in their interaction, Rumelhart has outlined a formalism based on the parallel computing applications found in current simulations of natural language processing (Kaplan, 1973; Lesser, Fennell, Erman, & Reddy, 1974). The model specifies that everything the reader needs in order to decode and understand print is organized into a series of six independent "knowledge sources," each of which is responsive to one dimension of a text. The textual input is classified according to the visual featural, letter, letter cluster, lexical, syntactic, and semantic information it represents. The bidirectionality of the system is such that information furnished from any knowledge source can affect current, past, and subsequent contributions from any other knowledge source.

The mechanism through which these independent knowledge sources interact is a structure called the "message center" to which the formidable task of textual interpretation is assigned. The system operates by generating hypotheses based on the content of each knowledge source; guesses as to the identity of the input on each of the six relevant dimensions are formulated and assigned a numerical probability value. The implications of the most probable interpretation at each level of analysis are then supposedly assessed relative to each other and to each successive input, necessitating a constant reevaluation of all existing hypotheses and their associated probability values. When the assigned values achieve some arbitrary criterion of "strength," further processing of that segment is abandoned and the message center's current hypotheses furnish the accepted interpretation or reading of the text.

Rumelhart's (1977) model maintains the conceptual gains of the analysis-by-synthesis approach—that is, the characterization of reading as an essentially cognitive activity achieved through a very active mode of perceptual processing; it is superior to this class of models generally, however, for its heuristic promise and particularly for its potential to generate testable hypotheses. To date, all treatments of reading as a hypothesis-testing operation appear to have been motivated by a desire to account for that increasingly persuasive literature documenting the nonlinearity of the process. In the analysis-by-synthesis tradition, the mechanisms to accommodate interactional feedback are unidirectional, operating exclusively from the top (i.e., most cognitive level) down. In contrast, Rumelhart's model is noteworthy for its complete bidirectionality and for the extent to which an interaction of processes truly defines the act of reading. Another central point of departure from the analysis-by-synthesis approach concerns the way in which partial processing has been conceptualized. Unlike the former models, partial processing here, instead of referring to textual segments which are or are not processed, refers rather to the extent and amount of processing required to verify the currently most probable interpretation. The interactive model thus appears to incorporate some of the best features of both its linear and its nonlinear predecessors.

Despite its potential for processing specificity and the attendant promise of testability, by his own admission, Rumelhart's model, at present, simply outlines a formalism within which more detailed models can be built. Much of the model's appeal derives from its description of an optimally interactive processing system; it should be recognized, however, that the description is formulated with no assumptions about attention allocation and thus presupposes few, if any, constraints on the number and type of processes which can simultaneously occur in parallel. Unless the reader is to be characterized as an information processing mechanism with infinite capacity, some parameters of the system must be estimated. Posner and Snyder (1975) have suggested that processes which are automatically activated should be distinguished from those directed by "conscious" attention; this distinction, if coupled with the assumption of different capacity restrictions in each category, might allow Rumelhart to specify in some detail and with some empirical credibility a system which can accommodate so much simultaneous activity.

Although it has yet to include enough processing detail to generate many specific performance predictions, it is possible to speculate on what aspects of the Rumelhart model may pose problems for those attempting to work within its framework. The data storage versus hypothesis generation components of the model seem to acknowledge implicitly the current distinction between "declarative" and "procedural" types of knowledge—that is, knowledge about facts as opposed to knowledge about procedures (Anderson, 1976; Winograd, 1975). Neither type has been specified in any discernible detail, however, either with respect to the way in which information is organized in the knowledge sources or with respect to what form activation of different procedures actually takes in the model. There is no indication, for instance, of the mechanism which allows each of the six knowledge sources to scan the message center for hypotheses relevant to their domain of specialization.

These issues are not explicitly addressed in Rumelhart's (1977) presentation. The model as it is presently outlined simply presupposes a series of fixed knowledge domains which interact or "communicate" through the highly structured data storage or message center. One might speculate that an informational base of each type will be represented in the knowledge sources and that the latter's communication with the message center will necessitate a representational system in which entries are dynamic rather than fixed.

The content of a recent proposal by Rumelhart (1979), however, suggests that further specification of the formalism may again deliberately abandon the declarative/procedural distinction in favor of a more economical representational model. Arguing that the declarative/procedural dichotomy can be bridged by any system which allows new procedures to be generated from old ones, Rumelhart now proposes a model in which procedural knowledge is represented as part of an "active semantic network." Analogical processing, seen as the common denominator in human learning and cast as the basic modus operandi of the system, provides the vehicle through which procedures can be altered and operated upon as previously only declarative knowledge was thought to be.

All of these speculations still await empirical support. Whether Rumelhart's (1979) recent theorizing can address the question of how the informational base of the knowledge sources changes in response to the textual input available in the message center remains unknown. In fairness, these issues pose a major problem for any model attempting to deal with the effect of current contexts and previously acquired knowledge on ongoing perceptual processes (see Anderson & Ortony, 1975); they are therefore not peculiar to Rumelhart's (1977) treatment of the topic, a fact which will be evident in following pages of this article. Although the general problem is shared to some extent by each of the models reviewed here, however, it is one of immediate concern to the Rumelhart model since processing specificity to the point of quantifiability is an explicit goal.

Another alternative to the concept of partial processing can be found in a model which discusses the role of attention in reading and emphasizes the importance of automatic information processing to the process. LaBerge and Samuels' (1974) model is based on the premise that all well-learned stimulus patterns can be encoded with or without attentional direction. They have contended that the development of automaticity (i.e., processing without attention) in all decoding processes is essential to fluent reading; and that fluency is established *only* when all levels of visual to semantic decoding proceed automatically, and attention is thereby freed for continuous processing at the semantic level.

At first glance, the LaBerge and Samuels model presents a form and structure similar to that of linear stage models. Encoding of letters, spelling patterns, words, and word groups proceeds in hierarchical fashion, with phonological translation an apparent prerequisite for memory access and semantic interpretation. Closer scrutiny of the model's attentional mechanism reveals two rather dramatic deviations from previous stage theory: (a) with sufficient perceptual learning, organization from the top of the hierarchy can dictate the size of a processing unit at the bottom; and (b) a minimum of five different processing routes are defined to account for the characteristic variability of reading behavior. Presented in descending order of complete automatization, reading can occur via any of these options. Fluent reading is restricted to automatic processing routes; however, the flexibility of the model allows the skilled reader to exercise a different processing option for an unfamiliar word or rarely encountered phrase.

LaBerge and Samuels adhered to a feature analytic model of perception at all levels of their reading hierarchy. Letter perception occurs by selection and rapid scanning of appropriate feature detectors and, subsequently, construction of a letter code. Each time features are organized into a particular code a new unit is established and some trace of the organization is laid down; these deepening traces as well as gains in scanning rate—both the result of practice—underlie the development of automaticity and the resulting possibility of higher level unitization. In essence, unitization permits an expansion of the reader's unit of perception. Just as the letter code is itself an organization of component features, it is also a component in a hierarchy of superordinate codes (e.g., spelling patterns, words, word groups). Automatization and unitization of all codes develop in an analogous manner.

The model assumes that efficient comprehension requires exclusive attention to the organization of meaning codes. It should be recognized that attention here is conceptualized as an all-or-none phenomenon, a mechanism that is turned "on" or "off" at a particular level of processing. As LaBerge and Samuels (1974) explained,

> The number of existing codes that can be activated by attention at a given moment is sharply limited, probably to one. But the number of codes which can be simultaneously activated by outside stimuli independent of attention is assumed to be large, perhaps unlimited. In short, it is assumed that we can only attend to one thing at a time, but we may be able to process many things at a time so long as no more than one requires attention. (p. 295)

Organization of word meaning codes is allegedly accomplished by fast scanning at the semantic level, just as fast scanning of letter features results in unitization of a letter code. The reader's upper processing limits are thought determined by the number of word meanings he can comprehend in one "chunk" of semantic memory.

LaBerge and Samuels acknowledged that the model lacks sufficient sophistication to account for the complexities of linguistic parsing, predictive processing, and contextual effects on comprehension. They were willing to speculate, however, on what may be involved in understanding and remembering textual information. It was recognized that language comprehension generally involves adding one's own associations to the pattern of meanings provided (Bransford & McCarrell, 1974). LaBerge and Samuels suggested that acts of semantic association would entail the switching of attention to other existing codes in semantic and episodic memory (Tulving, 1972). The final product of comprehension (i.e., the superordinate meaning code that is subsequently organized) presumably would then itself be stored in the semantic or episodic system.

The LaBerge and Samuels model is a significant contribution on a number of different fronts: (a) Similar to Rumelhart (1977), it addresses the possibility that "top down" (or more cognitive) and "bottom up" components of the process interact in reading; what is even more noteworthy, it presents the concept of such an interaction without completely sacrificing processing specificity—the recognized strength of linear stage theories and the source of their ability to generate testable hypotheses. (b) Acknowledging its areas of inadequacy, the model remains open-ended, allowing for future extension into more complex linguistic processing, presumably through the same strategy of feature analysis and code construction. (c) It surpasses existing models in its willingness to address the problem of variable reading behaviors. (d) Finally, a distinction is made between accuracy and automaticity as separate criteria of perceptual learning, a distinction with considerable impact for developmental theories of reading.

Direct empirical evaluation of the LaBerge and Samuels model has yet to be reported. Doehring (1976) provided evidence that processing time for different reading subskills decreases differentially with age, the more complex behaviors reaching asymptote only in the high school years. These data constitute indirect support of an automaticity-based definition of fluency. A direct test of the model would necessitate adoption of its own criterion of automaticity, which is that processing be carried out while attention is deployed elsewhere. The only clear demonstration of such automaticity to date has been on the level of letter perception (LaBerge, 1973) and color and tone recognition (LaBerge, Van Gelder, & Yellott, 1970). Although there is some recent evidence suggesting that word recognition can be achieved automatically (see Posner & Snyder, 1975), automaticity in the perception of higher order units has yet to be documented.

Finally, any discussion of reading theory must acknowledge the view that model-building is an inappropriate activity for reading researchers. Venezky *et al.* (1976) have contended that we know far too little of the component processes to warrant any attempt at a comprehensive model. Gibson and Levin (1975) dismissed as absurd the notion that there could be a single model of reading. In their words,

there are as many reading processes as there are people who read, things to be
read, and goals to be served. Reading is as varied and adaptive an activity as
perceiving, remembering, or thinking, since in fact it includes all these activities.
(p. 454)

Despite the essential heterogeneity of the activity, Gibson and Levin
(1975) have conceded that reading is "rule-governed" and that one can
articulate a few generic principles. Drawing upon Gibson's (1969, 1970,
1971, 1972) theory of perceptual learning, the reader is characterized as
an economical processor of information: one who seeks the least amount
of information required for his purpose and in the largest manageable
units. Fluent reading is described as a process of continual information
reduction. Informational alternatives in the yet unprocessed text are
reduced through the constraints of phonology, orthography, syntax, and
semantics—or more specifically, through the reader's knowledge of these
rule systems, in conjunction with his general knowledge of the world.
Adaptability is considered an integral part of the skill, allowing the behavior to change form as both the text and the reader's goals dictate.

This section has highlighted several aspects of our ignorance about
reading. The role of attention, the parameters of visual perceptual processing, the extent to which complete text is processed—all these issues
await empirical resolution. Nowhere is our ignorance more blatant, however, than in the area of semantic processing. Consideration of the models
just reviewed illustrates this point all too clearly. Gough (1972) abandoned
all pretense and dubbed his model's comprehension device "Merlin"
and the storehouse of its magical activity the "Place Where Sentences
Go When They Are Understood." More radical sampling theorists, such
as Kolers (1970), discussed meaning as a unitary concept, something the
reader is able to see in the graphic characters—a daring interpretation,
but one of little heuristic value. Rumelhart (1977) conceded that his
semantic knowledge source is the most difficult to characterize. LaBerge
and Samuels (1974) treated the encoding of meaning no differently than
that of graphic information; word meaning was defined in terms of semantic features, and feature scanning at the semantic level was analogous
to that at lower sensory levels. The problem is obvious: reading theorists
must address the issue of meaning, yet the theoretical controversy surrounding this topic makes it a particularly formidable task.

II. THE PROBLEM OF MEANING: WHAT IS REMEMBERED?

It is clear that while reading we are extracting meaningful information
that we may well remember for indefinite lengths of time. What remains

unclear is *how* we remember meaning. In what form and according to what principles of encoding, organization, and retrieval does semantic memory operate?

Until recently, most basic research in this area focused on the problem of word meaning; the search for semantic memory structures was initially restricted to our experiences with and knowledge about single words. Theorists such as Collins and Quillian (1969, 1972) addressed this issue by proposing a hierarchical model of lexical memory in which the meaning of a word is defined and remembered in relation to its superordinate and to its constituent properties. The hierarchical organization of their model is dictated by a principle which they designate "cognitive economy." In its strictest form, this principle postulates that each of a word's properties is represented at only one level, the most general possible. In considering the properties of *lion,* for instance, the model would place *mane* directly with *lion* because of its specificity, but would allocate the more generic properties of *fur* and *skin* to *mammal* and *animal,* respectively, superordinates of the *lion* entry (Nelson & Kosslyn, 1975). Collins and Quillian speculated that the greater the distance in the hierarchy between the subject of a sentence and the superordinate or property assigned it, the more processing time would be required for its verification. Posner, Lewis, and Conrad (1972) have described data consistent with this prediction, but, at the same time, have noted that some recent evidence (e.g., Conrad, 1972; Schaeffer & Wallace, 1970; Schulman, 1974) appears contradictory to the notions of cognitive economy and isolable subsystems. Nelson and Kosslyn (1975) reported that their subjects provided the fastest response times to properties of lowest specificity; these findings stand in direct opposition to Collins and Quillian's (1969) contention that low-specificity properties (e.g., *skin*) will be retrieved more slowly because they are accessed through a noun's superordinate (e.g., *animal*). Nelson and Kosslyn concluded that, rather than a nested hierarchy, lexical memory may be an interconnecting semantic network, similar to that described by Rumelhart, Lindsay, and Norman (1972), but organized according to the dimensions of saliency and specificity.

Recent discussions of lexical memory have favored more global representational structures, perhaps in reaction to Collins and Quillian (1969, 1972) and to the lexical marking advocates. Lexical marking theory specifies that word meanings are represented as semantic feature sets; in memory, "marked" features (e.g., as in *short*), because of their alleged linguistic complexity, are frequently forgotten, causing a shift in recall toward the less complex and corresponding "unmarked" form (e.g., *tall*) (Carpenter, 1974; Clark & Card, 1969). Brewer and Lichtenstein (1974) found, however, that when such shifts (from marked to unmarked forms) could not conserve sentence meaning, they almost never occurred. In a similar vein, Schulman (1974) reported that lexical memory is unaffected by a word's location in an attributive versus a superordinate query: only the congruous or meaningful context of a word affects later recall. He argued that congruous queries foster a relational encoding of words and thereby facilitate their recall. Both these results were interpreted as favoring a global "memory for meaning" approach over the "memory for marked semantic features" tradition.

In the past decade, specific interest in lexical memory has given way to widespread interest in sentence memory. Many investigations have focused on sentences embodying statements of propositional logic (Meyer, 1970; Schvaneveldt & Meyer, 1973), and have studied encoding, storage, and retrieval operations using verification tasks (Carpenter & Just, 1972; Clark & Chase, 1972). Carpenter and Just (1975) have contended that all sentences are represented in memory as "an ordered set of constituents in . . . abstract propositional format" (p. 45). Anderson and Bower (1973) have concurred, asserting further that *all* long-term memory information is in fact propositionally (i.e., declaratively) represented. In their model of Human Associative Memory (HAM), Anderson and Bower claimed that memory representation is fully accounted for by HAM's parsing of a sentence into functionally independent associations. Foss and Harwood (1975) have demonstrated, however, that HAM is limited in its capacity to deal with the encoding and retrieval of configurational information. Anderson's (1976) updated model, ACT, abandons the binary relational structure of HAM, a feature which required sentences with three or more arguments to be parsed into several simpler statements; in ACT, complex sentences can be accommodated by multi-argument relational structures. Like HAM, however, the representation of information in ACT is restricted to literal subject–predicate constructions.

The trend already discussed with respect to lexical memory is even more salient in current discussions of sentence memory. Interpretive or semantic feature theories are contrasted with constructive, assimilation models. Interpretive models (including the above-mentioned examples) assume that complete linguistic analysis of a sentence will render everything necessary for its memory representation. This class of models owes a significant theoretical debt to computational and transformational linguistics (Chomsky, 1965) and draws heavily upon a feature analytic approach to word meaning (Clark, 1969; Katz & Fodor, 1963). In general, such models have met with reasonable success in accounting for verification latencies to various complex sentences. Their applicability to the semantic processing involved in reading discourse, however, appears thus far quite limited (Gibson & Levin, 1975).

In contrast, assimilation theories of sentence memory contend that *what* is stored results from the interaction of sentential information with the reader's existing knowledge structures. The memory product may embody information not explicitly contained in the sentence and therefore not available from its linguistic analysis (Barclay, 1973). To illustrate the intuitive sense of this approach, consider the memory advantage enjoyed by chess masters. De Groot (1966) demonstrated that masters and novices do not differ in visual memory capacity; however, if both groups have to recall the pieces and their positions after only 5 seconds examination of a chess board, their performances are dramatically different. The chess master's memory advantage can be attributed to the interplay of his knowledge of chess with the new information presented on the board (Brewer, 1974).

An assimilation approach to memory is not new. In addition to the obvious influence of Piagetian constructs, the theory dates back to the pronouncement of Sir Frederick Bartlett (1932) that "an organism has somehow to acquire the capacity to turn around upon its own schemata and to construct them afresh" (p. 206). The evidence supporting a constructive approach to sentence memory is more recent. Bobrow and Bower (1969) found that when subjects were responsible for generating their own mnemonic sentences, they exhibited far better recall of a list of word pairs than when they rehearsed equally meaningful but experimenter-generated sentences. Kintsch and Monk's (1972) subjects read the same content but in passages of different structural complexity; when posed questions requiring inferences from passage content, subjects from different conditions did not differ in the latencies of their correct responses. Kintsch and Monk suggested that the same information acquired from structurally different sources assumes an equivalent representation in semantic memory.

Bransford, Barclay, and Franks (1972) have contended that subjects often go "beyond the information given" (Bartlett, 1932; Bruner, 1973) to the point of including implied information in their memory representation of a sentence. The subjects of Bransford *et al.* (1972) confused old and new sentences when the latter was a potential inference of the former, a demonstration which has become a classic in the assimilation tradition. The existence of derived information in sentence memory has been documented in both recognition and recall paradigms (Barclay, 1973), in reading (Lovett, 1977; Waller, 1976) and in listening tasks (Bransford & McCarrell, 1974), and for inferences involving spatial representation (Bransford *et al.*, 1972), ordinal position (Barclay, 1973), implied instrumentation and probable consequence (Johnson, Bransford, & Solomon, 1973). The replicability and apparent consistency of these data pose a serious problem for interpretive theory; it is difficult to imagine a linguistic analysis accounting for information not explicitly available in the sentence.

A more radical approach to the question of what is stored has been proposed. Kolers (1973, 1975a,b) has contended that it is not abstract representations of content that are stored, but rather the decoding procedures that constituted their comprehension. This suggestion is compatible with Neisser's (1967) theory. Speculating on what information the reconstructive activity of memory is based, Neisser claimed that it is "traces of prior processes of construction. There are no stored copies of finished mental events, like images or sentences, but only traces of earlier constructive activity" (1967, p. 285). According to Kolers (1975a), knowing how to encode a sentence accommodates knowledge of the statement or proposition it expresses.

As supporting evidence, Kolers has cited a series of experiments which indicate that graphemic features can predict recognition up to 4 weeks after a sentence is read (Kolers & Ostry, 1974); additional data suggested that in some instances graphemic memory facilitation can outlive the traditional semantic effect (Kolers, 1975b). The logic of these results stems from the rather curious task that was adopted: subjects learned to read sentences in geometrically inverted typography. Presumably the effort of decoding emphasized the visual pattern-analyzing component of the procedural memory representation, yielding the unusual facilitation for graphemic information. As subjects acquired fluency in reading inverted sentences, graphemically influenced recognition declined (Kolers, 1975b).

Kolers' procedural memory approach is compatible with (though not equivalent to) Craik and Lockhart's (1972) "depth of processing" hypothesis and Craik and Tulving's (1975) revised notion that the degree of elaboration of the encoded trace determines the strength of its representation. These theorists, however, did not address themselves to the issue of substantive versus procedural representation, and therefore align as easily with the constructive approach as with its operational or procedural counterpart. It is important to realize that the latter two positions are by no means mutually exclusive. Both constructive and procedural theory can account for Graesser and Mandler's (1975) finding that memory for surface structure varies with the level of initial processing. Similarly, both views can accommodate Moeser's (1976) suggestion that sentential information is sometimes encoded into a noninferential episodic system, rather than a higher level semantic network (Tulving, 1972).

At this point, it seems important that no artificial distinctions be drawn between the procedural and constructive traditions. Both share similar encoding constructs and subscribe to equally interactive theories of comprehension; in essence, the two traditions simply reflect different perspectives on the question of whether information assumes a declarative or a procedural representation in memory (Anderson, 1976; Winograd, 1975). As Rumelhart (1979) has recently suggested, however, a differentiation of the two representational models is often ambiguous; knowledge may eventually come to be better described as simultaneously procedural and declarative in nature. In any case, it is likely to be quite some time before any definitive data will resolve the issue of substantive versus operational representation in as enigmatic an area as semantic memory.

III. THE PROBLEM OF MEANING: THEORIES OF COMPREHENSION

Much of the controversy in semantic memory research reflects the search for an adequate theory of comprehension. Indeed most of the issues already discussed with respect to lexical and sentence memory reveal an attempt to redefine classical notions of knowledge and understanding.

Traditional accounts of meaning in some ways parallel the interpretive memory models outlined above. The meaning of a word was established through association with its referent and word meanings were for the most part treated in isolation (Bransford & McCarrell, 1974). The credibility of isolationist versus interactional theories has been the basis of some philosophical controversy for centuries. Burke (1969) traced the argument back to Aristotelian times.

> In Aristotle, each stone, or tree, or man . . . could be a substance, capable of being considered "in itself" . . . Thinking contextually, Spinoza held that each single object in the universe is "defined" . . . by the other things that surround it . . . in terms of its total context. (p. 25)

The advent of computational linguistics has, without question, contributed significantly to our understanding of language; at the same time, the theory has been somewhat zealously overinterpreted as a psychological performance model, rather than a formal competence model of language. The principles of computational linguistics have been wedded to semantic feature definitions of word meaning (Katz & Fodor, 1963; Katz & Postal, 1964), and have produced what Franks (1974) has characterized a symbol manipulation approach to comprehension. He has maintained that all symbol manipulation systems are tautologies: the symbols are defined in relation to other symbols, but neither symbols nor relations are ever explicitly linked to our knowledge of the world.

Bransford and McCarrell (1974) have argued that the preoccupation with surface and deep structural analysis has led us to ignore the obvious—cognitive analysis and alinguistic knowledge. Recognition of the semantic anomaly "My typewriter is embarrassed" need not invoke the complexities of a complete linguistic interpretation (Brewer, 1974); the contradiction is immediately available to the reader by virtue of its incompatibility with his knowledge of the world.

Frederiksen (1975a,b) has stated that models of language comprehension must be revised to include a constructive component and to acknowledge the influence of contextual knowledge. He described an experiment designed to evaluate different interpretations of the well-replicated finding of derived information in prose recall. The interpretive theories described earlier propose an "output" explanation of derived responses: during recall, subjects are attempting to fill in for nonretrievable information. Constructive, contextually based theories suggest an "input" hypothesis: derived information is considered a direct demonstration of inferential encoding strategies. Using repeated exposures and a free recall paradigm, Frederiksen reported an increase in derived responses with repeated presentation, and little or no correlation with the amount of reproduced information. In addition, the basic long-term memory change involved a substantial decrease in reproduced information; derived responses, in comparison, enjoyed significantly better retention a week later. These data are compatible with Tzeng's (1975) illustration of differential decay functions for inferential versus recognition memory. Frederiksen's results offer convincing support for the constructive-contextual hypothesis, suggesting that derived responses do in fact reflect assimilation into existing knowledge structures.

There is much current interest in developing a theory of comprehension that can accommodate the findings of Frederiksen (1975a,b) and those of other assimilation theorists (see Weimer & Palermo, 1974). Almost by consensus, recent attempts have focused on the relational nature of comprehension. Bransford (1974) has claimed that knowledge is not a state, but rather "an activity of relatedness" (p. 302). Franks (1974) has defined meaning as relations constructed from the interaction of knowledge relations and a particular environmental context; understanding is thus described with respect to the quality of the meanings that are activated in that context. Rejecting the notion that "something" is stored in memory, Franks has contended that what is remembered is a modification of our knowledge system—an assimilation of, or accommodation to, the relational activation that occurred in response to stimulation. Bransford has concurred, concluding that this approach virtually eliminates the distinction between remembering and knowing.

In retrospect, it is not surprising that reading theorists have been sometimes vague, sometimes flippant, and sometimes negligent in their treatment of the comprehension process. It seems clear that a theory of reading comprehension must await further developments in our general understanding of language comprehension.

IV. THE DEVELOPMENT OF READING COMPETENCE:
A THEORETICAL PERSPECTIVE

While the past decade has witnessed a large-scale effort to provide a convincing theoretical account of skilled reading, explanations of the process of *learning* to read have failed to keep pace. The traditional emphasis on lower order perceptual operations, sound–symbol correspondences, intra- and intersensory transfer have not led to any clear understanding of the basic ingredients of successful reading acquisition. One can speculate as to what has contributed to preventing the emergence of a sound developmental theory of reading. The field of cognitive development generally has been slow to incorporate the new principles and methodologies offered in work with adult subjects. In addition, most discussions of reading acquisition have invariably stressed the discontinuities between the early process and its mature form, failing to capitalize upon what has been discovered about skilled reading.

It seems appropriate at this point to examine how existing models attempt to treat the acquisition process. Gough (1972) claimed that the prereading child already has at his disposal a lexicon, a comprehension device, and a phonological system. He has simply to acquire a character recognition device and a decoder which will convert the characters it yields into systematic phonemic representations. There are inconsistencies in Gough's position, however. Along with his insistence on letter-by-letter processing, he claimed that pauses between words disrupt comprehension; so to understand what he is reading, the child must try to read rapidly. If the beginning reader cannot immediately identify a word, Gough (1972) suggested that he must guess—a suggestion contrary to the main thesis of his model, that is, that "the Reader is not a guesser" (p. 354). The model does not lend itself well to developmental issues. In fact, its architect seems to find the acquisition phenomenon itself somewhat incredible: "How the child solves the decoding problem is a mystery, but many do!" (p. 353).

Analysis-by-synthesis theorists (e.g., Goodman, 1973; Kolers, 1970, 1972; Smith, 1971, 1973) have encountered equal difficulty in this area.

The continuity/discontinuity issue is nowhere more dramatically presented than in their treatment of reading acquisition: Smith (1971) has contended that the beginning reader has to acquire special skills which will be relatively useless once he becomes fluent. The skilled reader is said to enjoy immediate comprehension, being able to derive meaning directly from the graphic input. In contrast, mediated processes of word identification are said to precede comprehension for the beginning reader, and, being considered more complex, they entertain a greater risk of overloading short-term memory and exceeding visual processing boundaries before comprehension is achieved. This argument focuses on the cognitively uneconomical nature of early reading relative to later fluency. The validity of these claims and their utility to the developmental theorist are questionable; as with other issues, the model's lack of processing specificity precludes any meaningful evaluation.

It can be speculated that the mediated processes described by Smith (1971) are in fact inherent to the development of perceptual automaticity and therefore the *basis* of eventual fluency. The LaBerge and Samuels (1974) model appears better equipped than its predecessors to handle developmental questions. The advantage lies in its specification of two criteria of achievement in skill development: accuracy and automaticity. In defining reading as a structure of initially interdependent component processes, the model dictates that all readers go through the same stages of learning to read, although at different rates. Pedagogically, a demonstration of accurate performance has always been taken as sufficient indication of skill acquisition. The contribution of this model is its prediction that the child will not progress if he still requires attentional direction to execute lower subskills accurately. Although the LaBerge and Samuels model requires further elaboration on the mechanics of acquisition, its theoretical base should generate testable hypotheses and sound developmental research.

Without question, the most comprehensive treatment of reading acquisition to date has been provided by Gibson and Levin (1975), theorists who disavow any model-building aspirations. Gibson (1969, 1970, 1971) described perceptual learning as the discovery of distinctive features and higher order invariance. In defining reading acquisition as a perceptual learning phenomenon, Gibson and Levin suggested development to be an increasing ability to perceive text economically. Economy in reading is considered the perception of extended units according to the redundancy afforded by graphological, orthographic, syntactic, and semantic features. In each of these feature classes, discrimination learning proceeds over time and some aspects of development can extend into adolescence. There is evidence to indicate that certain types of syntactic ambiguity, for instance, are not reliably perceived before the age of 12 years (Shultz & Pilon, 1973).

Theoretically more conservative than the model builders, Gibson and Levin are credible sources from an empirical perspective. Over the years, they have amassed a body of evidence which demonstrates clear developmental changes in children's responsiveness to textual features. Extensive investigations of graphological (Gibson, Schapiro, & Yonas, 1968), orthographic (Gibson, Osser, & Pick, 1963; Gibson, Shurcliff, & Yonas, 1970), and syntactic learning (Gibson & Guinet, 1971; Levin, Grossman, Kaplan, & Yang, 1972; Levin & Kaplan, 1968) have supported Gibson's perceptual learning principles and the general hypothesis that higher order structure is critical to reading early in its development. One aspect of this developmental framework still lacking substantial support, however, is that concerning the perceptual learning of semantic features. Both Gibson and Levin (1975) and LaBerge and Samuels (1974) have defined word meaning as semantic feature sets, and have, therefore, implicitly aligned themselves with interpretive theories of meaning. In a manner parallel to that discussed in previous sections, it appears that developmental theory will have to reexamine its approach to linguistic meaning to accommodate recent evidence supporting the constructive position.

V. THE DEVELOPMENT OF READING COMPETENCE: AN EMPIRICAL PERSPECTIVE

Although correlational studies of reading achievement and various subskills have been conducted for decades, their impact in terms of reaching a clear understanding of the learning involved has been negligible. What appears needed at this point in time are extensive investigations of cognitive, language, and memory development and their influence on the course of normal reading acquisition.

Abundant evidence can be cited to suggest that the period between 5 and 7 years is a particularly fertile one for developmental change in basic aspects of cognition (Hale, Taweel, Green, & Flaugher, 1978; Halford & Macdonald, 1977; Kemler, 1978). One can predict that these qualitative changes in the child's ability to perceive and organize his experiences will play an important role in the ease with which reading will be acquired. Some indirect evidence exists to indicate that this may be so. Biemiller (1970) observed oral reading errors and found that first graders make different types of errors at different stages of development.

In essence, early errors are dictated by contextual constraints alone, while later errors reflect an increasing ability to coordinate both the contextual and the graphemic dimensions of text. This finding is compatible with Halford's (1978) contention that children at this stage are acquiring the capacity to construct representational systems with two or more relationships. Kuhn and Phelps (1976) have demonstrated that comprehension of causal direction (expressed in sentences) develops rapidly between kindergarten and Grade 2. The available data suggest that this question merits further examination: in the 5- to 7-year period, there are undoubtedly many interactions between cognitive development and normal reading acquisition that have yet to be explored.

There is also reason to propose that the interdependence of oral language competence and successful reading acquisition should be more thoroughly investigated. From a theoretical standpoint, the relationship between spoken and written language fluency is self-evident (Kavanagh & Mattingly, 1972); yet developmental data on normal populations are scarce. Rodgers, Slade, and Conry (1974) reported preliminary evidence that oral language competence in Grade 1 predicts reading proficiency in Grade 2; their conclusions may be somewhat complicated by socioeconomic and general intellectual differences, however. Drawing upon a normal sample, Perfetti and Goldman (1976) reported a substantial correlation ($r = .66$) between vocabulary and reading comprehension measures in Grades 3 and 5. Lovett and Rabinovitch (1976) have provided evidence to indicate that the more precocious the Grade 1 reader, the greater his tendency to capitalize upon the morphological structure of written language; the recognition memory performance of these young beginners was superior when pseudowords featured morphological (e.g., -ing) rather than control endings (e.g., -uct). Although no cause–effect statements can be made on the basis of cross-sectional or correlational designs, there is ample indication that further exploration of the interdependence of oral and written language development is justified.

Carol Chomsky (1969) has contended that major changes in syntactic competence occur after the age of 6 years, the age at which children normally begin to acquire reading. O'Donnell, Griffin, and Norris (1967) have concurred, having documented the acquisition of new grammatical transformations between Grades 3 and 7. Parallel to the development of grammatical competence in this age range, there are indications of significant change in performance and control parameters. Entwisle and Frasure (1974) reported development between the ages of 6 and 9 in children's exploitation of syntactic cues and subsequent enhanced performance on an auditory recall task. By Grades 2 and 3, children were able to repeat grammatically acceptable anomalous sentences more ac-

curately than randomized word strings of equal length, a difference which failed to reach significance in the performance of younger subjects.

One can speculate that rate of syntactic development will be an important factor in the ease with which reading is acquired. It is important to recognize, at the same time, that reading acquisition may also increase the child's general level of linguistic awareness and contribute to his syntactic development. There is clear evidence that superior readers by Grade 4 are better able to use syntactic cues than their less advanced peers (Weinstein & Rabinovitch, 1971). The evidence on younger readers is scarce by comparison. While Doehring (1976) has contended that syntactic–semantic structure facilitates and speeds oral reading as early as Grade 1, Levin and Turner (1968) have suggested that Grade 2 children in the eye–voice span situation behave, to some extent, like word-by-word readers.

The critical importance of memory to reading is intuitively obvious and a third major focus of concern in our consideration of reading acquisition. Skilled reading necessitates what Conrad (1972) termed "a massive short-term memory operation" (p. 218): for comprehension, the reader must retain at the end of a sentence, paragraph, or page, the meaning of what he read at the beginning. The basis of developmental changes in memory has been hotly debated for much of this century. In 1916, Terman demonstrated that memory span was related to chronological age (Hagen, Jongeward, & Kail, 1975); since that time, age differences in memory performance have been explored from a number of different perspectives and with a variety of tasks. Hall and Pierce (1974) have estimated that while recognition memory increases only slightly from the age of 8 or 9 to adulthood, there is roughly a threefold increase in free recall performance over the same period. Similar trends have been reported for the Kindergarten to Grade 4 population, suggesting that recognition processes develop early and rapidly (Hall & Pressley, 1973). There is no consensus on the underlying mechanisms of memory development; however, current evidence does suggest that the development of organizational and control processes accounts for more developmental variability in memory performance than any concurrent change in capacity (Hagen et al., 1975; Morrison, Holmes, & Haith, 1974). To date, the control processes indicated involve aspects of encoding (Waters & Waters, 1976), rehearsal (Kellas, McCauley, & McFarland, 1975), and retrieval access (Eysenck & Baron, 1974).

There has been little systematic work relating memory processes to normal reading acquisition. There is evidence indicating that children who are poor readers are also more susceptible to short-term memory interference (Leslie, 1975), experience general short-term memory deterioration over time (Farnham-Diggory & Gregg, 1975), are at a higher risk for memory overload (Cohen & Netley, 1978), and are less consistent in their use of rehearsal strategies (Kastner & Rickards, 1974; Torgesen & Goldman, 1977). These data have questionable value from the perspective of normal development, however, owing to the inevitable heterogeneity of poor reader samples (Doehring & Hoshko, 1977; Mattis, French, & Rapin, 1975). There is one notable exception in this area. Perfetti and Goldman (1976) have reported that Grade 3 and 5 children who are superior in reading comprehension are also superior in probed recall on a discourse memory task; no significant differences were found in probed digit recall, leading these investigators to hypothesize that reading skill in this age range implicates a language-specific memory advantage. The fact that Perfetti and Goldman's skilled comprehenders produced more paraphrases in recall suggests that different encoding and/or retrieval processes may be available to these children.

In conclusion, it seems clear that there is much to be gained from the pursuit of further normative data. One major priority in developmental investigations of reading must be the study of *normal* acquisition as it relates to our understanding of the development of language, memory, and cognition in general. It is disappointing that so much of the available research on children's reading has employed the good and poor readers paradigm. This standard methodology is at best an indirect method of investigation: any technique of studying what a process is through examining the deficiencies of those who lack the ability to enact it is highly suspect. In addition, this paradigm carries with it two disturbing assumptions: (a) that the reading process is an all-or-none phenomenon, not observable at different levels of achievement or in its component parts; and (b) that a poor reader sample may be considered homogeneous with respect to their reading deficits.

It is clearly beyond the scope of this article to provide a comprehensive review of the available evidence relating early reading skill to indices of cognitive, language, and memory competence; entire volumes have been prepared which address this topic in some detail (e.g., see Resnick & Weaver, 1979). A cursory consideration of the question has been included here, however, because of the frequent failure to study reading acquisition from a normal developmental perspective and because of its consequence—our present inability to theorize from a sound data base.

VI. TOWARD A CONTINUOUS THEORY OF READING DEVELOPMENT

The conclusion that current models of skilled reading cannot account for the phenomenon of reading development was reached in a previous section; little attention has been directed, however, to the reason for this shared inability to extend down the developmental scale. Despite the profound differences which characterize their descriptions of skilled reading, virtually all adult models embrace the same implicit assumptions in their approach to the early process. From the analysis-by-synthesis advocates (e.g., Smith, 1971, 1973) to the linear stage proponents (e.g., Gough, 1972), the almost universal assumption is that beginning reading is a strictly linear or bottom-up process—that access to higher order, more "cognitive" influences awaits the automatization of basic decoding skills and is, therefore, the sole preserve of the fluent reader. Given the persuasive evidence cited earlier documenting the nonlinearity of skilled reading, this approach to reading development carries with it the presupposition of a basic discontinuity between the early process and ultimate fluency.

Although little experimental attention has been directed to testing the developmental predictions of the adult models, there is recent evidence to suggest that early reading is not the totally bottom-up process it is assumed to be. Using reading time as his dependent measure and differentially constrained texts as the experimental materials, Doehring (1976) charted the acquisition of rapid reading responses from Kindergarten to Grade 11. The results of this comprehensive cross-sectional study suggest that reading is facilitated by higher order structure as early as Grade 1. Statistical approximations to meaningful discourse were read more rapidly than words in random order by first-grade children, and words in meaningful sentences were decoded at greater speeds than the statistical approximations as early as Grade 2. In a similar vein, Siler (1974) found that sentences with syntactic violations were read more slowly than semantically violated sentences, and the latter more slowly than intact sentences, by second grade. Through an analysis of oral reading errors, Weber (1970) and Biemiller (1970) earlier demonstrated the supremacy of contextual factors over graphemic ones from the first year of reading experience. These data support the hypothesis that higher order constraints influence the act of reading very early in the course of its development.

A direct appraisal of the discontinuity assumption was undertaken in a recent study by the author (Lovett, 1979). Many adult reading models (e.g., LaBerge & Samuels, 1974; Perfetti & Lesgold, 1977) suggest that a higher order processing of extended textual segments (e.g., the sentence) will be jeopardized if increased attention must be allocated specific lexical operations such as decoding. The developmental implications of this prediction might be expressed in the following way: the more time and attention a child requires in sounding out individual words, the longer he will be in getting to the stage where structural and exact wording information can be discarded because they are no longer needed to encode the meaning of a sentence. A sentence memory paradigm, similar to that reported by Sachs (1974), was adopted to assess the developmental aspects of this prediction with 80 Grade 1 and Grade 2 children selected to represent four levels of early reading competence. The experiment was designed to determine (a) whether beginning readers exert clear informational priorities during prose reading in a manner parallel to that observed in skilled adult performance (Perfetti & Garson, 1973; Sachs, 1974); and (b) whether children at different levels of decoding skill differ in their access to higher order structure while reading sentences in text.

The children were tested in their recognition of semantic, syntactic, or specific lexical change in sentences which they had just decoded during prose reading. Semantic change sentences differed from the original target by a single word; that one-word substitution, however, altered the meaning of the entire sentence. In the syntactic change sentences, content and wording remained the same but sentence structure was modified either by a change in word sequence or by a cleft or pseudocleft transformation. Lexical change sentences preserved the meaning and structure of the target sentence, but introduced a single word substitution in which the new word was functionally synonymous with that which it replaced. A final set of test sentences were identical to the original target sentences. By manipulating the amount of story material which intervened between reading of the target sentence and presentation of the recognition item, it was possible to assess the children's immediate, short-term, and long-term retention of these sentential features.

The beginning readers demonstrated definite informational priorities during prose reading, exhibiting a pattern of informational selectivity essentially parallel to that observed for skilled adult readers (Sachs, 1974). The children were able to recognize semantic change in most instances (M = 73%), syntactic change in some cases (M = 52%), and lexical change only rarely (M = 29%), while identical test sentences were accurately recognized on almost every occasion (M = 86%). The hierarchical status of semantic, syntactic, and lexical information was evident at each retention interval, but the relative impact of these linguistic features changed dramatically over a very short period of time. The syntactic features of a target sentence, initially quite accessible to the reader, appeared to be discarded with the reading of an additional sentence or two; while specific lexical information was poorly recognized even upon immediate exposure, suggesting that these features may well be discarded as soon as or even before the reader finishes decoding the sentence.

The finding of greatest relevance to our present discussion is that *all* of the children adhered to this informational hierarchy, regardless of their grade placement or actual level of decoding competence. Thus sophisticated discourse processing skills appear to direct reading long before decoding becomes a fully accurate or automatic procedure. Sentential information can be selectively and hierarchically encoded despite the increased time and attention the beginning reader must devote to lower order decoding operations, a finding which fails to support the developmental predictions of current adult models and which is clearly contrary to prevailing assumptions of discontinuity. Instead these data underline the extent to which early reading behavior is directed by higher order cognitive and linguistic constraints and illustrate just how "top-down" the normal process is for these Grade 1 and 2 children.

If beginning reading can be characterized as an essentially cognitive activity, one might ask what it is that changes with the course of reading development? While the paucity of normative data as yet precludes any definitive response to this question, some suggestions can be offered on the basis of recent developmental findings. A cross-sectional investigation of normal reading development was undertaken in conjunction with a comparison study using skilled adult readers (Lovett, 1977, 1981; Lovett & Rabinovitch, 1977). As in the work reported above, a sample of 84 Grade 1 and Grade 2 children was selected to represent four levels of early reading competence. In these studies, an eye–voice span (EVS) paradigm was adopted; the EVS measure—basically the distance in word units that the eyes precede the voice in oral reading—has long proven a sensitive tool with which to examine the linguistic structures to which the reader attends (Levin *et al.,* 1972; Levin & Kaplan, 1968; Resnick, 1970). In its present application, this procedure was used to assess whether decoding by beginning readers is facilitated by certain sentential constraints; of particular interest were the questions of whether this facilitation could be observed in children at various levels of decoding skill and how it might compare with that observed in skilled adult readers.

Both child and adult subjects read texts of four different types, with textual condition varying in the degree to which materials were semantically and/or syntactically constrained. Condition 1 texts contained sentences which embodied the natural semantic and syntactic constraints of English prose. Condition 2 texts were the same as those in Condition 1 but with word order disrupted and randomized. Condition 3 texts were constructed using the sentence frames of Condition 1, but with the subsequent manipulation that all content words were replaced with highly pronounceable pseudowords; in Condition 4, the Condition 3 texts were presented in randomly scrambled sequence. The conditions were designed to make it possible to examine the influence of normal semantic and syntactic structure (Condition 1), with the controls of examining the same words without sentential constraints (Condition 2) and the same sentential cadences without the familiar and meaningful words (Condition 3). Prior to EVS testing, all of the children were trained to criterion in identifying the individual words and pseudowords used in the experimental texts; this precaution was considered important as the purpose of the experiment was to examine differential responsiveness to sentence structure, and not decoding differences on the single word level.

Results from the developmental study indicate that the more precocious the young reader, the greater his reported span; the better readers' advantage was more dramatic, however, the more linguistically constrained the reading material. Children at each level of decoding competence, and in both grades, were able to extend their spans to a significant degree when meaningful words were arranged in a syntactic (Condition 1) rather than random sequence (Condition 2); the extent of this facilitation, however, increased in direct relation to the child's level of decoding competence. Interestingly, only the most precocious young readers were able to exploit syntactic structure in the absence of conventional meaning; children in the top two reading groups reported longer spans for pseudowords arranged as "sentences" (Condition 3) than for the same items without sentential constraints (Condition 4). This suggests that syntactic features make some seemingly independent contribution to early reading, a contribution which apparently increases with increasing reading competence.

When the spans of the child and adult readers were compared, the advantage of adult fluency could be observed in each textual condition, suggesting a general enhancement of all reading functions (as would be expected). The *greatest* changes with the development of ultimate fluency—as was the case with early reading precocity—were observed when texts were constrained by higher order semantic and/or syntactic structure (i.e., Conditions 1 and 3, respectively). Although fluency provides an overall extension of the EVS, the areas of greatest developmental gain appear to involve the reader's capacity to use the linguistic information available in textual structure.

These data suggest that many of the same processes that facilitate fluency for the accomplished adult reader also underlie reading success in the Grade 1 and 2 population. That the most critical of these processes, even for the youngest and least competent readers, appears to have a cognitive–linguistic base is theoretically important. This evidence supports our earlier characterization of beginning reading as a process with considerable top-down capacity; these data, in addition, clearly demonstrate the continuity between the early behavior and its mature form.

The EVS data summarized above are compatible with Gibson and Levin's (1975) definition of reading development as an increasing ability to perceive text economically. The more precocious young readers and the adults of the present sample were able to perceive text in larger units when they could capitalize upon the higher order constraints that relate words in meaningful prose. But their advantage, although greatest in the sententially constrained texts, was not confined to them. These readers also possessed some advantage relative to their less skilled peers when decoding the random arrangement of pseudowords presented in the Condition 4 passages—the latter texts being bound only by the lower order constraints of graphology, phonology, and orthography—strictly *intra*-word decoding constraints. The extended spans of the better readers, and ultimately of the adults, in this condition might be attributed to an increased automaticity in lower order decoding operations. (It should be recalled that the children were trained to an accuracy criterion before EVS testing; no controls were attempted with respect to the automaticity with which decoding skills were acquired.) Doehring (1976) found consistent decreases in response times for all of the component reading functions that he studied developmentally. Although neither Doehring's data nor the present EVS findings constitute a direct test of LaBerge and Samuels' (1974) dual criteria for skill acquisition, both sets of data are compatible with their suggestion that the second criterion, automaticity, is important to our understanding of the perceptual learning involved in reading acquisition. These data might be best accommodated by a model which defines reading development in terms of an increased capacity for higher order unitization coupled with an increasing automatization of lower order or intraword decoding skills.

It appears that reading begins as a process with considerable top-down capacity. Normal children bring sophisticated discourse processing skills to their first encounters with text—skills which they have presumably developed in the context of oral language experience. The reading behavior of these young children appears directed by the same principles of informational selectivity and processing economy that guide the skilled reader; the ultimate goal of facilitating discourse comprehension seems shared by both novice and master in this sense. Thus early reading behavior is an interactive phenomenon almost from its inception and probably never resembles the linear, bottom-up process that has commonly been depicted.

Throughout the course of this discussion, the need for an interactive model of reading development has become clear. To accommodate recent data on normal reading development, we require a model which can simultaneously account for the bottom-up changes which must accompany the acquisition of automatic decoding skills, while also allowing for the top-down influences which, from the first year of reading experience, enable the child to realize his purpose of reading for meaning. No existing models can accommodate developmental change in both directions. The formalism recently outlined by Rumelhart (1977), however, might eventually be of some heuristic value to developmental theorists; the principles which he has adopted to capture the interactive flavor of fluent reading could be extended to a consideration of the acquisition phenomenon. Rumelhart's concept of reading as the simultaneous implementation of highly interactive, parallel processes need not be restricted to a description of the fluent process alone; the same formalism could also be applied to the emergent skills of early acquisition and to the developmental course which follows. In addition to the greater explanatory power afforded by an interactive rather than a serial model, application of the same theoretical principles to both fluency and acquisition has enormous appeal on still another level: it allows us to abandon traditional notions of a processing dichotomy between early reading and later fluency in favor of modeling the process along a developmental continuum. Most of the evidence considered in earlier sections of this article offers little justification for the dichotomous theorizing which has characterized treatments of reading behavior at both ends of the developmental scale.

While we await the provision of a detailed developmental model, the available data reviewed here provide some basis for suggesting three general principles on which a continuous model of reading development might eventually be formulated. These principles presuppose an interactive definition of skilled reading—that is, that all acts of reading fluency reflect the essential interdependence of higher and lower order processing skills. Based on this premise, it can be suggested that:

1. All reading behavior must be modeled along a continuum which encompasses both the minimal skills of earliest acquisition and the consummate product of adult fluency, for behavior at all points on the continuum is at least partially determined by the same general factors.

2. Early reading behavior must be defined interactively; traditionally conceived lower order components of the early reading process are subject to the same class of higher order, cognitive-linguistic constraints that govern later fluency.

3. The course of reading development must also be conceptualized as

an interactive phenomenon; that is, with development, reading becomes an increasingly interactive process. Although the exact mechanisms of the learning involved are as yet unknown, perceptual learning, consolidation, and the development of automaticity in lower order reading functions appear to free up greater capacity for, or in some other manner facilitate, a multidimensional appreciation of the text. Increasing reading skill reflects an increasing interdependence of the myriad of cognitive and perceptual processes which define the act of reading.

At the end of these deliberations, armed with more questions than answers, we are reminded of Huey's thought at the beginning of the century. The telling of what we do know of the reading process more than 70 years later is indeed a "tangled story," and our consideration of what remains unknown reveals how far we remain from what Huey so aptly characterized as "the acme of a psychologist's achievements." The new perspectives afforded in current models of cognition, particularly in the realm of language comprehension, will undoubtedly have considerable impact on the direction of future reading theory. It is hoped that some of the speculations offered in these pages will stimulate further experimental interest in reading development and will contribute to a changing theoretical perspective on what the normal child achieves in the course of reading acquisition.

ACKNOWLEDGMENTS

The support of the Medical Research Council of Canada is gratefully acknowledged; the final version of this manuscript was prepared during tenure of an MRC Centennial Fellowship. I especially thank Donald G. Doehring, Gordon D. Logan, Michael R. Seitz, and Sharon W. Stamm for their insightful comments on an earlier version of the chapter.

REFERENCES

Anderson, J. R. *Language, memory, and thought.* Hillsdale, New Jersey: Erlbaum, 1976.
Anderson, J. R., & Bower, G. H. *Human associative memory.* New York: Holt, 1973.
Anderson, R. C., & Ortony, A. On putting apples into bottles: A problem of polysemy. *Cognitive Psychology,* 1975, **7,** 167–180.
Barclay, J. R. The role of comprehension in remembering sentences. *Cognitive Psychology,* 1973, **4,** 229–254.
Bartlett, F. C. *Remembering: A study in experimental and social psychology.* Cambridge, Massachusetts: Cambridge University Press, 1932.
Biemiller, A. J. The development of the use of graphic and contextual information as children learn to read. *Reading Research Quarterly,* 1970, **6,** 75–96.
Bobrow, S., & Bower, G. Comprehension and recall of sentences. *Journal of Experimental Psychology,* 1969, **80,** 455–461.

Bransford, J. D. Bransford-McCarrell-Franks discussion. In W. B. Weimer & D. S. Palermo (Eds.), *Cognition and the symbolic processes.* Hillsdale, New Jersey: Erlbaum, 1974.

Bransford, J. D., Barclay, J. R., & Franks, J. J. Sentence memory: A constructive versus interpretive approach. *Cognitive Psychology, 1972, 3,* 193–209.

Bransford, J. D., & McCarrell, N. S. A sketch of a cognitive approach to comprehension: Some thoughts about understanding what it means to comprehend. In W. B. Weimer & D. S. Palermo (Eds.), *Cognition and the symbolic processes.* Hillsdale, New Jersey: Erlbaum, 1974.

Brewer, W. F. The problem of meaning and the interrelations of the higher mental processes. In W. B. Weimer & D. S. Palermo (Eds.), *Cognition and the symbolic processes.* Hillsdale, New Jersey: Erlbaum, 1974.

Brewer, W. F., & Lichtenstein, E. H. Memory for marked semantic features versus memory for meaning. *Journal of Verbal Learning and Verbal Behavior, 1974, 13,* 172–180.

Bruner, J. S. *Beyond the information given: Studies in the psychology of knowing.* New York: Norton, 1973.

Burke, K. *A grammar of motives.* Berkeley: University of California Press, 1969.

Buswell, G. T. An experimental study of the eye-voice span in reading. *Supplementary Educational Monographs,* No. 17. Chicago, Illinois: Department of Education, University of Chicago, 1920.

Carpenter, P. A. On the comprehension, storage, and retrieval of comparative sentences. *Journal of Verbal Learning and Verbal Behavior, 1974, 13,* 401–411.

Carpenter, P. A., & Just, M. A. Semantic control of eye movements during picture scanning in a sentence-picture verification task. *Perception and Psychophysics, 1972, 12,* 61–64.

Carpenter, P. A., & Just, M. A. Sentence comprehension: A psycholinguistic processing model of verification. *Psychological Review, 1975, 82,* 45–73.

Cattell, J. M. Ueber die Zeit der Erkennung und Benennung von Schriftzeichen, Bildern und Farben. *Philosophische Studien, 1885, 2,* 635–650.

Chomsky, C. *The acquisition of syntax in children from 5 to 10.* Cambridge, Massachusetts: MIT Press, 1969.

Chomsky, C. Reading, writing, and phonology. *Harvard Educational Review, 1970, 40,* 287–309.

Chomsky, N. *Aspects of the theory of syntax.* Cambridge, Massachusetts: MIT Press, 1965.

Clark, H. H. Linguistic processes in deductive reasoning. *Psychological Review, 1969, 76,* 387–404.

Clark, H. H., & Card, S. K. Role of semantics in remembering comparative sentences. *Journal of Experimental Psychology, 1969, 82,* 545–553.

Clark, H. H., & Chase, W. G. On the process of comparing sentences against pictures. *Cognitive Psychology, 1972, 3,* 472–517.

Cohen, R. L., & Netley, C. Cognitive deficits, learning disabilities, and WISC Verbal-Performance consistency. *Developmental Psychology, 1978, 14,* 624–634.

Collins, A. M., & Quillian, M. R. Retrieval time from semantic memory. *Journal of Verbal Learning and Verbal Behavior, 1969, 8,* 240–247.

Collins, A. M., & Quillian, M. R. Experiments on semantic memory and language comprehension. In L. W. Gregg (Ed.), *Cognition in learning and memory.* New York: Wiley, 1972.

Conrad, C. Cognitive economy in semantic memory. *Journal of Experimental Psychology, 1972, 92,* 149–154.

Conrad, R. Speech and reading. In J. F. Kavanagh & I. G. Mattingly (Eds.), *Language by ear and by eye*. Cambridge, Massachusetts: MIT Press, 1972.

Craik, F. I. M., & Lockhart, R. S. Levels of processing: A framework for memory research. *Journal of Verbal Learning and Verbal Behavior*, 1972, **11**, 671–684.

Craik, F. I. M., & Tulving, E. Depth of processing and the retention of words in episodic memory. *Journal of Experimental Psychology: General*, 1975, **104**, 268–294.

de Groot, A. D. Perception and memory versus thought: Some old ideas and recent findings. In B. Kleinmuntz (Ed.), *Problem solving: Research, method, and theory*. New York: Wiley, 1966.

Doehring, D. G. Acquisition of rapid reading responses. *Monographs of the Society for Research in Child Development*, 1976, **41**, Serial No. 165.

Doehring, D. G., & Hoshko, I. M. Classification of reading problems by the Q-technique of factor analysis. *Cortex*, 1977, **13**, 281–294.

Entwisle, D. R., & Frasure, N. E. A contradiction resolved: Children's processing of syntactic cues. *Developmental Psychology*, 1974, **10**, 852–857.

Eysenck, M. W., & Baron, C. R. Effects of cuing on recall from categorized word lists. *Developmental Psychology*, 1974, **10**, 665–666.

Farnham-Diggory, S., & Gregg, L. W. Short term memory function in young readers. *Journal of Experimental Child Psychology*, 1975, **19**, 279–298.

Foss, D. J., & Harwood, D. A. Memory for sentences: Implications for human associative memory. *Journal of Verbal Learning and Verbal Behavior*, 1975, **14**, 1–16.

Franks, J. J. Toward understanding understanding. In W. B. Weimer & D. S. Palermo (Eds.), *Cognition and the symbolic processes*. Hillsdale, New Jersey: Erlbaum, 1974.

Franks, J. J. Bransford-McCarrell-Franks discussion. In W. B. Weimer & D. S. Palermo (Eds.), *Cognition and the symbolic processes*. Hillsdale, New Jersey: Erlbaum, 1974.

Frederiksen, C. H. Acquisition of semantic information from discourse: Effects of repeated exposures. *Journal of Verbal Learning and Verbal Behavior*, 1975, **14**, 158–169. (a)

Frederiksen, C. H. Effects of context-induced processing operations on semantic information acquired from discourse. *Cognitive Psychology*, 1975, **7**, 139–166. (b)

Gibson, E. J. *Principles of perceptual learning and development*. New York: Appleton, 1969.

Gibson, E. J. The ontogeny of reading. *American Psychologist*, 1970, **25**, 136–143.

Gibson, E. J. Perceptual learning and the theory of word perception. *Cognitive Psychology*, 1971, **2**, 351–368.

Gibson, E. J. Reading for some purpose. In J. F. Kavanagh & I. G. Mattingly (Eds.), *Language by ear and by eye*. Cambridge, Massachusetts: MIT Press, 1972.

Gibson, E. J., & Guinet, L. The perception of inflections in brief visual presentations of words. *Journal of Verbal Learning and Verbal Behavior*, 1971, **10**, 182–189.

Gibson, E. J., & Levin, H. *The psychology of reading*. Cambridge, Massachusetts: MIT Press, 1975.

Gibson, E. J., Osser, H., & Pick, A. A study in the development of grapheme-phoneme correspondences. *Journal of Verbal Learning and Verbal Behavior*, 1963, **2**, 142–146.

Gibson, E. J., Schapiro, F., & Yonas, A. Confusion matrices for graphic patterns obtained with a latency measure. In *The analysis of reading skill: A program of basic and applied research*. (Final Rep., Project No. 5-1213). Cornell University and U. S. Office of Education, 1968.

Gibson, E. J., Shurcliff, A., & Yonas, A. Utilization of spelling patterns by deaf and hearing subjects. In H. Levin & J. P. Williams (Eds.), *Basic studies on reading*. New York: Basic Books, 1970.

Goodman, K. S. Reading: A psycholinguistic guessing game. *Journal of the Reading Specialist*, 1967, **4**, 126–135.

Goodman, K. S. Psycholinguistic universals in the reading process. In F. Smith (Ed.), *Psycholinguistics and reading*. New York: Holt, 1973.

Gough, P. G. One second of reading. In J. F. Kavanagh & I. G. Mattingly (Eds.), *Language by ear and by eye*. Cambridge, Massachusetts: MIT Press, 1972.

Graesser, A., & Mandler, G. Recognition memory for the meaning and surface structure of sentences. *Journal of Experimental Psychology: Human Learning and Memory*, 1975, **104**, 238–248.

Hagen, J. W., Jongeward, R. H., & Kail, R. V. Cognitive perspectives on the development of memory. In H. Reese (Ed.), *Advances in child development and behavior* (Vol. 10). New York: Academic Press, 1975.

Hale, G. A., Taweel, S. S., Green, R. Z., & Flaugher, J. Effects of instructions on children's attention to stimulus components. *Developmental Psychology*, 1978, **14**, 499–506.

Halford, G. S. Toward a working model of Piaget's stages. In J. A. Keats, K. F. Collis, & G. S. Halford (Eds.), *Cognitive Development*. New York: Wiley, 1978.

Halford, G. S., & Macdonald, C. Children's pattern construction as a function of age and complexity. *Child Development*, 1977, **48**, 1096–1100.

Hall, J. W., & Pierce, J. W. Recognition and recall by children and adults as a function of variations in memory encoding instructions. *Memory and Cognition*, 1974, **2**, 585–590.

Hall, J. W., & Pressley, G. M. *Free recall and recognition memory in young children*. Paper presented to the annual meeting of the Psychonomic Society, St. Louis, November, 1973.

Halle, M., & Stevens, K. N. Speech recognition: A model and a program for research. In J. A. Fodor & J. J. Katz (Eds.), *The structure of language: Readings in the philosophy of language*. New York: Prentice-Hall, 1964.

Halle, M., & Stevens, K. N. Remarks on analysis by synthesis and distinctive features. In W. Wathen-Dunn & L. E. Woods (Eds.), *Models for the perception of speech and visual form: Proceedings of a symposium*. Cambridge, Massachusetts: MIT Press, 1967.

Hochberg, J. Components of literacy: Speculations and exploratory research. In H. Levin & J. P. Williams (Eds.), *Basic studies on reading*. New York: Basic Books, 1970.

Hochberg, J., Levin, H., & Frail, C. *Studies of oral reading: VII. How interword spaces affect reading*. Ithaca, New York: Cornell University, 1966 (mimeographed).

Huey, E. B. *The psychology and pedagogy of reading*. New York: Macmillan, 1908; republished by MIT Press, 1968.

Johnson, M. K., Bransford, J. D., & Solomon, S. K. Memory for tacit implications of sentences. *Journal of Experimental Psychology*, 1973, **98**, 203–205.

Kaplan, R. M. A general syntactic processor. In R. Rustin (Ed.), *Natural language processing*. New York: Algorithmics, 1973.

Kastner, S. B., & Rickards, C. Mediated memory with novel and familiar stimuli in good and poor readers. *Journal of Genetic Psychology*, 1974, **124**, 105–113.

Katz, J. J., & Fodor, J. The structure of a semantic theory. *Language*, 1963, **39**, 170–210.

Katz, J. J., & Postal, P. M. *An integrated theory of linguistic descriptions*. Cambridge, Massachusetts: MIT Press, 1964.

Kavanagh, J. F., & Mattingly, I. G. (Eds.). *Language by ear and by eye*. Cambridge, Massachusetts: MIT Press, 1972.

Kellas, G., McCauley, C., & McFarland, C. E., Jr. Developmental aspects of storage and retrieval. *Journal of Experimental Child Psychology*, 1975, **19**, 51–62.

Kemler, D. G. Patterns of hypothesis testing in children's discriminative learning: A study of the development of problem-solving strategies. *Developmental Psychology*, 1978, **14**, 653–673.

Kintsch, W., & Monk, D. Storage of complex information in memory: Some implications of the speed with which inferences can be made. *Journal of Experimental Psychology*, 1972, **94**, 25–32.

Kolers, P. A. Three stages of reading. In H. Levin & J. P. Williams (Eds.), *Basic studies on reading*. New York: Basic Books, 1970.

Kolers, P. A. Some problems of classification. In J. F. Kavanagh & I. G. Mattingly (Eds.), *Language by ear and by eye*. Cambridge, Massachusetts: MIT Press, 1972.

Kolers, P. A. Remembering operations. *Memory and Cognition*, 1973, **1**, 347–355.

Kolers, P. A. Specificity of operations in sentence recognition. *Cognitive Psychology*, 1975, **7**, 289–306. (a)

Kolers, P. A. Memorial consequences of automatized encoding. *Journal of Experimental Psychology: Human Learning and Memory*, 1975, **1**, 689–701. (b)

Kolers, P. A., & Ostry, D. Time course of loss of information regarding pattern analyzing operations. *Journal of Verbal Learning and Verbal Behavior*, 1974, **13**, 599–612.

Kuhn, D., & Phelps, H. The development of children's comprehension of causal direction. *Child Development*, 1976, **47**, 248–251.

LaBerge, D. Attention and the measurement of perceptual learning. *Memory and Cognition*, 1973, **1**, 268–276.

LaBerge, D., & Samuels, S. J. Toward a theory of automatic information processing in reading. *Cognitive Psychology*, 1974, **6**, 293–323.

LaBerge, D., Van Gelder, P., & Yellott, J. I. A cueing technique in choice reaction time. *Perception and Psychophysics*, 1970, **7**, 57–62.

Leslie, L. Susceptibility to interference effects in short-term memory of normal and retarded readers. *Perceptual and Motor Skills*, 1975, **40**, 791–794.

Lesser, V. R., Fennell, R. D., Erman, L. D., & Reddy, D. R. *Organization of the HEARSAY II speech understanding system*. (Working papers in Speech Recognition III). Pittsburgh, Pennsylvania: Carnegie-Mellon University, 1974.

Levin, H., Grossman, J., Kaplan, E., & Yang, R. Constraints and the eye-voice span in right and left embedded sentences. *Language and Speech*, 1972, **15**, 30–39.

Levin, H., & Kaplan, E. L. Eye-voice span (EVS) within active and passive sentences. *Language and Speech*, 1968, **11**, 251–258.

Levin, H., & Turner, A. Sentence structure and the eye-voice span. In H. Levin, E. J. Gibson, & J. J. Gibson (Eds.), *The analysis of reading skill*. (Final Rep., Project No. 5-1213). Cornell University and U. S. Office of Education, 1968.

Lovett, M. W. *Early reading competence: The perception and memory of sentential information*. Unpublished Ph.D. thesis, McGill University, 1977.

Lovett, M. W. The selective encoding of sentential information in normal reading development. *Child Development*, 1979, **50**, 897–900.

Lovett, M. W. *Sentential structure and the perceptual span in normal reading development*. Submitted, 1981.

Lovett, M. W., & Rabinovitch, M. S. *Reading acquisition and the perception of word features*. Paper presented at the 84th annual meeting of the American Psychological Association, Washington, D.C., September, 1976.

Lovett, M. W., & Rabinovitch, M. S. *A study of early reading competence: Linguistic structure and the eye-voice span.* Paper presented at the 38th annual meeting of the Canadian Psychological Association, Vancouver, B.C., June, 1977.

Mackworth, N. H., & Morandi, A. The gaze selects informative details within pictures. *Perception and Psychophysics,* 1967, **2**, 547–552.

Mattis, S., French, J. H., & Rapin, I. Dyslexia in children and young adults: Three independent neuropsychological syndromes. *Developmental Medicine and Child Neurology,* 1975, **17**, 150–163.

Meyer, D. E. On the representation and retrieval of stored semantic information. *Cognitive Psychology,* 1970, **1**, 242–300.

Miller, G. A. Some preliminaries to psycholinguistics. *American Psychologist,* 1965, **20**, 15–20.

Miller, G. A. A psychological method to investigate verbal concepts. *Journal of Mathematical Psychology,* 1969, **6**, 169–191.

Miller, G. A. English verbs of motion: A case study in semantics and lexical memory. In A. W. Melton & E. Martin (Eds.), *Coding processes in human memory.* New York: Holt, 1972.

Moeser, S. D. Inferential reasoning in episodic memory. *Journal of Verbal Learning and Verbal Behavior,* 1976, **15**, 193–212.

Morrison, F. J., Holmes, D. L., & Haith, M. M. A developmental study of the effect of familiarity on short-term visual memory. *Journal of Experimental Child Psychology,* 1974, **18**, 412–425.

Morton, J. The effects of context upon speed of reading, eye movements and the eye-voice span. *Quarterly Journal of Experimental Psychology,* 1964, **16**, 340–354.

Neisser, U. *Cognitive psychology.* New York: Appleton, 1967.

Neisser, U. *Cognition and reality.* San Francisco, California: Freeman, 1976.

Nelson, K. E., & Kosslyn, S. M. Semantic retrieval in children and adults. *Developmental Psychology,* 1975, **11**, 807–813.

Nodine, C., & Lang, N. Development of visual scanning strategies for differentiating words. *Developmental Psychology,* 1971, **5**, 221–232.

Nodine, C., & Steuerle, N. Development of perceptual and cognitive strategies for differentiating graphemes. *Journal of Experimental Psychology,* 1973, **97**, 158–166.

Norman, D. A. Toward a theory of memory and attention. *Psychological Review,* 1968, **75**, 522–536.

Norman, D. A. *Memory and attention: An introduction to human information processing.* New York: Wiley, 1969.

O'Donnell, R. C., Griffin, W. J., & Norris, R. C. *Syntax of kindergarten and elementary school children: A transformational analysis.* (Res. Rep. No. 8). Champaign, Illinois: National Council of Teachers of English, 1967.

Perfetti, C. A., & Garson, B. Forgetting linguistic information after reading. *Journal of Educational Psychology,* 1973, **65**, 135–139.

Perfetti, C. A., & Goldman, S. R. Discourse memory and reading comprehension skill. *Journal of Verbal Learning and Verbal Behavior,* 1976, **14**, 33–42.

Perfetti, C. A., & Lesgold, A. M. Discourse comprehension and sources of individual differences. In M. Just & P. Carpenter (Eds.), *Cognitive processes in comprehension.* Hillsdale, New Jersey: Erlbaum, 1977.

Posner, M. I., Lewis, J., & Conrad, C. Component processes in reading: A performance analysis. In J. Kavanagh & I. G. Mattingly (Eds.), *Language by ear and by eye.* Cambridge, Massachusetts: MIT Press, 1972.

Posner, M. I., & Snyder, C. R. R. Attention and cognitive control. In R. L. Solso (Ed.),

Information processing and cognition: The Loyola symposium. Hillsdale, New Jersey: Erlbaum, 1975.

Rayner, K. The perceptual span and peripheral cues in reading. *Cognitive Psychology,* 1975, **7,** 65–81.

Resnick, L. B. Relations between perceptual and syntactic control in oral reading. *Journal of Educational Psychology,* 1970, **61,** 382–385.

Resnick, L. B., & Weaver, P. A. *Theory and practice of early reading.* Hillsdale, New Jersey: Erlbaum, 1979.

Rodgers, D., Slade, K., & Conry, R. Oral language, reading ability, and socioeconomic background in three grade one classes. *Alberta Journal of Educational Research,* 1974, **20,** 316–326.

Rumelhart, D. E. Toward an interactive model of reading. In S. Dornic (Ed.), *Attention and performance VI.* Hillsdale, New Jersey: Erlbaum, 1977.

Rumelhart, D. E. *Analogical processes and procedural representations.* (Tech. Rep. No. 81) La Jolla, California: University of California, San Diego, Center for Human Information Processing, February 1979.

Rumelhart, D. E., Lindsay, P. H., & Norman, D. A. A process model for long-term memory. In E. Tulving & W. Donaldson (Eds.), *Organization of memory.* New York: Academic Press, 1972.

Sachs, J. S. Memory in reading and listening to discourse. *Memory and Cognition,* 1974, **2,** 95–100.

Schaeffer, B., & Wallace, R. The comparison of word meanings. *Journal of Experimental Psychology,* 1970, **86,** 144–152.

Schulman, A. Memory for words recently classified. *Memory and Cognition,* 1974, **2,** 47–52.

Schvaneveldt, R., & Meyer, D. E. Retrieval and comparison processes in semantic memory. In S. Kornblum (Ed.), *Attention and performance IV.* New York: Academic Press, 1973.

Shultz, T. R., & Pilon, R. Development of the ability to detect linguistic ambiguity. *Child Development,* 1973, **44,** 728–733.

Siler, E. R. The effects of syntactic and semantic constraints on the oral reading performance of second and fourth graders. *Reading Research Quarterly,* 1974, **9,** 583–602.

Smith, F. *Understanding reading.* New York: Holt, 1971.

Smith, F. *Psycholinguistics and reading.* New York: Holt, 1973.

Smith, F., & Holmes, D. L. The independence of letter, word, and meaning identification in reading. In F. Smith (Ed.), *Psycholinguistics and Reading.* New York: Holt, 1973.

Sperling, G. A. Short-term memory, long-term memory, and scanning in the processing of visual information. In F. Young & D. Lindsley (Eds.), *Early experience and visual information processing in perceptual and reading disorders.* Washington, D.C.: National Academy of Sciences, 1970.

Torgesen, J., & Goldman, T. Verbal rehearsal and short-term memory in reading-disabled children. *Child Development,* 1977, **48,** 56–60.

Tulving, E. Episodic and semantic memory. In E. Tulving & W. Donaldson (Eds.), *Organization of memory.* New York: Academic Press, 1972.

Tulving, E., & Gold, C. Stimulus information and contextual information as determinants of tachistoscopic recognition of words. *Journal of Experimental Psychology,* 1963, **66,** 319–327.

Tzeng, O. J. L. Sentence memory: Recognition and inferences. *Journal of Experimental Psychology: Human Learning and Memory,* 1975, **1,** 720–726.

Venezky, R. L., Massaro, D. W., & Weber, R. M. Modelling the reading process. In H.

Singer & R. B. Ruddell (Eds.), *Theoretical models and processes of reading*. Newark, Delaware: International Reading Association, 1976.

Waller, T. G. Children's recognition memory for written sentences: A comparison of good and poor readers. *Child Development,* 1976, **47,** 90–95.

Wanat, S. F. *Linguistic structure and visual attention in reading*. Newark, Delaware: International Reading Association Research Reports, 1971.

Waters, H. S., & Waters, E. Semantic processing in children's free recall: Evidence for the importance of attentional factors and encoding variability. *Journal of Experimental Psychology: Human Learning and Memory,* 1976, **2,** 370–380.

Weber, R. M. First graders' use of grammatical context in reading. In H. Levin & J. P. Williams (Eds.), *Basic studies on reading*. New York: Basic Books, 1970.

Weimer, W. B., & Palermo, D. S. (Eds.) *Cognition and the symbolic processes*. Hillsdale, New Jersey: Erlbaum, 1974.

Weinstein, R., & Rabinovitch, M. S. Sentence structure and retention in good and poor readers. *Journal of Educational Psychology,* 1971, **62,** 25–30.

Winograd, T. Frame representations and the declarative-procedural controversy. In D. G. Bobrow & A. M. Collins (Eds.), *Representation and understanding: Studies in cognitive science*. New York: Academic Press, 1975.

TOWARD A MODEL OF SKILLED READING: AN ANALYSIS OF PERFORMANCE IN TACHISTOSCOPIC TASKS

D. J. K. MEWHORT AND A. J. CAMPBELL[1]

Psychology Department
Queen's University at Kingston
Kingston, Canada

I. INTRODUCTION

Reading—the process by which people acquire meaning from print—is a multicomponent skill of great importance. Cattell (1885b), one of the first to apply experimental methods to the study of reading, considered it to be "one of the largest factors in our modern life" and acknowledged

---

[1] Present address: Behavioural Studies Group (Department 2Z12), Bell-Northern Research Ltd., Ottawa, Canada.

its cultural basis by suggesting that it is "a thoroughly artificial act" (p. 306).

In spite of its importance, current understanding of reading is primitive, a failure which results from a more general problem: we do not have consensus concerning how to build a theory to assist in the study of reading. Because basic theory is primitive, and in spite of wide-spread and well-intentioned concern for poor readers, current understanding of reading offers little of substance to those responsible for teaching the skill. Indeed, as Chall (1967, 1970) documents, lack of an adequate theory has created enough of a vacuum that several disciplines can claim remedial authority.

The present work concerns theory and theory construction. In the article, we shall discuss the kind of theory required for complex skills such as reading. In addition, we shall offer a model which describes some of the mechanisms which underlie the skill of the adult reader. Finally, we shall discuss empirical work associated with the model. The article, then, illustrates the kind of thinking needed to deal with reading, offers the kernel of a theory, and describes empirical support for the theory.

Our perspective on models and on model building has been influenced by work associated with the artificial-intelligence community. Within the artificial-intelligence community, models are computational, i.e., they are formal accounts which have been implemented on a computer. From the outset, however, we acknowledge that our model is both informal and incomplete. It is incomplete because it accounts for only a subset of the skills associated with reading, and it remains informal because it requires liberal assumptions about the reader's skill at problem solving and at language comprehension. Despite its informality, however, the account has been built with the need to provide a formal statement in mind. As a result, its structure addresses a relatively detailed view of a range of behavior and provides a firm base for expansion. Thus, while not a formal model, i.e., a working system capable of simulating the task, we prefer to describe it as not-yet-formal rather than as informal.

While advice to the teacher remains a long-term goal for our work, in light of our primitive knowledge of the reading process, we prefer to avoid preaching to teachers and to await better information. There are two main reasons to wait for better information before offering advice. First, premature advice is bad advice and is likely to lead to mischief: advice to teachers leads to intervention in the classroom. Without a relatively complete theory, it is hard to connect specific interventions to particular theoretical considerations. If we do not link an intervention to theory, however, change becomes its own goal; we think it unlikely that wise changes can be made for random reasons. Thus, intervention in the absence of complete theory, even well-intentioned intervention, risks the education of the student/subject.

Second, as Chall (1967, 1970) documents, advice to teachers leads to premature "professionalism," i.e., to the delivery of remedial service without the intention of (and, perhaps, the objectivity required for) development of a better theory. More important from the student's perspective, successful intervention is more an art than a science, and premature professionalism allows a failure of art to hide behind the mask of scientific respectability.

II. SOME THEORETICAL CONSIDERATIONS

Reading is based on language and depends on the reader's use of knowledge, i.e., on his skill at manipulating symbols. By knowledge we mean to include both the reader's knowledge of his language and his general knowledge, i.e., his knowledge of the world surrounding him.

Knowledge, and the study of its influence on behavior, has a mixed heritage in psychology. Behaviorism banished it, along with other mentalistic concepts. The perspective we have adopted, the perspective of the artificial-intelligence community, makes use of knowledge within an information-processing analogy: we see performance and skill in terms of the manipulation of symbols. A behaviorist may not accept the analogy. Discussing memory from the behaviorist's position, for example, Neisser (1967) asked, "If memory consists of transformations, what is transformed?" He answered the question from the information-processing perspective by asserting, "*information* is what is transformed, and the structured pattern of its transformations is what we want to understand" (p. 8). Newell (1980) has provided a thorough statement of the reasoning underlying the information-processing analogy.

Reading is a complicated skill, and construction of a complete theory is a large task. The theory would have to include an account of subjects' language skills, their general knowledge, and, finally, the visual aspects of reading. Representing the language prerequisites to reading is a major problem by itself (Winograd, 1980). It is convenient, therefore, to break the analysis of reading into component analyses. Without much controversy, we can distinguish separate analyses for word identification, for sentence comprehension, and for story, i.e., paragraph-level, appreciation.

Literature on the topics within the three aspects of reading—word identification, sentence comprehension, and paragraph understanding—is scattered over several disciplines. Each discipline uses distinct methods, and discussions within each subfield usually center on concepts with different computational power than those in adjacent subfields. Even within subfields, the literature is often divided into separate communities, each using different methods and different explanatory concepts.

Studies of word recognition, for example, are associated with several levels of analysis. Some studies concern aspects of sensory physiology and center on concepts such as retinal sensitivity, lateral masking, and the timing differences associated with sustained versus transient channels (e.g., Breitmeyer & Ganz, 1976; Estes, 1978). Such concepts are based on simple threshold and sensitivity ideas, and studies motivated by the concepts are associated with classical psychophysical methods, typically those appropriate to threshold and signal-detection technology.

Other studies of word identification eschew sensory factors and apply concepts in a relatively abstract way. Hanson, Riseman, and Fisher (1976), for example, consider the application of letter-frequency relations. Their analysis is mathematical and is not based on ideas derived from underlying physiological structures. In particular, Hanson *et al.* consider word recognition in terms of an initial letter-recognition stage followed by a mechanism to assemble the letters into words. The letter-recognition analysis is based on the shape of the segments comprising each character, and the assembly operation involves a Bayesian decision mechanism. The Bayesian mechanism evaluates the output of the letter-recognition mechanism in terms of letter-frequency relations, i.e., the word is determined by the combination of visual and frequency information (see also Toussaint, 1978; Shinghal & Toussaint, 1979).

Studies in sentence- and paragraph-level comprehension are, typically, indifferent to input modality and use the concepts of computational linguistics (see Anderson, 1976; Anderson & Bower, 1973). Words are abstract entities and form the fundamental building blocks for sentence and paragraph comprehension. The main problems for analysis, then, concern how memory deals with words and how meaning and knowledge can be represented. Typical discussions concern the structure of various kinds of linking representations and control processes. Goldstein and Papert (1977) provide an excellent overview of the general design and philosophy of current knowledge-based systems. Unfortunately, while the design requirements for knowledge systems are clear, other aspects of knowledge-based systems remain cloudy. We do not, for example, have consensus concerning how to build a knowledge-based theory: the study of meta-systems for construction of knowledge-based theory is in its infancy. Bobrow and Winograd (1977), for instance, have provided a preliminary example of a meta-system in their KRL, their knowledge representation language, but as Lehnert and Wilks (1979) note, basic issues remain controversial (see also the reply by Bobrow & Winograd, 1979).

Like the preferences for various theoretical constructs within different communities, experimental methods differ both across the three levels of analysis and, sometimes, within a level of analysis. Studies of letter and word recognition, for example, characteristically involve experimental situations featuring good control over both visual and performance factors likely to influence behavior. Studies of sentence and paragraph comprehension tend to involve informal displays, trick sentences, and loose control over performance. Instead of emphasis on experimental control, then, work from the computational-linguistic perspective sacrifices experimental control in defense of formidable theoretical work.

A. Familiarity Effects

The work we shall report, here, concerns word-identification processes, and it is based on an information-processing analysis. Our main experimental tool is the tachistoscopic-identification task, and the bulk of the empirical work concerns the familiarity effect associated with report of nonsense materials. Some readers may question the utility of an analysis based on tachistoscopic presentation of pseudowords, but, as we shall argue later in detail, word-identification processes include mechanisms used in tachistoscopic tasks involving nonsense material. In particular, the mechanisms responsible for the familiarity effect in a simple free-recall tachistoscopic task are also used in word identification. Before considering the familiarity effect and its theoretical implications, however, a comment on the basic tachistoscopic technique is needed.

Tachistoscopic presentations are brief visual displays lasting 150 milliseconds or less. Such displays permit an experimenter to mimic a single brief glimpse from the normal reading process. Similar procedures are also used to limit the energy available to the visual system. For such purposes, however, one usually arranges the luminance, the duration, and the subject's state of adaptation to yield performance at, or near, the subject's threshold. We use tachistoscopic procedures for the first reason, i.e., to limit the subject to input from a single fixation, a single "look." Thus, we seldom restrict the energy available to the visual system.

Both historically and in terms of our account of word identification, the main experimental problem centers on familiarity effects in tachistoscopic recognition. Briefly, letters arranged as words are reported more easily than when they are arranged as nonwords (e.g., *COMPUTER* versus *TMOUPRCE*). The benefit indicates that subjects are able to exploit their knowledge of language during the task. Thus, the main theoretical problem concerns how subjects acquire, maintain, and apply their knowledge.

How does a letter's context determine our recognition of it? Several answers have been suggested, including the theory urged here, and the specific answers differ in several ways. Perhaps the most important is that they represent different classes of underlying theory.

In general perceptual theory, familiarity—the consequence of prior experience—is atomic, i.e., it cannot be analyzed into component concepts. As a result, accounts of the familiarity effect based on general perceptual theory are couched in global terms, and examples of familiarity effects obtained in different tasks, or with different materials, are treated as if they reflected the same mechanism. The treatment is wrong, however. As we shall illustrate later in detail, different processing mechanisms can yield quite different familiarity effects from the same materials in different tasks.

In contrast to general perceptual theory, however, information-processing theories start by considering the knowledge represented by various familiarity effects. The use of different knowledge implies use of different processing mechanisms. Information-processing theories assume performance can be explained in terms of a structured arrangement of modular processing components. The processing modules, then, are the atoms of the theory (e.g., Simon, 1979), but, in contrast to general perceptual theory, the atoms of an information-processing account represent much smaller components.

The earliest analysis of familiarity effects obtained with alphabetic stimuli concerned the relation of individual letters to words. To explain the benefit of a word presentation over its anagram, for example, Cattell (1885a) suggested that, when we learn to read, we acquire templates of each word. His concept of a template included aspects of the word's visual shape, a position retained by more recent theorists (e.g., Kolers, 1972). Presumably, given such a hypothesis, the benefit of a word context for letter identification reflects our ability to use the template in reading the word, and then to use the word to derive the letter.

From the earliest demonstrations of the phenomenon, then, explanations of "the" familiarity effect have focused on the whole word. Such focus, in turn, suggests that when we learn to read, we learn individual words and templates for them. In addition, the focus has prompted educators to stress the "look–say" method of reading instruction. The latter drills the student/subject on skills associated with reading single whole words aloud.

There is, however, evidence to suggest that an account based on whole-word templates is not complete. In particular, an account based on the whole-word or template idea is not consistent with a classic experiment reported by Miller, Bruner, and Postman (1954). They showed that subjects are able to use letter and letter-cluster information and, thereby, that subjects use subword data.

Miller *et al.* (1954) exploited the fact that some letters are used more frequently in English than others; *e*, for example, appears more frequently than *z*. Similarly, letter clusters do not appear equally often in English; *th* is a common letter combination but *tq* is not. Miller *et al.* capitalized on the stable pattern of letter and letter-combination frequencies by constructing pseudowords which conformed to the pattern in graded degrees. The various degrees have been termed orders of approximation to English.

To illustrate the familiarity associated with increased order of approximation to English, consider some examples. *UCQXSAWV* and *NJKEMLDX* were generated using the zero-order rules. *HEDICKNG* and *WATHIPRE* are second-order approximations to English. Finally, *POLICKET* and *DICTORES* are fourth-order approximations to English. Note that the higher order examples are familiar in the intuitive sense that they look like English words and are pronounceable.

Pseudowords of zero-order approximation to English are generated by sampling letters at random from the alphabet; first-order approximations are generated by sampling at random from a text. Because they preserve the letter-frequency constraints of the text, first-order strings are more predictable than zero-order. Higher order pseudowords preserve constraints from larger letter groups; second-order strings preserve bigram frequency, third-order preserve trigram frequency, and so forth. Because of the increased constraint, the higher order sequences are more familiar.

Miller *et al.* (1954) used the pseudowords in a simple free-recall tachistoscopic task: subjects saw one eight-letter pseudoword per trial and were required to report as many of the letters as possible. The results were straightforward: as the order of approximation to English increased, i.e., as the pseudowords conformed to the pattern in English, subjects were able to report more letters.

Miller *et al.* (1954) accounted for their results by appealing to information theory (Shannon & Weaver, 1949). The relative information associated with a letter depends on its context. For each order of approximation to English, Miller *et al.* derived a measure of the relative information per letter, i.e., a quantitative measure of the sequential redundancy of the various orders of approximation to English (cf. Tulving, 1963). Applying the measure of sequential redundancy to the accuracy-of-report data, they showed that the information reported from the display was constant for all orders of approximation to English.

Garner (1962, pp. 252–254) has argued that Miller *et al.* (1954) mis-
applied information theory. His point is that their experiment manipulated
the form, not the amount, of redundancy. The distinction, however, is
not critical for present purposes. Moreover, independent of their reliance
on information theory, Miller *et al.* demonstrated an important empirical
relationship: performance on higher order pseudowords is proportional
to that on zero-order material.

Mewhort and Tulving (1964) confirmed the proportional relationship
and showed that it is independent of limitations imposed by the display
energy. They used zero-, first-, second-, and fourth-order approximations
to English and varied display energy by manipulating both the exposure
duration and exposure illuminance. Their results, previously unpublished, are shown in Fig. 1. The top panel shows the proportion of letters
identified correctly as a function of approximation to English, illuminance, and exposure duration. The bottom panel shows the same data

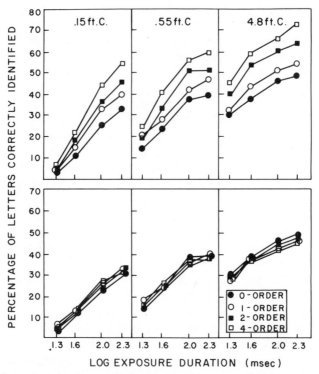

Fig. 1.   Accuracy of report as a function of approximation to English, exposure illuminance, and exposure duration. The data, previously unpublished, are taken from an
experiment reported by Mewhort and Tulving (1964).

after the higher order scores have been corrected by weighting them with an estimate of sequential redundancy, i.e., an estimate of the relative information per letter. The weights, taken from Tulving (1963), were 1.0, .85, .73, and .63 for zero- to fourth-order material, respectively.

As is clear in the figure, accuracy increases with increased energy in the display, where energy was contributed by increased illuminance or by increased exposure duration. More important, across the range of energy levels, the benefit of higher order pseudowords over zero-order letter strings remained proportional to the performance on the zero-order material.

Garner (1974, pp. 153–157) has distinguished *state* from *process* limitations to performance, and the data in Fig. 1 illustrate both kinds of limitation. State limitations are imposed when the representation of information is inadequate. Process limitations are encountered when subjects are unable to manipulate or transform information successfully.

In the present context, a state limitation to performance is illustrated by the effects of the energy manipulations. Energy controlled the overall level of performance. The control of performance is illustrated by the data shown in the bottom panel of Fig. 1, the scores corrected for information per letter.

A process limitation to performance is shown by the effects of the various orders of approximation English. Order of approximation altered performance, but the change was proportional to the level set by the energy factors. Thus, while the energy level controls overall level of performance, the familiarity effect is limited by the match between the material and subject's knowledge of English.

One implication of the pattern shown in Fig. 1 concerns the experimental design needed for studies of the familiarity effect. Because performance on each order of approximation to English is proportional to performance on zero-order material (across a wide range of energy levels), to show that a manipulation reduces the familiarity effect by introducing a processing limitation to performance, one must reduce the effect by an amount greater than the proportional constant. The latter requirement, in turn, calls into question studies which measure the familiarity effect while adjusting the energy level to match a designated performance level (e.g., Purcell, Stanovich, & Spector, 1978; see also Campbell & Mewhort, 1980, pp. 150–152).

The Miller *et al.* (1954) demonstration, along with the replication shown in Fig. 1, shows a clear familiarity effect which is independent of the subject's prior experience with the particular stimulus. As the demonstration involves nonsense material, the effect is also independent of the meaning of the stimulus. The combination indicates that the familiarity effect involves much more than use of simple whole-word templates: to explain the effect, one needs to think in terms of a system which uses knowledge of the statistical structure of letter use in English. Such knowledge may take the form of simple statistical relationships, or it may include the rules underlying English orthography (see Venezky, 1970, for an account of the latter rules).

B. Approaches to Theory

The familiarity effect illustrates a major role for prior knowledge in controlling performance, but it raises several major problems for theory: in particular, how do subjects represent and use knowledge? Obviously the knowledge is indirect—it is not prior experience with particular stimuli, as in standard learning tasks. Further, it does not reflect simple stimulus generalization when applied to novel stimuli. A related question is equally troublesome; namely, what class of theory can accommodate a knowledge-based model?

The questions can be approached from several directions. Some authorities suggest that perceptual systems find relevant stimuli while arriving at a representation of the world. J. J. Gibson (1966), for example, has defended the view that the world contains adequate stimuli; the job of past experience is to assist the developing organism in its search for higher order stimulus invariants. Knowledge or prior experience, for such a theory, helps the perceptual system find the relevant stimulus dimension so that the organism can react to particular stimuli.

Gibson's (1966) position is that perceiving is a matter of attaching meaning to stimuli; one learns, first, how to select the meaningful and, then, to react to it. Our position, in contrast, is that "stimuli" (in the sense of determinants of behavior) are constructs, they represent a blend of current input and past knowledge. The job of past experience, then, is relatively more radical; it determines the current input by adding information (not just by helping to select information).

Given that past knowledge contributes information to the analysis of current input, the next question concerns the architecture of the system which uses the knowledge. An understanding of the architecture prompts other questions. Where in the system, for example, is the user's knowledge stored? Architecture does not, by itself, indicate the type of information supplied at each stage or submechanism. As each submechanism may apply different knowledge, one must inquire separately about the knowledge for each.

Given an understanding of where the system applies knowledge—and how much information is used at various stages—the next question concerns how it is used. Traditional psychological theory is relatively uninformative on the point; accordingly, recent theory has adopted concepts from outside the discipline, for example from computational linguistics (Bobrow & Collins, 1975).

The work discussed here is concerned primarily with the problem of defining system architecture. The problem is complicated by historical circumstances: there are two distinct and major theoretical perspectives which guide current empirical work. The first, which we shall call the visual-science tradition, seeks a catalogue of empirical generalizations from which to predict performance. The emphasis is empirical, and it focuses on prediction of effects from known functional relations. The second, which we call the cognitive-science tradition, treats the organism as an abstract machine and seeks an explanation of behavior in terms of mechanisms which can reproduce the behavior. The emphasis is theoretical, and it focuses on development of theory adequate to produce the behavior in question.

1. The Visual-Science Tradition

The visual-science tradition reflects the perceptual interests of its proponents. Scientists working in the visual-science tradition identify themselves with several disciplines, including ophthalmology, optometry, and sensory physiology. When applied to questions of general behavior theory, the tradition directs one to a narrow range of questions. In terms of the familiarity effect in tachistoscopic presentation, for example, the question of main interest concerns whether or not the familiarity effect reflects perceptual or later processes. Typically, the question is raised in terms of a loose model implying a flow of information through (1) an input coding stage which has both extraction and interpretation components, (2) a storage stage, and (3) an output coding stage which has both report and comparison components (e.g., Krueger, 1975).

A perceptual locus for the familiarity effect is one affecting the first stage, the extraction of visual features. Visual features are usually considered in global terms. No distinction is made, for example, between the type of knowledge used when extracting features from a picture and that used when identifying letters (e.g., Kaufman, 1974, Ch. 12). Thus, the possibility of different forms of knowledge at the feature-extraction level is not usually addressed: features are atoms for the visual-science analysis. Krueger, for example, asserts "the question remains as to whether familiar visual objects, *such as words and faces,* [emphasis added] yield up their features any more readily to the experienced eye than do unfamiliar objects'' (Krueger, 1975, p. 949). Curiously, Krueger concluded that there is more than one familiarity effect, but he did not explore the implications of that view.

From the perspective of general behavior theory, the bias of the visual-science tradition is too narrow. Accordingly, the tradition has little to offer a theorist interested in behavior of the whole system. Nevertheless, its methodology has become popular in general psychology, and some aspects of the methodology deserve comment.

Investigators pursuing a purely perceptual familiarity effect frequently restrict themselves to forced-choice methodology, i.e., to tasks limited to yes–no or same–different judgments. In a representative forced-choice task, subjects would be shown a target letter at or near their visual threshold. The subjects would be required to indicate which letter had been presented by selecting it from a pair of response alternatives (e.g., Reicher, 1969; Wheeler, 1970).

In addition to the limitation on the range of responses, forced-choice methodology usually involves adjustment of performance by manipulating the stimulus energy. Such manipulations are tricky: they limit the generality of the results. It is not clear, for example, what issues relevant to reading are addressed in an energy-limited task: normal reading does not occur in the dark. Limiting the stimulus energy may well preclude use of word-identification processes used under normal circumstances and, as a consequence, may well force the use of desperate strategies to match the energy crisis.

An example of the difficulty raised by a mismatch of an experimental technique and its putative application is provided by the well-known study of the word-frequency effect by Goldiamond and Hawkins (1958). The word-frequency effect refers to the lower threshold for frequent words than for rare ones. Goldiamond and Hawkins argued that the effect is due entirely to the subject's guessing strategy. In support of their view, they showed an effect of response bias by omitting the stimulus in a simulated threshold study. While the response-bias effect in their task is clear, it is not clear that a parallel effect would occur in a situation with an adequate display: why should subjects adopt such a strategy when bona fide stimuli are present?

We suspect that subjects do not adopt such a guessing strategy, and there is experimental evidence to support our position. Mewhort (1970) and Lefton (1973) measured the contribution of response-bias to the familiarity effect for situations which provide an adequate stimulus; both studies found the contribution of response bias too small to account for more than about 25% of the effect which occurs in typical tachistoscopic experiments.

In light of the problems associated with paradigms involving energy-limited forced-choice displays, why are such paradigms popular? Their popularity reflects the aims and meta-theory of investigators in the visual-science tradition: the technique permits one to examine sensory factors contributing to the familiarity effect by minimizing memory-related, output-related, and all other so-called "artifactual" factors (see Smith & Spoehr, 1974, p. 238, for a defense of the position).

Use of forced-choice methodology, however, restricts one's view of the whole system. In particular, one cannot evaluate the flow of information through successive stages. Similarly, one cannot examine how successive stages interact. Instead, the methodology implies that memory, response, and bias factors—indeed, all of the factors controlled by its use—are neutral with respect to the "interesting" perceptual effects.

The ability to restrict the view of the system is, of course, exactly why the methodology is used. While the visual scientist's strong division between perception and later processes has some appeal, such a dichotomy is simplistic: too much of the system which produces behavior—the part controlled by use of forced-choice methods—is hidden from view. Thus, the methodology hides behavioral complexity and, once lost, it is hard to fit isolated parts into a whole model capable of producing behavior.

The problem is a traditional one with experimental psychology. Experimental psychology attempts to manage the complexity of behavior by adopting simplified measurement schemes. A bar-press does not capture the richness of a rat's behavior, but, according to radical behaviorists (e.g., Skinner, 1974) and those influenced by their posture, it provides a useful, i.e., complicated enough, measure of performance. Even unsophisticated models of the flow of information, however, acknowledge more than one transformation of data before "sensations" are converted to responses (e.g., Haber & Hershenson, 1973, p. 162). Realistic models require a sequence of stages which lead to a response, and several of the data-transformation stages could involve application of acquired knowledge (see Fodor, 1981, for a discussion of systematic approaches to behavior theory). The division between perception and later processes, nevertheless, underscores the major differences between the visual-science tradition and the cognitive-science position, to be discussed next.

2. The Cognitive-Science Tradition

The second tradition is concerned with performance in the task as a whole. In contrast to the visual-science approach, the aim is not to study particular sensory, i.e., early visual, processes. Rather, it treats experimental tasks as complete units of behavior; thus, the aim is to trace the flow of information through successive stages underlying performance, i.e., to develop an operational model of the processing in a task as a whole. In short, the goal is not to eliminate subprocesses from perceptual tasks; instead, it is to describe how the stages are connected and how information is handled at each stage. From the cognitive-science perspective, then, all aspects of performance in a task require explanation and are potentially salient for attempts to reproduce behavior in the task.

In a free-recall task, for example, subjects report in a left-to-right order. The preference for a left-to-right order is strong, and, as will be elaborated later, a body of data links it to the familiarity effect. Accepting the link, an explanation of an advantage for familiar sequences over random ones is sensible only if it includes a mechanism which also explains how subjects accomplish an ordered report for simultaneously presented material. Because the behavior is produced by one machine, it is risky to explain subphenomena in a piecemeal fashion; a piecemeal approach is likely to distort the relative importance of various mechanisms and to provide subcomponents which cannot fit together.

The example linking the familiarity effect to ordered report provides an excellent illustration of the gulf separating the visual- and cognitive-science traditions: the visual-science tradition is mute when faced with sequential behavior or with behavior attributable to mechanisms following the initial feature processes. Indeed, the sequential behavior implies a question which cannot be asked from within the visual-science tradition: What kind of processing system would yield a familiarity effect, a left-to-right report et cetera?

To answer the question, we start with the architecture of the system implied by the question. By architecture, we mean a general outline, a framework, of the system. The framework influences how particular mechanisms are structured, not how they accomplish particular tasks, i.e., the architecture indicates the logical structure of functions which must be performed. With an emphasis on system architecture, we use experiments to corroborate the general structure of the model. Presumably, the details of each component can be elaborated after the broad structure of the system has been outlined.

While our emphasis, and the emphasis within the cognitive-science community in general, is on theory construction, the corresponding emphasis within the visual-science community is on empirical generalization. The difference in emphasis has a parallel in two larger intellectual communities, the experimental-psychology and the artificial-intelligence communities. Experimental psychology approaches problems of behavior in much the same way as the visual-science tradition approaches the problem of seeing. The artificial-intelligence community, especially the part residing in departments of computing science, approaches theory construction with much the same emphasis we have described for the cognitive-science tradition.

Unfortunately, interaction between the experimental-psychology and the artificial-intelligence communities is minimal. Both groups suffer because of the lack of contact. Further, taking their respective positions to the extreme, both groups are wrong: experimental psychology clearly lacks adequate theory (Newell, 1973), and it could acquire useful theoretical tools from the artificial-intelligence community; Raphael (1976, chapters 2–5) has provided an excellent introduction to such techniques. Recent artificial-intelligence work does not pay sufficient attention to experimental work and, to an alarming extent, suffers an unfortunate reputation for armchair speculation. Experimentation is needed, for example, to illuminate the architecture which a formal model must have. Indeed, one artificial-intelligence worker, Hunt (1973), has come close to suggesting that such corroboration of a system's architecture is a necessary step in the development of a formal model.

Commenting on the gulf between the artificial-intelligence and the experimental-psychology communities, L. Miller (1978) has suggested that the two have different definitions of "success" in science. He characterizes the experimenter's approach as an attempt to establish classes of viable theories by eliminating classes of explanations for a particular phenomenon. Experimental workers assume, presumably, that there exists an abundance of adequate theory and that experimentation is needed to reduce the number of serious contenders. Artificial-intelligence workers, in contrast, attempt to build competent working models of circumscribed problems. Such work is needed, presumably, because adequate models of performance do not exist. As Miller notes, most artificial-intelligence theorists believe that, once working models have been developed, experimental tests of their adequacy to explain human behavior should be straightforward.

3. Comparing Models

Given a mix of experimental and theoretical work, the role of experimentation remains cloudy. When proposing an account of a particular set of data, we occasionally forget that other models can also explain the same data and that no single set of results can confirm a theory. A single set of results can only fail to disconfirm the theory. Parenthetically, we should note that throughout our discussion we have ignored the distinction sometimes made between a theory and a model.

If experiments cannot, strictly speaking, confirm a theory, how can we narrow the range of theories which contend for our attention? The answer lies in the complexity, i.e., the number of separate phenomena, which we ask the theory to explain simultaneously. As the body of data to be explained simultaneously is increased—by requiring the model to remain consistent with new (and old) evidence—the number of models competent to the task decreases. It is the increasing complexity of the fit between the world and competent models of the world which reduces the number of alternate solutions.

If experiments cannot confirm a theory, then, a series of experiments which conform to predictions from a theory can corroborate the theory (see Popper, 1935/1968, Ch. 10, for an extended discussion of corroboration versus verification). Such corroboration lends credibility to a theory by increasing the complexity of the body of data with which a competitive theory must deal. Theories, even if true, cannot be proven to be true; at best, a theory predicts well. A theory, then, is a summary of knowledge about the world, and its value is epistemological, not ontological.

If a model is to be considered a legitimate alternate to an incumbent theory, it should deal with the same data explained by the incumbent. If it does not, comparison of the two theories is like a comparison of apples to oranges: the domain of the evidence, i.e., the body of data to be explained, should match. If one account explains only a subset of that explained by the other, the preferred model is the one which explains the larger body of data. If both competitors explain the same data equally well, the model preferred is the one which minimizes preconditions and assumptions, i.e., the more elegant of the two.

While theory comparison in ideal situations is straightforward, such situations are, unfortunately, seldom encountered. Instead of a contrast between two equally competent and equally comprehensive accounts, we usually encounter a contrast between barely competent accounts which involve imperfectly overlapping empirical domains.

If two theories do not explain equivalent bodies of evidence, proponents for either position usually resort to a defense based on extra-data considerations. Estes (1978), for example, suggests that theories based on structural factors are to be preferred over theories based on cognitive factors. His reasons reflect a philosophic bias rather than corroboration by experiment.

Estes (1978) acknowledges that both early visual and subsequent cognitive factors can play a role in determining performance. He suggests, however, that "a shift to linguistically meaningful stimuli . . . does not reduce the importance of continuing attention to the basic physical parameters" (p. 165). As a consequence, he argues that "it must be a sound strategy routinely to consider the degree to which phenomena arising in studies of letter or word perception can be interpreted in terms of more basic visual processes before considering the introduction of hypotheses . . . of higher-order processes or mechanisms" (p. 166).

Estes's (1978) position has long-standing precedent. Cattell (1885b) considered the role of visual acuity to be axiomatic: "Experiments are not necessary to show that books ... should be printed in large clear type" (p. 306). Nevertheless, Estes's position is in doubt on empirical grounds. Following an extensive review of the earliest literature, Woodworth (1938/1950) concluded that "the speed and accuracy of reading are determined more by the central meaning-getting process than by peripheral factors. The normal eye, and even the eye with slight optical defects . . . are [sic] more than adequate for reading" (p. 736). Also, in a modern study of reading which included measurements of both sensory and cognitive factors, Jackson and McClelland (1979) "failed to find any reason to reject Woodworth's conclusion" (p. 170).

Our point is not based on the empirical evidence, however. Estes's (1978) position implies a sequential rule, and the major difficulty imposed by the rule is theoretical. The sequential rule gives reductionist mechanisms a privileged status and betrays a considerable reluctance to accept the role of higher order mechanisms. To paraphrase W. L. M. King (a former Prime Minister of Canada), not necessarily higher order variables, but higher order variables if necessary.[2] Unfortunately, because a mechanism can be shown to have an effect once, it does not follow that it should be considered a likely candidate in every situation. Further, such a strategy can lead to serious error. Like a radical behaviorist, a theorist bound by the sequential rule may defend the indefensible too long (see also Harcum, 1970, for an elaboration of the point).

The point can be illustrated, in concrete terms, with reference to the bar-probe partial-report task. In the bar-probe task, subjects are shown a row of letters followed by a bar probe indicating which letter to report. Accuracy of report in the task usually takes a W shape across the letter array.

To illustrate the reductionist approach, Estes (1978, pp. 188–189) derived the W shape of the stimulus-position curve for the bar-probe experiment from an analysis of two factors, lateral masking (lateral inhibition) and the retinal-sensitivity gradient. Retinal sensitivity decreases monotonically from the center to the periphery. But, neighboring letters are subject to lateral masking, i.e., to inhibition due to the proximity of their contours. Estes argues that "the lateral masking effects would necessarily be greatest in the interior of the display, where all letters

---

[2] The reference is to a remark by King in the House of Commons on June 19, 1942. He was discussing a controversial matter, the possibility of overseas war-time service by men conscripted into the Canadian Armed Services, and suggested, "Not necessarily conscription but conscription if necessary."

have neighbors, and least at the ends, where each terminal letter has only a single neighbor and blank space on the other side. Combining these considerations, we are prepared for the W shape" (p. 188).

Estes's (1978) derivation of the W-shaped accuracy curve focuses on identification processes, and his preferred theory discourages investigation of other aspects of behavior in the task. As Mewhort and Campbell (1978) have demonstrated, however, the shape of the accuracy curve reflects difficulty in localization, not difficulty in letter identification (see also Campbell & Mewhort, 1980, Expt. 1; Mewhort, Campbell, Marchetti, & Campbell, 1981). Further, Mewhort and Campbell (1978, Expt. 1) show the W-shaped function under conditions which minimized misidentification. Thus, their demonstration leaves little room for theoretical maneuver: Estes's derivation focused on the wrong class of mechanism.

III. A MODEL FOR TACHISTOSCOPIC TASKS

Consider a typical tachistoscopic experiment from the subject's point of view. Arriving in the laboratory, he is given a verbal description of the task, a few practice trials, and he sets to work.

To carry out the task, the subject applies a set of processing mechanisms which execute the behavior. If the task requires, for example, report of several letters following the tachistoscopic presentation, he will require mechanisms for seeing the material, for naming the items, for organizing and storing the material until report, and for producing the report itself. The set of mechanisms combine to produce the behavior. Thus, understanding how the subject performs the task can be accomplished by understanding how each mechanism functions, both alone and in combination.

The experimenter keeps an edited record of the subject's behavior. By suggesting that he keeps an edited record, we acknowledge that the experimenter records the letters reported by the subject while ignoring other aspects of his behavior, such as coughs, complaints, exclamations, questions, et cetera. Thus, we acknowledge that the experimenter collects an abstraction of the subject's behavior in a task. The abstraction is a first-order measure of behavior.

Abstractions based on the first-order measure provide, of course, compact summaries of the behavior. One should not lose sight, however, of the initial data reduction: the choice of the initial measure reflects the experimenter's biases concerning the causes of the behavior. Teller (1980) reminds us of the same point in slightly different terms. Describing a principle she calls the "Nothing Mucks It Up Proviso," she suggests that it is useful to list "things that have to *not* happen [emphasis added] in order for a simple, elegant theory to do the work one wants it to do" (p. 176). To her list, one should add a list of potential behavior which could, had a broader measurement scheme been used, disqualify the theory (see Butler, 1980a, 1980b, for examples).

A. The Role of Instructions

Instructions and practice are essential parts of a task. Their importance follows from the nature of the tasks which we ask subjects to perform during an experiment: from the subject's perspective, the tasks we require in experiments are like games. The experimenter contrives the environment and provides instructions defining the rules of the game, i.e., the task and the legal responses. Subjects use the instructions to decide how to carry out the task.

To decide how to carry out a task, a subject must first understand the task, i.e., he must build an internal representation of the problem implied by the task. The internal representation, in turn, guides the subject's strategy for carrying out the task. Without instructions (and practice to confirm his choice), then, a subject's behavior is unlikely to map onto the set of responses which the experimenter has defined to be legal; indeed, without instructions a subject is more likely to leave in boredom than to supply responses of the sort required by an experimenter.

Without instructions and practice, then, subjects are unlikely to provide useful experimental data. The role of instructions is, nevertheless, usually neglected in accounts of subjects' performance. The neglect is not haphazard; simply put, it reflects the difficulty of the topic. It also reflects a bias, typical of the visual-science tradition, to associate experimental manipulations with particular components of a system on the basis of meta-theoretic considerations.

To explain how subjects use instructions, one would have to include enough detail to show how a subject could build an internal representation of the task from the instructions and, then, show how he could use the representation to solve the problem implied by the task (cf. von Königslöw, 1974). Such an account would have to describe both language-comprehension and problem-solving skills in depth. Both problems, however, are major research topics, and although advances have been made in understanding aspects of problem solving (e.g., Newell & Simon, 1972), our understanding of language comprehension is in its infancy. Thus, a model for tachistoscopic tasks which details how a subject uses instructions is well beyond the scope of most literature on reading and visual processing.

We do not intend to offer a complete account, i.e., one including the relevant language-comprehension and problem-solving skills. Nevertheless, it is important to consider the role of instructions in the analysis of performance, even in an account which does not explain in detail how instructions are used. The point gained by considering the role of instructions is a matter of theoretical perspective and concerns the artificial nature of the processing system.

The view that subjects assign resources to solve an experimental problem implies an active problem-solving mechanism. In effect, the problem-solving mechanism builds an information-processing system to execute the task from the repertoire of submechanisms at its disposal. We shall call the problem-solving mechanism the *executive*.

Inasmuch as it is derived in response to both the goals of the executive and the environment in which it is placed, both of which can change, the system which actually executes the behavior is artificial (artificial in the sense defined by Simon, 1969, 1980). When we describe performance in terms of an information-processing model, then, we mean a model within a model, i.e., we mean the artificial system established by the executive.

For the reasons mentioned earlier, we cannot describe the executive in detail. Nevertheless, some general characteristics are clear. For example, to be able to assign resources the executive must have both reflective knowledge and the ability to act. It must "know," for example, the capabilities of each submechanism, and it must know how sets of submechanisms cooperate when assembled into a system. Finally, it must be able to assess the demands of the task and set a particular set of resources into place, i.e., it must be able to set up a system within a system.

The suggestion that tasks are executed by an artificial system, i.e., a system within a system, raises several major theoretical problems. Three are particularly troublesome.

1. If the executive has available a large repertoire of submechanisms, the number of combinations of submechanisms must also be large, and an experimental analysis of performance based on a small number of tasks must fail because it cannot explore the full range of possible systems. Indeed, if the repertoire is large, analysis of even a large subset of tasks is unlikely to involve all combinations of the components. As a result, if the repertoire available to the executive is large, a model for performance in a particular task risks becoming a theoretical farce, an appeal to a unique assignment of resources, an assignment resembling a deus ex machina.

One implication of the large number of combinations of submechanisms associated with complex systems concerns the role of experimentation. As noted earlier, some scientists use experiments to build sets of empirical generalizations from which predictions can be derived. A strategy which seeks empirical generalizations—the empirical laws of behavior—is futile when dealing with large systems: it is infeasible to test all combinations of submechanisms in a complex system, and it is impossible to define the number of combinations without a full knowledge of the system. In addition, as Simon (1969, 1980) has argued, the quest for laws of behavior often confuses the description of adapting processes in an artificial science with the search for invariants in a physical science.

2. Even with a moderate number of assignable resources, an account derived from an empirical analysis cannot escape the ad hoc unless the theoretical basis for assignment of resources is clear. Freudian theory illustrates the problem. It entails a small number of major factors, but it permits a too flexible assignment with the result that one cannot predict behavior but can "explain" almost any behavior after the fact. In short, lacking a formal description of the executive, the rules for assignment of resources must provide reasonable constraints or the resulting account is likely to be too flexible to be plausible.

3. The final problem reflects the historical character of the information processing involved in reading. It is a subtle problem and, for that reason, is more difficult than the earlier ones. The executive requires knowledge, particularly knowledge of the capabilities of each submechanism or set of subprocesses. In addition, the subprocesses may require local knowledge. Because the system involves knowledge, it faces two problems which we call the bootstrap and variance problems.

Formal description of knowledge-based systems is a focus for current theory, and, as noted earlier, development of an appropriate language in which such systems may be described is a major research topic in itself. Even if a detailed description of knowledge-based systems were possible, however, the developmental details of such a system would not necessarily follow from the account. Thus, knowledge-based systems face a "bootstrap" problem—the development of a system from simple resources across growth and practice (cf. Fodor, 1976, p. 90ff).

In addition to the bootstrap problem, knowledge-based systems also face a "variance" problem: knowledge does not enjoy a genetic code to limit the number of solutions to problems, especially across practice with problem-solving situations. Thus, the fact that people adopt similar solutions, i.e., assign similar resources, is, by itself, remarkable.

The bootstrap and variance problems are, of course, not unique to the information-processing perspective. Nevertheless, that perspective quickly encourages a realistic appraisal of the problems. We suspect that part of the appeal of simplistic views, such as behaviorism and the learning theory it spawned, is the difficulty of solving the variance problem exposed by more complete views.

B. Resources and Tasks

To outline the model, we shall describe a series of processing resources available to the executive and discuss their role in an artificial processing system. To organize the description, it is convenient to outline the resources in the context of several simple tachistoscopic tasks, in particular, the whole-report free-recall task and the partial-report bar-probe task.

Some tasks can be performed in several ways, depending on the particulars of the situation. Others do not permit the same flexibility. From our perspective, tasks which can be performed in several ways involve different artificial systems, i.e., systems based on a different assignment of resources. The choice of a particular assignment depends, presumably, on the details of the situation.

The tasks selected to illustrate the components of the model, the free-recall and bar-probe cases, are relatively inflexible in terms of the resources they require. Indeed, the two tasks are used to introduce the model because they share some of the same mechanisms and because their use of particular mechanisms is relatively immune to changing circumstances.

1. The Free-Recall Task

The free-recall task is, perhaps, the most straightforward tachistoscopic task. In the free-recall case, subjects are shown a row of letters for a brief interval and are required to report as many of the letters as possible. No restrictions are placed on the order of report; indeed, order of report is a principal dependent measure describing performance.

The basic task is often complicated with extra demands, such as special instructions concerning report. Before considering such complications, however, several aspects of unconstrained performance deserve mention. First, the task yields a healthy familiarity effect; subjects report more letters from a familiar letter string than from a string of random letters (e.g., Miller *et al.*, 1954). Second, subjects report in a left-to-right fashion; the tendency to report from left to right is greater for familiar sequences than for randomly derived ones (e.g., Bryden, 1966b; Mewhort, 1966, 1974). Finally, report involves runs of letters, a characteristic which suggests that the material reported has been organized into subunits corresponding to the runs (e.g., Campbell, 1979; Campbell & Mewhort, 1980).

Tracing the flow of information on a typical free-recall trial, our theoretical analysis starts at the level of visual features. In particular, it begins with a feature buffer which stores the set of features which have been extracted from the display.

Visual features represent the object shown. For a series of letters, they involve subletter units—line segments, the presence of curves, of angles and intersections, and of similar elements—held in a real space. By real space, we mean that the features represent the visual display in a way which preserves information concerning the spatial arrangement among the features.

Visual features need not be extracted simultaneously. Some current theories consider extraction of features—the process by which characters are filtered by the nervous system to yield elementary and subletter units—to be of basic interest (e.g., Bjork & Murray, 1977; Chastain, 1977). Our account, in contrast, starts with the collection of features taken together, the set stored in the feature buffer.

Starting the analysis with the set of features taken together is somewhat arbitrary. The position precludes consideration of a number of interesting sensory phenomena. Granting that feature extraction is extended in time, features may shift from one location to another during the extraction process (Wolford, 1975). Because feature-shift occurs before the features are stored on the buffer, it is invisible to the model, i.e., the model does not deal with events prior to the feature buffer. Furthermore, the feature buffer absorbs time-of-arrival differences associated with feature extraction—a characteristic of buffers in any real-time system. Thus, the arbitrary starting point should not cause trouble provided that the theory is not asked to address events associated with feature extraction over time.

The initial stage in any analysis is arbitrary. A theory which starts with single features, for example, could be accused of ignoring subfeature units, and so forth. Nevertheless, our starting position is not theoretically neutral. Theories which focus on feature extraction over time usually invoke a decision mechanism which can act on partial, i.e., not-yet-complete, information. Our position reflects some unease with accounts which suggest a decision mechanism set to respond on the basis of partial information. Such a mechanism is tuned for speed rather than for accuracy and, as a result, has difficulty assessing feature information in light of extra-feature knowledge, such as letter-frequency information. The problem is similar to the one raised in connection with Goldiamond and Hawkins's (1958) suggestions concerning response bias: just as response bias may not apply when subjects have adequate perceptual information, a system tuned for speed may not parallel the system used in more relaxed circumstances.

In common with all feature models, the kind of elementary unit which can serve as a feature is fixed; it is a subcharacter unit. The latter point is basic: without agreement on fundamental units, feature analysis becomes a metaphor for pattern recognition. In other words, if one were free to change the kind of unit which can comprise a feature, e.g., from a subletter to a letter, or from a subletter to a supraletter element, the idea of a feature analysis becomes a deus ex machina rather than a testable hypothesis concerning pattern recognition.

The basic feature data held in the feature buffer are used by a character-recognition mechanism. The character-recognition mechanism carries out a series of logically distinct operations. The first operation is a feature-bundle operation which, like a figure-ground calculation, sorts the features into bundles associated with discrete characters. The bundles are formed on the basis of global properties of the stimulus configuration.

The next operation concerns character recognition. A recognition operator notes the presence and the absence of particular features. The pattern of presence/absence is used to build a list of candidate letters, one for each position represented by a feature bundle. Choice of a letter from each candidate list is based on spatially conditioned letter-frequency information. In particular, letter-frequency information serves as the prior distribution to a Bayesian operator (see Hanson et al., 1976, for an excellent discussion of such a mechanism). By spatially conditioned information, we mean frequency information taking into account the position of the character in the letter string (cf. Mason, 1975).

The letter-recognition mechanism, then, uses two kinds of information: the basic feature data and letter-frequency knowledge. The use of letter-frequency information is responsible for a familiarity effect, i.e., the recognition mechanism will be more accurate when dealing with familiar strings (see Campbell & Mewhort, 1980; Mewhort et al., 1981). Nevertheless, it is important not to overstate the familiarity effect associated with the character-recognition mechanism. As Campbell and Mewhort discuss at length, a later processing mechanism—one which uses rules of orthography instead of simple frequency information—is responsible for the bulk of the familiarity effect illustrated in the simple free-recall task.

The output of the letter-recognition process is stored in a character buffer. The representation in the character buffer is abstract. By abstract, we mean that the character buffer holds identified characters, items with labels, not basic features. Further, the characters, themselves, are abstractions not images. The character-recognition mechanism defines a blank character, for example, in terms of the height/width relation of the characters, and the blank character is stored in the character buffer as a labeled item, not as a linear distance. Thus, although it preserves the relative spatial position of the characters in the string, the buffer is not a pictorial representation.

The character buffer is the second major data representation suggested in the model (the first is the feature buffer). Like the feature buffer, the character buffer absorbs time-of-arrival differences associated with processing operations which precede it. But, it acknowledges events during the preceding operations. An example is provided by a study reported by Davidson, Fox, and Dick (1973). They presented a row of five letters followed by a single-character masking stimulus. The mask followed a voluntary eye movement which moved the subject's point of fixation two letter positions to one side. The perceived location of the masking stimulus did not match the position of its informational effect: the mask reduced report from one letter position but appeared to be at another position. The informational disruption was in retinal space, reflecting the impact of the mask at the feature buffer. The perceived location was in real space, reflecting compensation at the character-buffer for the voluntary eye movement.

Letter recognition implies data reduction; not all details of the image representation at the feature buffer are preserved at the character buffer. But, the letter-recognition process also implies data generation; a blank character, as an abstraction, is a "generated" item. Similarly, the use of letter-frequency information during letter recognition adds information.

While the feature and character buffers are major storage systems, the character-identification mechanism requires some local storage within the process itself. The local storage is of two types: the first is the working memory needed by the process itself, and the second is stored knowledge. The latter memory is particularly important inasmuch as it represents aspects of the knowledge subjects have acquired by learning to read.

The character buffer provides basic data for the next processing operator, the scan-parse mechanism. The scan-parse mechanism accepts the character string and applies a series of orthographic rules to derive new units. The derived units range from single-letter units to multiletter units, depending on the familiarity of the character string. That is, the units reflect an interaction of the rules and the particular letter string.

The scan-parse mechanism passes the units to short-term memory, the third major storage system involved in the task. The transfer normally involves a left-to-right order. By ordering the units, the scan-parse mechanism converts the data from a parallel (spatial) array in the character buffer to a temporal string in short-term memory. The conversion to temporal form provides the basis for orderly rehearsal and sequential report.

The orthographic rules used by the scan-parse mechanism concern higher order spelling constraints and are not simple letter-frequency relationships. The rules, for example, distinguish vowels from consonants and require knowledge different from the frequency-based information used in letter recognition. Thus, there are two separate types of orthographic information involved in the task.

The scan-parse mechanism has much in common with a mechanism suggested by Smith and Spoehr (1974). Following an extensive and thoughtful review of the literature, they suggest a basic architecture similar to that suggested here. Specifically, they propose that subjects parse a word into basic units, called vocalic center groups. The parser acts on postcategorical data, and the derived units serve as basic data for lexical access. Their parser, like the scan-parse mechanism, involves a grammar of the sort outlined by Hansen and Rodgers (1968).

Although Smith and Spoehr (1974) suggest views similar to ours, there are a number of differences. Consistent with the present account, for example, they argued that the parser requires identified letters, i.e., postcategorical data, as input, but they did not expand on the implications of that view. Such a view implies, for example, two data storage systems, a pre- and a postcategorical system. The presence of two systems raises the possibility that some manipulations, such as visual masking, can affect the two systems differently. They treat visual masking methodologically, however—in the spirit of the visual-science tradition—without considering the implications of the manipulation in a dual-buffer system. As we shall describe later in detail, a mask does not act in a unitary fashion; it has different effects on the feature and character buffers.

In the Smith and Spoehr (1974) theory, the parser is responsible for familiarity effects. In our view, by contrast, there are three separate familiarity effects, one associated with letter-recognition, one associated with the scan-parse mechanism, and one associated with rehearsal at the short-term memory level. In addition, while Smith and Spoehr stressed the construction of derived units and related the units to speech, they did not recognize the data-structure implication of the new unit. In particular, they did not discuss the change from a parallel or spatial representation to a sequential form. The change, however, is basic to understanding order-of-report phenomena in free-recall.

Finally, Smith and Spoehr (1974) rely exclusively on a grammar developed by Hansen and Rodgers (1968) for a study of speech production.

We have extended the rules by including aspects of English orthography. Venezky's (1970) work has been particularly helpful in guiding the extensions. The Hansen and Rodgers (1968) grammar treats a word as a string of consonant and vowel symbols, and forms vocalic-center groups by dividing the string into units according to six simple rules. For a word with a VCCCV series embedded within it, for example, the rules suggest a split into either . . .VC/CCV. . . or . . .V/CCCV. . . . In both examples, leading and trailing consonants would be attached to the initial and final vowel, respectively.

Because it was developed for an application concerning speech production rules, the Hansen and Rodgers (1968) grammar cannot be applied directly in reading. Consider the impact of diphthongs, e.g., the *ai* in *paint*. Because it does not deal with adjacent vowels, i.e., a . . .VV. . . string, the grammar could not apply to such words. Similarly, the grammar has no rules for *diphthong* or *diphtheria* because of the juxtaposition of the central four consonants, *phth*. Finally, because it would treat both the *e* in *love* and the *e* in *context* equivalently, the grammar does not apply to words involving a "silent" *e*. Smith and Spoehr (1974) did not discuss such awkward cases and, consequently, did not indicate how they would handle the problem. Such neglect, however, is not a serious criticism: their interest was expository, and provided their illustrations are well edited, the thrust of their account is clear without becoming lost in the detail of a formal model.

For the scan-parse mechanism, we have extended the rules for parsing by including a series of preliminary orthographic and word-level syntactic rules. For example, our model recognizes certain diphthongs and some consonant clusters, e.g., the *th* in *thinking,* the *ch* and *ck* in *check,* and the *ph* in *telephone.* In addition, it recognizes the silent *e* in *love,* and, by applying adverbial and plural decomposition rules, it recognizes the same relation in *loves* and *lovely.*

Preliminary experimental work using a computer program to simulate the scan-parse mechanism has provided encouraging results. Mewhort and Campbell (1977), for example, applied the scan-parse mechanism to the pseudowords listed by Hirata and Bryden (1971, Table 2). Their list includes examples for several orders of approximation to English and, as one might expect, the scan-parse mechanism produced syllable-like units when applied to the familiar strings and a long string of unconnected letters when applied to the randomly derived strings. Using a simple free-recall task, Mewhort and Campbell showed that the number of units derived by the scan-parse mechanism predicted the rank for performance on individual pseudowords relatively well.

It is easy to overstate the success of a single simulation of the scan-parse mechanism. In the illustration provided by Mewhort and Campbell (1977), for example, it is not clear that alternate parsing schemes—even a simple vowel-counting algorithm—might not predict remarkably well. Also, there are a number of cases for which the extended rules do not apply. For example, while *th* forms a familiar consonant cluster in *father,* it does not cluster in *sweetheart.* We sincerely wish that spelling could retain the hyphen, as in sweet-heart. Similarly, we note a deplorable trend to create adjectives from two nouns without including the hyphen and to create ambiguous vowel clusters by leaving the hyphen out of words such as re-evaluate and re-establish. The result creates trouble for our simulation of the scan-parse mechanism, for our own reading speed, and, likely, for the beginning reader.

The scan-parse mechanism passes material to short-term memory for storage until report. We assume that material in short-term memory must either be refreshed by a rehearsal operation or be lost. The units for rehearsal are those created by the scan-parse mechanism. Further, rehearsal is extended in time, and the usual organization for rehearsal is taken from the order-of-arrival to short-term memory, i.e., it takes a left-to-right order. Our conception of rehearsal and its role in organization of report owes much to the model suggested by Feigenbaum and Simon (1962).

With appropriate instructions, subjects can delay rehearsal for a brief period. By delaying rehearsal, subjects can organize material in an order other than the usual left-to-right order. But, if the instructions are delayed too long (about 500 to 1000 milliseconds) rehearsal must start without the benefit of instructions, and subjects typically default to the order implied by the time of arrival.

Rehearsal is one of several operations which can be carried out concurrently. Other examples of operations which can be carried out concurrently include listening, switching attention, and the act of reporting itself (see Mewhort, Thio, & Birkenmayer, 1971). Such time sharing, however, is done at cost: there is a limited capacity to carry out operations (cf. Moray, 1967; Posner & Rossman, 1965). Although rehearsal and report can coexist, for example, report causes interference to rehearsal and vice versa. Such interference, in turn, causes loss of information during report.

Finally, the data passed to short-term memory—now in temporal form—serve as basic data for several processes, e.g., for pronunciation processes and for lexical-access processes. Note that the derived units are not, strictly speaking, in a speech code. Similarly, although lexical access uses the same data used to pronounce the word, the look-up process is not mediated by speech mechanisms.

2. The Bar-Probe Task

The bar-probe paradigm was created by Averbach and Coriell (1961). They wished to study early visual processes and developed the task to minimize limitations to performance imposed by short-term memory. In the bar-probe task, subjects are shown a row of letters. Instead of instructions to report as much as possible, the subjects are required to report one item. The item required is indicated by a bar marker, usually an arrow placed above the relevant item.

Accuracy of report is greater with familiar letter strings than with random ones. The bulk of subjects' errors are location errors; across a linear letter display, accuracy of report takes a W shape, while location errors assume a complementary M shape. Finally, most of the location errors reflect report of items adjacent to the letter probed, and, although accuracy of report increases with increased familiarity of the material, the occurrence of location errors is not affected by the familiarity of the material (Mewhort *et al.*, 1981).

Tracing the flow of information during a trial, our theoretical analysis starts, as in the corresponding free-recall case, at the feature buffer. As noted in connection with the free-recall task, the feature buffer stores the basic feature data and provides input to the character-identification mechanism. The identification mechanism combines the feature data with letter-frequency knowledge, and its output is stored in the character buffer. Thus, to the level of the character buffer, processing is similar for both the free-recall and the bar-probe tasks.

In a free-recall task, the next stage of processing is the scan-parse mechanism. In the bar-probe task, however, the scan-parse mechanism is not used. Instead, an attentional mechanism is used to transfer an item to short-term memory. The attentional mechanism acts on data represented spatially, i.e., it searches material in the character buffer. Accuracy of its search depends on several factors such as the number of items in the array and the existence of local anchors (e.g., Mewhort & Campbell, 1978). After finding an item in the character buffer, the attentional mechanism moves it to short-term memory for storage until report.

Why does the executive assign the scan-parse mechanism to the free-recall task and the attentional mechanism to the bar-probe task? The answer reflects the different demands of the two tasks. In a bar-probe task, subjects are required to report one item, and the instruction concerning which item to report is provided by a direct spatial indicator, the bar probe. Thus, the subjects are encouraged to use the spatial data representation. For the free-recall task, in contrast, subjects are required to report several items. The requirement to report several items forces the subjects to organize a verbal report. Such a report is sequential and requires that the data be in a temporal form. To convert the material to the required temporal form (by transferring it to short-term memory), the executive requires the scan-parse mechanism.

Like the scan-parse mechanism, the attentional mechanism passes material from the character buffer to short-term memory. Although the two devices provide similar services—both are transfer mechanisms— they differ on a number of other dimensions. The attentional mechanism, for example, keeps individual items separate whereas the scan-parse mechanism integrates individual letters into supraletter units. (An exception, of course, occurs for difficult letter strings, such as a series of consonants.) Also, whereas the scan-parse mechanism uses orthographic rules and, thereby, contributes to the familiarity effect, the attentional mechanism does not change the status of the items and does not contribute to the familiarity effect. Thus, whereas the familiarity effect found in free-recall reflects the contribution of both the character-identification mechanism and that of the scan-parse mechanism, the effect in a corresponding bar-probe task reflects only the contribution of the identification mechanism.

C. An Overview of the Model

The two tasks illustrate the main components of the model. A diagram illustrating the flow of information for both tasks is presented in Fig. 2.

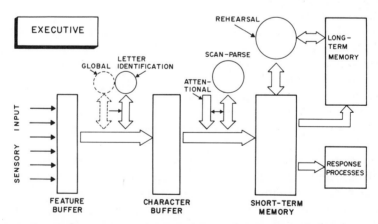

Fig. 2. A schematic outline of the model. Data buffers are indicated by rectangles and the data move from left to right as indicated by the broad arrows. Processors which move data and which contain knowledge are indicated by circles. Control signals which permit one processor to lock out another are indicated by line arrows, and the arrowheads indicate the direction of control.

Data are assumed to move from left to right across the figure as represented by the broad arrows. Processes which move data and which include knowledge, i.e., the global mechanism, the letter-identification mechanism, the scan-parse mechanism, and rehearsal processes, are represented by circles. The major data buffers are indicated by rectangles. Control signals which permit one mechanism to lock out another are indicated by line arrows.

Lacking a formal description of the executive—the mechanism responsible for assembling the systems for the two tasks—the steps by which the executive assigns the different resources must remain obscure. Nevertheless the outcome can be predicted for a particular task by considering the set of mechanisms available to the executive along with the nature of the processing required to complete the task.

The executive uses the scan-parse mechanism in a free-recall case because that mechanism provides services which match the demands of the task. Consider the demands first: a free-recall task involves a sequential report. A sequential report requires organization, and organization of report, particularly a report extended in time, implies rehearsal. Rehearsal involves processing at the short-term memory level; thus, the task requires a mechanism which can facilitate the flow of information through to the short-term memory level. Next, consider the services offered by the scan-parse mechanism: it prepackages material for efficient rehearsal and transfers material more quickly than the attentional mechanism. Both features match the requirement of the task, and because the match is good, the executive assigns the scan-parse mechanism in a free-recall case.

The bar-probe case, in contrast, requires subjects to report a single element and provides a direct spatial cue indicating which element to report. The demands are quite different from those associated with the free-recall case: instead of the sequential report and the rehearsal operations demanded in the free-recall case, the subject needs to report only one letter. Further, as the probe is spatial, there is a clear incentive to use the spatial data representation (the character buffer) rather than the temporal representation (short-term memory)—such use facilitates indexing with the probe. Because it provides services which match the requirements of the task, the executive uses the attentional mechanism in the bar-probe case.

The relation between the task demands and the processing system used to satisfy the demands is not straightforward. Suppose, for example, that one were to change the bar-probe task to a digit-probe example. In the digit-probe case, instead of using an arrow to index a particular letter, a digit is provided to index the letter. For example, instead of an arrow over the letter fourth from the left of a linear array, the digit four (4) would be presented to indicate the same element. Because both tasks present the same material and require the same response, one might think that the executive would assign the same processing mechanisms to both the digit- and the bar-probe cases. Such an assignment, however, would ignore a major factor separating the tasks. While the probe is a direct spatial indicator in the bar-probe example, it is an indirect indicator in the digit-probe case. To use the digit probe, one must count items.

Counting, like rehearsal, can be accomplished easily at the short-term memory level. The attentional mechanism—the mechanism which uses the spatial indicator in the bar-probe case—cannot count and, thus, cannot use the digit probe. Therefore, although the tasks are similar in some respects, they cannot be executed with the same processing mechanisms. Instead, because the digit-probe case requires counting to use the probe, the material must be transferred to short-term memory, and the executive will use the scan-parse mechanism to move the material to short-term memory. Despite the similarity of the stimulus and response, then, the resources required in the digit-probe and the free-recall tasks are closer than those required in the digit- and the bar-probe cases.

IV. EVIDENCE RELATING TO THE MODEL

Word identification and reading were among the first topics addressed by the new psychology in the late 1880s, and both topics remained in the mainstream of experimental psychology until the advent of behaviorism in the second decade of this century. The early work was motivated by interest in educational applications and focused on the process of reading (see Kintsch & Vipond, 1979). In the latter respect, it resembles modern cognitive psychology. When behaviorism banished cognitive processes in the second decade of this century, however, emphasis on the process of reading was lost, and research on reading came to be dominated by work on curriculum, i.e., by work contrasting one curriculum against another.

During the prebehaviorist period, experimental debate centered on the nature of the stimulus used to identify a word. In particular, debate concerned a whole-word versus a letter-unit account of word identification. Reviews of the early work are provided by Woodworth (1938/1950) and by Huey (1908/1968). For our purposes, examples of work by Cattell and by Pillsbury illustrate the kind of argument attempted.

Pillsbury (1897) studied reading by asking subjects to read words containing misprints. Cattell (1885a, 1885b) studied the process by considering the time required to identify words, letters, and nonsense letter strings. Both studies were carried out against a background of opinion which assumed that subjects read in a letter-by-letter fashion, literally spelling to themselves. In contrast to the background opinion, however, both lines of evidence pointed to a whole-word account of the reading process.

Pillsbury (1897), for example, noted that subjects could identify a word even when it contained a misprint, such as *fashxon* for *fashion*. He also noted that, while they can read over such a misprint, subjects do notice the misspelling, i.e., subjects do notice fine visual detail. Nevertheless, the ability to read over misprints suggests that reading is not a simple letter-by-letter spelling-like process, and Pillsbury argued that subjects do not use a letter-by-letter spelling-like strategy. He remained agnostic, however, concerning the nature of subjects' strategy.

Cattell (1885a, 1885b) adopted a more extreme position by arguing for a whole-word account. His position was derived mainly from an analysis of reading-time measurements; he showed both that subjects take less time to name a word than to name a single letter and that reading unrelated letters takes longer than reading the same letters arranged as a word. Because one can read a word as rapidly as one of its constituent letters, Cattell argued that we do not construct words on a letter-by-letter basis and suggested, instead, that we read words as wholes.

Both Cattell's (1885a, 1885b) position and the logic of his argument are remarkably modern: as Haber and Hershenson (1973, pp. 256–264) document, similar arguments are associated with the well-known word-superiority effect (e.g., Reicher, 1969; Wheeler, 1970). Massaro (1975, pp. 382–398) has rejected the word-unit view on the grounds that the experimental design used in modern demonstrations does not provide an appropriate test of the whole-word view. Nevertheless, because the modern variant has wide support, the logic of the argument deserves careful consideration.

The conclusion that we use a whole-word unit—a stronger conclusion than a simple argument against the use of letter-size units—does not follow from an advantage for words over single letters in either reading speed or accuracy unless we assume that the possibilities are mutually exclusive and exhaustive. It is clear, however, that the alternatives are not exhaustive: consider the point in terms of the model described in the previous section.

Word identification requires integration of the letters, a responsibility of the scan-parse mechanism. Identifying a single letter, like the item-isolation requirement in the bar-probe task, involves the attentional mechanism, not the scan-parse mechanism. The speed advantage for reading a word rather than a letter would cause trouble for the model only if one argues that the speed of the attentional mechanism exceeds that of the scan-parse mechanism. As Mewhort and Campbell (1980) have argued, however, the opposite is the case; the scan-parse mechanism transfers material to short-term memory more efficiently than the attentional mechanism can move a single character. Their argument was based on estimates of word integration using an overprinting paradigm, not on reading times per se, and they suggested that the difference in speed reflects both the relative familiarity of the two situations—reading an isolated letter (the indefinite article excepted) is a relatively rare event—and the data-type conversion implied by use of the parser. Thus, without suggesting either a letter-by-letter process or a whole-word unit, because the time required to read a letter versus a word is based on the timing of different submechanisms, the advantage cited as evidence for use of whole-word units does not prove the conclusion.

Despite the difficulties inherent in the original argument, the idea that we use word-level units in reading is held widely (e.g., Johnson, 1975, 1977). Indeed, its influence popularized several corollary ideas. In the prebehaviorist period, for example, it was taken as evidence that subjects do not require fine visual detail when identifying a word—a view consistent with the threshold technology favored by the visual-science tradition but inconsistent with Pillsbury's observations on the point. More important, it motivated the look–say approach to instruction in reading.

As the influence of behaviorism started to wane at mid-century, three important trends emerged from the interregnum. Behaviorism, the interrex, implies a simulus-bound organism. Hebb (1949) was among the first to acknowledge the difficulties associated with such a view, and he imported ideas from neurophysiology to reintroduce processing-mechanism concepts to theoretical psychology. In particular, he suggested that elementary knowledge units develop from sensory–motor interactions and that the units can be incited to action by both internal and external stimuli. In addition, he resurrected the concept of attention to organize internal processing. Second, the "New Look" in perception (see Bruner & Anglin, 1973) expanded the conception of performance in tachisto-scopic-recognition experiments. Instead of a simple method for studying sensory events, the expansion forced consideration of memory, response, and various kinds of bias and set as determinants of performance. Finally, the seminal work of H. A. Simon and his associates (see Feigenbaum & Feldman, 1963) introduced the information-processing analogy and, thereby, the possibility of simulation models.

The dual-buffer parsing model grew out of an earlier account proposed by Heron (1957) and extended by both Bryden (1967) and Harcum (1967). Heron's position, which we call classic scanning theory, combined topics from the New Look in perception with concepts derived from Hebb's (1949) neurophysiological theory. In particular, Heron developed the idea of a distribution-of-attention operator to explain aspects of performance during identification of tachistoscopically presented letter strings.

Heron's (1957) account focused on a number of issues related to the study of visual processing in tachistoscopic tasks. In addition, it has influenced the study of lateralization of function in the brain (Bryden, 1966a; Kimura, 1959; but see Harcum & Filion, 1963); we will concentrate, however, on the role the work played in the study of letter and word identification.

A. Classic Scanning Theory

Heron's (1957) experiments were designed to clarify results reported by Mishkin and Forgays (1952). They used subjects who could read both Yiddish and English, and, on each trial, the subjects saw a single word presented to either the left or the right visual field. From trial to trial, the subjects did not know which language was to be presented or on which side the word was to appear. Mishkin and Forgays found that English words which had been presented in the right visual field were reported more accurately than when the same words were presented in the left visual field. For Yiddish words (which are written in Hebrew characters from right to left), however, the field superiority reversed (see also Harcum & Friedman, 1963).

Mishkin and Forgays (1952) interpreted their experiment in terms of stimulus equivalence and neural organization. In particular, they considered their experiment in terms of a question of neural equipotentiality versus neural specialization of function. They took the side-specific performance superiorities as evidence for corresponding cortical specialization, a specialization dependent on learning. Although they speculated that an attentional mechanism might contribute to cortical specialization, they did not discuss such a mechanism in any detail.

Heron (1957) extended the Mishkin and Forgays (1952) experiment by including conditions involving presentation of letters to both visual fields simultaneously. Replicating Mishkin and Forgays, he also showed that when groups of letters are exposed on successive trials to either the left or the right visual field, a right-field superiority appears. When the same material is presented across the fixation point to both visual fields simultaneously, however, a left-field superiority emerges. To obtain the left-side advantage, both sides must contain similar material. If a horizontal line is presented to one field while letters appear in the other, for example, a right-field superiority appears; thus, the left-field superiority requires presentation of letters to both fields. Moreover, for the case of letter presentation to both fields, subjects report the letters in a left-to-right order, usually starting from the leftmost position (see Bryden, 1966b, and Mewhort, 1966, for a discussion of order of report).

Heron (1957) argued that the right- and left-field superiorities reflect use of an internal attentional mechanism which has been acquired as part of the reading skill. The attentional mechanism is a postexposural process which permits a sequential analysis of persisting stimulus traces; it was thought to develop in the way suggested by Hebb (1949) for a phase sequence, i.e., it starts as sensory–motor interaction, but it evolves into an internalized process. The beginning reader's strategy of moving his eyes in a step-by-step fashion, for example, becomes an internal "sweep" of attention as he learns to read. While it does not include overt eye movements themselves, the attentional mechanism was thought to involve central neural activity which is associated with control of overt eye movements. In effect, then, a shift of attention is an internalized eye movement.

The internal mechanism allows subjects to distribute attention in two ways, a fast shift to the beginning of a line and a slower left-to-right sweep, i.e., internalizations of the two main eye movements used in reading. To explain the right-field superiority found when material is presented to the fields separately, Heron (1957) suggested that the material in the right field requires only a simple left-to-right shift of attention whereas the material in the left field requires both a shift to the left and a left-to-right scan. As a result, the material in the right field has the advantage. For the case involving simultaneous presentation to both fields, he suggested that "the dominant tendency to move the eyes to the beginning of the line would result in more letters being recognized in the left field" (p. 47).

Terrace (1959) used material presented successively to either the left or the right visual field and confirmed the corresponding part of Heron's (1957) experiment. Like Heron, he showed better recognition for words presented in the right visual field than for those presented in the left field. In addition, he failed to show a corresponding field superiority when forms were used as stimuli. Because both the visual field and the kind of material for successive trials were selected randomly, he argued that the visual-field superiority found with alphabetic material cannot be explained in terms of potential set effects; instead, he argued, in agreement with Heron, for an account involving a postexposural scanning operation. In addition, he suggested that the scanning operator is preceded by an operation which determines the nature (i.e., alphabetic versus form) of the material, a point mentioned by Heron only in passing.

Harcum and Finkel (1963) also confirmed a portion of Heron's (1957) experiment; they showed a right-field advantage when letter strings were presented in either the left or the right visual field successively. Like Heron, they explained the right-side superiority in terms of a sequential postexposural analysis of the stimuli. Heron had argued that starting a left-to-right scan at the fixation point would be easier than a skip left (back to start a new line) followed by a left-to-right scan. Thus, he argued, the right-side superiority reflects a difference in the difficulty of the skip-to-the-left and the simple left-to-right cases. Harcum and Finkel accepted Heron's point but argued that the direction of the scan is also related to directional properties of the stimulus itself. Their experiment included a mirror-image reversal of the stimulus, and the results showed a modest advantage for mirror-image letters presented on the left over the case involving mirror-image letters presented on the right. In addition, while subjects reported normal sequences from left to right, they used a right-to-left report for mirror-image letters. Accordingly, Harcum and Finkel suggested that subjects chose the direction of the scan based on the orientation of the letters comprising the stimulus string. Like Heron (1957) and Terrace (1959), then, Harcum and Finkel acknowledge that the scanning operation, i.e., the sequential analysis, can occur only after enough perceptual analysis has been performed to determine the characteristics of the stimuli.

Harcum (1964) took up the question of the directionality of the stimulus itself in a supplementary experiment. He presented eight-letter pseudowords, centered at the fixation, i.e., with four letters in both fields, and asked subjects to report as many letters as possible. Two kinds of pseudowords were used; one kind was constructed from bilaterally asymmetric letters, and the other was composed of symmetric letters. Overall, accuracy of report was better for the material presented to the left of fixation, and the majority of the subjects reported from left to right. About one-quarter of the subjects reported more material from the right, presumably because they reported from right to left. For the pseudowords composed of bilaterally asymmetric letters (B, G, J, K, N, R, and S), performance on the side yielding best scores (presumably the side reported first) was enhanced relative to performance for a corresponding set of bilaterally symmetric letters balanced for frequency of use in English (H, M, T, V, W, X, and Y). Harcum argued that "since there was no chance of establishing a differential set to perceive the two classes of stimuli before their exposure . . . the direction of the process must be established in part by a direction inherent in the stimuli themselves" (p. 605).

Bryden (1968) extended Harcum's (1964) argument concerning the directionality of asymmetric letters. First, he replicated the basic finding: free-recall performance is greater for a string of asymmetric letters than for a string of symmetric ones. In addition, he showed that with increased spacing between letters, the advantage for asymmetric material is reduced. Finally, using a single-letter presentation (with the letter occupying the same retinal positions used in the first experiment) he showed that there is no advantage for asymmetric letters when they are presented alone. The benefit of asymmetry, then, appears to be related to a mechanism associated with processing the string of letters, not to one associated with identification of a single character.

A second aspect of directionality concerns the class of stimulus. Bryden (1960) asked subjects to report a row of material from left to right or from right to left. The instruction indicating the direction of report was provided after the display, and when subjects reported a row of letters, accuracy was better for the material on the left side, regardless of the direction of report. The left-side superiority, of course, corroborates Heron's (1957) data and illustrates left-to-right processing independently of left-to-right report. When the subjects reported a row of nonalphabetic forms (such as a square, a triangle, or a star), however, accuracy was better for material on the side reported first, regardless of the direction of report (see Cornett, 1972, for a replication). Letter strings appear to involve directional processing, but a string of forms does not; the difference reinforces Heron's idea that the left-to-right scan is related to reading habits (see also Bryden, Dick, & Mewhort, 1968). It also reinforces his suggestion that "before the post-exposural process operates discrimination of the stimulus-materials must occur" (p. 47), a point consistent with the effects of letter asymmetry noted earlier.

The evidence presented so far points to the use of a postexposural analysis, a process which can be thought of as a temporal distribution of attention across space. The idea of distributed attention, and of the scanning mechanism itself, was derived from Hebb's (1949) ideas concerning the development of functional neural structures from sensory–motor interaction. Evidence concerning the role of the motor component was obtained by Bryden (1961) and, independently, by Crovitz and Daves (1962). In both studies, subjects were shown a row of letters tachistoscopically, and the direction of the first postexposure eye movement was recorded. Although the two studies differed in technical details (e.g., details concerning the recording of eye movements and the calculation of relative performance for the left versus the right side), both showed a strong positive correlation between the side yielding better performance and the direction of the eye movement. The data are particularly striking inasmuch as the eye movement occurs well after the stimulus had been removed: the correlation points directly to a link between attention and motor processes, exactly as predicted from Heron's (1957) theory (see also Hall, 1974).

With the success of the Bryden (1961) and the Crovitz and Daves (1962) experiments, Heron's (1957) theory had achieved a considerable success. Nevertheless, it was not without some critics. The critics took two main lines of argument, each related to a particular experimental procedure. Both procedures challenged the idea of a sequential scan: the first involved an ordered-recall technique and concerned the possibility of an ordered-report artifact in the evidence supporting Heron's proposed scanning mechanism. The second involved a partial-report technique and dealt with a related argument concerning the order in which letters are identified.

1. Ordered-Processing and the Artifact of Ordered-Report

Heron (1957) argued that the left-field superiority associated with free-recall of material presented simultaneously to both visual fields reflects a postexposural attentional process. In particular, he argued that subjects first shift their attention to the beginning of the row and then scan the row from left to right. Similar arguments were made by Bryden (1960), by Harcum and Dyer (1962), and by Ayres and Harcum (1962).

Ayres (1966) took exception to the role assigned a postexposural shift of attention. In reporting tachistoscopically presented letter strings, subjects prefer to use a left-to-right direction. Ayres argued that, instead of postulating a postexposural perceptual mechanism, one needs only to suggest that subjects recall best those items which they recall first. His view claims, then, that the left-field advantage Heron sought to explain in terms of a postexposural attention mechanism reflects, instead, an artifact of ordered report.

In support of the artifact argument, Ayres (1966) presented patterns tachistoscopically and required subjects to report the material in several designated orders. The orders included a left-to-right report, a top-to-bottom report, and the reverse of each. In each case, the material reported first was reported best.

Ayres's (1966) data represent a severe challenge to the idea of a postexposural scan: the scanning view would appear to predict a left-field superiority for material presented to both visual fields simultaneously regardless of the order of report. Indeed, that prediction accurately reflects results reported by Bryden (1960). With hindsight, it is clear that Ayres' results depend on subtle aspects of his procedure, a point to be considered shortly. First, however, we shall consider a logical flaw in his argument.

Ayres (1966) found that items reported first are reported best, and he used the relationship to explain the left-field superiority without the extra baggage, the postexposural attentional mechanism, suggested by Heron (1957). Notice, however, that Heron's account explains how subjects order their report, i.e., how they convert a parallel spatial array into a sequence ordered temporally. The difficulty for Ayres's argument is that it leaves unexplained how subjects order their report. Without explaining how subjects organize their report, however, it is not clear that one can eliminate the idea of an attentional shift. At best, one can only switch the location of the ordering mechanism from a perceptual locus to one based on rehearsal or other short-term memory functions. Ayres did not attempt such a switch; instead, he denied the need for such a mechanism. It is difficult to understand what was gained by denying the scanning idea—particularly by using the idea of an ordered report—if it must be replaced with an alternate mechanism.

In Ayres's (1966) experiment, subjects were told the direction of report in advance of the display, and they reported best the material which they reported first, regardless of the direction of report. As mentioned earlier, Ayres's results appear to contradict those reported by Bryden (1960). In Bryden's experiment, subjects were asked to report a string of letters from left to right or from right to left; the instruction was provided after the display. Accuracy of report was better on the left side regardless of the order of report. Harcum, Hartman, and Smith (1963) reported both patterns of results: subjects were asked to report from left to right or from right to left (along with other report conditions). When the instructions were given in advance of the display, the subjects reported best the material which they reported first. When the instructions were given after the display, the subjects were best on the left side, regardless of the order required. Freeburne and Goldman (1969), however, used a postdisplay order-of-report instruction and found subjects were best on the side reported first, a sharp contrast to both the Bryden and the Harcum *et al.* studies.

At face value, the results for ordered-report experiments are contradictory. Part of the contradiction, however, reflects the timing of the order-of-report instructions. Ayres (1966) presented the instructions before the display. Bryden (1960) and Harcum *et al.* (1963) provided both pre- and postexposure order-of-report instructions, but the instructions were presented verbally, i.e., the experimenter called out the direction of report. In a more recent study, Scheerer (1972) presented a row of letters and provided order-of-report instructions by means of a precisely timed cue. With predisplay instructions, subjects were able to report in both directions, and accuracy of report was best on the side reported first, a result confirming the pattern of all three earlier studies involving the predisplay case. With postdisplay instructions, however, Scheerer found that the side superiority depended on both the direction of report and the timing of the order-of-report instruction. If the instruction was immediate, subjects reported best the material from the side reported first. When the instruction was delayed beyond about 700 milliseconds, however, accuracy of report was better for the material on the left, regardless of the direction of report (see also Cornett, 1972, and Scheerer, 1973). For an "immediate" postdisplay order-of-report instruction in the earlier studies, the effective cue must have been delayed by at least 750 milliseconds (a minimum estimate considering the experimenter's reaction time and the length of the utterance required). If we assume such a delay, both the Bryden and the Harcum *et al.* studies are consistent with the results reported by Scheerer (1972).

In connection with the timing question, Freeburne and Goldman (1969) presented their postdisplay order-of-report instruction 128 milliseconds after the display. For the left-to-right case, they found a strong left-side advantage; for the right-to-left report, however, there was a right-side superiority which failed to reach significance. Such a pattern is exactly what one might expect at an intermediate timing interval, i.e., at a value for which subjects start to switch from an advantage for the material reported first to a left-side advantage. Thus, although their study appears to contradict the Bryden (1960) and the Harcum *et al.* (1963) studies, close examination of the timing parameters resolves the conflict.

In summary, ordered report has been used as a technique to study the idea of a left-to-right postexposure scanning mechanism. After some false starts, the evidence presents a clear picture. If the cue indicating how to report is available in time, subjects have a good deal of flexibility in organizing their report. If the instruction has been delayed, however, subjects adopt a default ordering, i.e., they use a left-to-right order. Thus, it is clear that one cannot explain the left-side superiority associated with a simple free-recall task in terms of ordered report without including a mechanism to explain the default (left-to-right) ordering. The evidence leaves open the nature of the mechanism, however. One possibility is that an order-of-report instruction is used to change the direction of the scan, a position urged by Scheerer (1972, 1973). A second possibility is that the flexibility in ordered report reflects short-term memory and rehearsal processes, rather than the scan itself. Mewhort (1974), for example, has argued that scanning orders letter groups in short-term memory by passing them in a left-to-right fashion; the scan, then, provides the default organization, but the default organization can be overridden if one receives an instruction in time to restructure rehearsal and organization of the report.

2. Ordered-Processing in the Absence of Ordered Report

The second line of argument questioning the idea of a left-to-right scan involves the partial-report technique. In a partial-report task, subjects are shown a row of letters and are provided a second stimulus to indicate which of the elements in the row is to be reported. Typically, the row of material is presented simultaneously to both visual fields, i.e., it is centered about a fixation point, as in the simple free-recall task.

The argument is similar to that suggested by Ayres (1966) and was developed independently by Smith and Ramunas (1971) and by Merikle, Lowe, and Coltheart (1971; see also Merikle, Coltheart, & Lowe, 1971). Assuming that the left-side superiority associated with the simple free-recall task is due to an artifact of ordered report, Ayres used the forced-order technique to control the bias resulting from ordered report and, thereby, to expose the artifactual nature of the left-side superiority. Similarly, if the left-side superiority associated with a simple free-recall task reflects an order-of-report artifact, a partial-report task should illustrate the point by eliminating the bias along with ordered report. In the Smith and Ramunas (1971) study, six-letter displays were presented tachistoscopically and a partial-report cue, a vibrotactile stimulus, followed the display after a delay of zero to 2000 milliseconds. In the Merikle, Lowe, and Coltheart (1971) study, seven-letter displays were followed by a visual marker indicating which letter to report. For both studies, the accuracy of report took a symmetrical W shape across the stimulus array, and both concluded that the left-side advantage associated with the free-recall experiment reflects an artifact of ordered report.

The partial-report experiment provides very clear results. It is not clear, however, what issues the experiment addresses. Heron's (1957) account involved a sequential process, but, as we have noted, it is not clear what unit (preidentification features or postidentification letters) is subject to the sequential analysis: Heron suggested enough processing to decide upon a class of material, a position confirmed by Harcum and Finkel (1963). Is the processing needed to decide upon classes of material tantamount to identification? If not, what unit is subject to scanning? If it is a preidentification unit, the partial-report task provides a rebuttal to the position. If the unit subject to scanning is a postidentification unit—as in the model defended in this article—the partial-report task requires an extra assumption before it can serve as a test for the sequential-analysis postulate. In particular, one must assume that processing in both the free-recall and the partial-report tasks involves the same sequential analysis after letter identification. The assumption has been tested experimentally and, as we shall discuss in detail later, has been shown to be false (Campbell & Mewhort, 1980; see also Scheerer, 1974).

The results of the partial-report task do not provide a fair test of Heron's (1957) position, but part of the reason follows from ambiguity in the theory. Such ambiguity is, at best, a weak defense. Nevertheless, the defense is important because it points to a meta-theoretical problem, a clash between two empirical traditions. Scanning theory was motivated by an interest in eye movements and sensory–motor interaction. Independently, Neisser's (1967) book, *Cognitive Psychology*, popularized similar work derived from an information-processing perspective.

Working from the information-processing perspective, Sperling (1963) presented letters for various durations, and followed the letters with a patterned masking stimulus. As the exposure time increased, subjects were able to report more letters. The rate of gain was about one letter for every 10 milliseconds of exposure up to a limit at about 100 milliseconds. Sperling suggested that letters are identified sequentially and are passed from a temporary visual representation to a more permanent auditory form at a rate of about one letter per 10 milliseconds (cf. Sperling, 1967, 1970). Further, he attached the label "scanning" to the two operations, i.e., to the operations involved in identifying the items and passing them to auditory memory.

Sperling's (1963) use of the term scanning is, clearly, quite different from that of Heron (1957). Nevertheless, given Sperling's usage, it is easy to read into Heron's concept the idea that letter identification proceeds in a left-to-right manner, i.e., that the unit subject to scanning is a preidentification unit. Indeed, discussing the letter recognition processes, one theorist associated with Heron suggested that in "identifying a series of letters the subject starts with the leftmost letter . . . and proceeds from there towards the right" (Bryden, 1966b, p. 271). Similarly, Smith and Ramunas (1971) connected Heron's concept of a scanning mechanism to Sperling's work quite explicitly. Referring to Sperling's account, they explain the left-side advantage discussed by Heron as follows: "while the initial scan of the visual image is very rapid, read in of this information to a 'rehearsal center' occurs at a much slower rate. If there is a tendency to read the information into this center in a left-right order, . . . there is some possibility of a fading of the image before all the items have been read in" (p. 27). Subsequent reviews appear to have accepted their reading of Heron's position (e.g., Butler, 1981).

While Heron's (1957) statement of his theory leaves the question open, the view that letter identification involves a left-to-right process has been defended occasionally (e.g., Gough, 1972; Gough & Cosky, 1977; Massa, 1967). In general, however, it seems more often to serve as a straw man (e.g., Brewer, 1972).

Sperling's (1963) technique does not provide strong evidence on the problem of serial identification. Indeed, his evidence for a sequential analysis, regardless of the direction, is circumstantial: the experiment appears to involve a sequential analysis inasmuch as more letters become available as the processing time is increased. But, appearances may be deceptive: suppose that all letters in an array were to be processed in parallel, i.e., that work on the identification of each letter starts at the same time. Provided that all letters do not become available simultaneously (an unlikely possibility if one accepts differences in difficulty based on the letter's context or its retinal position) Sperling's trick of delaying a mask over a reasonably small range of temporal intervals is bound to yield a letter-by-letter increase in report.

The idea of serial analysis during letter identification includes the notion that one distributes effort sequentially across space. To demonstrate sequential letter identification, then, one needs to combine Sperling's delay-of-mask technique with a manipulation which involves the distribution of effort across space.

Mewhort, Merikle, and Bryden (1969, Expt. 2) presented a row of letters followed by a mask arranged to cover half of the row. The delay of the mask was varied systematically. Masking on the left had both a local effect on the left and an effect on the right, especially when it followed the target relatively quickly. Masking on the right, however, had only a local effect on the right, regardless of the delay. Because of the asymmetry in combination with the temporal relation underlying it, Mewhort et al. (1969) concluded that processing includes a left-to-right component. Lefton and Spragins (1974) have provided similar results using the same technique.

Harcum and Nice (1975, see also Nice & Harcum, 1976) presented two compound words one after the other on the same spatial location. The compounds were selected so that the left half of the first word fit the context of the right half of the second word, and vice versa. With appropriate exposure durations, subjects often reported the left half of the first word combined with the right half of the second word, but not vice versa. Again, the asymmetry combined with the temporal relation strongly suggests subjects process from left to right.

Both the technique used by Mewhort et al. (1969) and that explored by Harcum and Nice (1975) show a strong left-to-right bias. Nevertheless, although they show a sequential operation, it is still not clear what unit is processed. In particular, it is not clear that the experiments point to a letter-by-letter sequential process. In both cases, the left-to-right mechanism could operate at the level, for example, of a postidentification character buffer.

The problem illustrated by the preceding examples is a problem for theory: issues such as parallel versus serial processing are sensible only when placed in context. While one can illustrate both kinds of processing, such work is not informative until there is corresponding information about the unit processed, the nature of the data, et cetera. Indeed, Townsend (1974) has argued that the parallel/serial issue cannot be decided, but, presumably, he means it cannot be decided without the constraints imposed by the context. His point is that one can always mimic a parallel process with an arbitrarily fast serial one. But, of course, the ability to mimic one process with another implies flexibility of design, flexibility which data-representation constraints may deny for a particular situation.

The importance of the problem can be illustrated in another way. We started this section by considering Heron's (1957) concept of a left-to-right postexposure process in light of "tests" of the idea based on the partial-report task. If one conceives of the left-to-right scan as an operation on precategorical features, i.e., as a mechanism responsible for letter recognition itself, the tests provided by partial-report tasks deny the idea of a left-to-right mechanism. Alternately, if one conceives of the scanning mechanism as an operation on postidentification units, the tests provided by partial-report tasks are inconclusive.

The fundamental thrust of the test provided by the partial-report task concerns the putative impact of ordered report: the partial-report task tests a theory based on free-recall experiments by eliminating the artifact of ordered report. Further, inasmuch as the task shows a symmetrical distribution of errors across the stimulus array, it denies the theory. Krueger (1976) attacked the same problem in another way. Rather than limiting report from a row of letters to one item by means of a partial-report technique, he used a search procedure and asked subjects to indicate, as rapidly as possible, whether or not a designated item had appeared in the row. Thus, like the partial-report technique, Krueger's technique tests the sequential letter-identification idea by eliminating the putative effects of ordered recall. Unlike the partial-report tests, however, Krueger's data provided results consistent with the left-to-right scanning account. Further, his study included a mirror-image condition of the sort used by Harcum and Finkel (1963), and when faced with mirror-image letter strings, Krueger's subjects took the direction of their scan from the stimuli themselves. Thus, in line with the position adopted by Harcum and Finkel, Krueger found that subjects use a sequential strategy during a search task but that considerable preprocessing is required to establish an appropriate unit of search.

The problem for theory is now clear. Both the search and the partial-report tasks were used to gain control over the putative effects of ordered report. Even though they were undertaken with similar goals, the conclusions differ dramatically. Thus, instead of a contrast of free-recall versus partial-report, or of free-recall versus search (with the second task in each pair serving as a control for the ordered-report condition), we have a contrast between the two controls (cf. Campbell, 1979, Ch. 7). The remarkable point is that the two tasks were used in good faith to control the same artifact but yielded, paradoxically, quite opposite conclusions. The contrast implies that both the original theory and the experimenter's intuition are insufficiently precise. Thus, instead of a situation in which experiments test a theory by confirming or denying predictions derived from it, the experiments raise problems of definition internal to the theory. Is the sequential process involved in a search task, for example, the same as that described by Heron (1957)? Given that a mirror-image manipulation controlled the direction of the scan in both tasks, we must assume that Harcum and Finkel (1963) would agree. Certainly, Krueger (1976) assumed so, but if he is correct, why does a partial-report task suggest that left-to-right bias is added well after letter identification? Perhaps more in line with Heron's original position, we might ask whether or not to treat a cell-assembly as a pre- or post-categorical unit. Whatever gains the neurophysiological language might have provided the early scanning theorists—and we concede a direct prediction concerning postexposure eye movements (Bryden, 1961; Crovitz & Daves, 1962)—it also provided an imprecise theoretical language.

The complexity of the experiments, combined with the inadequacy of the neurophysiological language, lead Harcum (1966, 1967) to propose an information-translation theory. The theory involved a multilayered series of processing steps, including differentiation of stimulus elements, intrinsic organization based on spatial and temporal primacy, element selection, element coding, semantic coding, and finally response selection. The theory attempted, in the fashion illustrated by Feigenbaum and Simon (1962), to account for performance in terms of a small number of elementary information-translation postulates. For example, it sought to explain the serial-position curve in both tachistoscopic identification experiments and serial paired-associate learning experiments in terms of the same mechanisms for serial order.

Harcum's (1966, 1967) information-translation theory brought into classic scanning theory the ideas of the information-processing metaphor represented by H. A. Simon and his colleagues and, thereby, expanded the range of the theory. While Harcum's account moved classic scanning ideas in a fruitful direction, he was reluctant to abandon the neurophysiological metaphor completely. Nevertheless, his approach acknowledged the complexity of behavior in a tachistoscopic experiment (and the complexity of the evidence accumulated to date) by postulating a number of more or less discrete processing layers. Unfortunately, he lacked empirical evidence to support the distinctions which he claimed.

Harcum's (1967) account, nevertheless, is pivotal: the work which he summarized includes most of the experimental work we have described under the title, classic scanning theory. In addition, it pointed the direction for the work to follow. In particular, he set a theoretical criterion by acknowledging the complexity of the evidence, and he established the need to distinguish layers of processing empirically.

B. Modern Scanning Theory

Modern scanning theory sets out to obtain experimental evidence illustrating the stages thought to be involved in tachistoscopic tasks. In contrast to approaches which start by considering initial visual processes, the strategy used to build modern scanning theory involves working forward from the response to the front end. With a response-forward strategy, one builds a model to accomplish the basic response and adds only the complexity needed to explain that response. If guessing can explain performance in a particular task, for example, one needs to postulate only a guessing mechanism and its supporting processes. If there were only one result to explain, of course, the minimum-complexity idea would make little sense, but as one increases the number of experiments to be explained simultaneously (and, thereby, the complexity of their interconnections), simple explanations fall aside in favor of an account based on an integrated set of mechanisms.

Of course, one introduces simple mechanisms first, but simplicity is a controversial topic. In contrast to a reductionist position, we consider simplicity in terms of the complexity of the model, not in terms of the hope that one can associate simple mechanisms with sensory factors.

The strategy of working forward from the response introduces different problems from the strategy of working from the stimulus to the response. When working from the stimulus backward, one has to assume that a good deal of the system can be neutralized, i.e., that it can be prevented from having an impact on the behavior, at least during the course of an experiment. The assumption is Teller's (1980) nothing-mucks-it-up proviso, and it usually forces one to restrict behavior by using a simple response, such as a latency-to-respond measurement or a yes/no decision (Teller's MMph versus MM-MMph).[3] The response-forward strategy, in contrast, does not require behavior-limiting assumptions. Indeed, it requires a relatively rich response: the account is determined by the richness of the behavior one seeks to explain.

The two strategies face different kinds of potential error. The response-forward strategy risks attributing too much explanatory power to later mechanisms at the expense of front-end mechanisms, and the stimulus-to-response strategy risks the converse, i.e., it risks attributing too much to early visual processes. The solution to both problems is similar, as indicated in the discussion of complexity and theory verification (Section II,B,3). Nevertheless, we should add a comment to explain our preference for the response-forward position. To the extent that front-end mechanisms—the objects of study for a stimulus-to-response theorist—are difficult to link to behavior, they are like the mental objects banished by behaviorism. While the behaviorist position faces serious philosophical problems, one lesson is well taken: explanatory concepts must be easy to link to the behavior they seek to explain or risk achieving the status of a ghost in the machine (cf. Ryle, 1949).

To illustrate the response-forward approach, let us reconsider the free-recall task involving presentation of pseudowords of various orders of approximation to English. The response can be characterized in several ways: accuracy of report takes an asymmetric U shape across the stimulus array; the number of letters reported correctly increases with the order of approximation to English; the subjects tend to report in a left-to-right order; and the report includes runs of letters, suggesting an organization into subunits (cf. Reitman & Rueter, 1980). Finally, both the tendency to report from left to right and the size of the runs increase with increases in the order of approximation to English. Details of performance in a free-recall task have been provided by Campbell (1979); Campbell and Mewhort (1980) present an abbreviated account.

In theoretical terms, all aspects of the report reflect one or another characteristic of the final stage of processing. For our purposes, the final stage is associated with rehearsal at the level of short-term memory. Thus, the order of report reflects a corresponding order during rehearsal, and the U-shaped stimulus-position curve (including the left-side advantage) also reflects rehearsal (see Feigenbaum & Simon, 1962, for an account of how rehearsal generates the characteristic U curve). Similarly, the runs reflect units used during rehearsal.

To note that all aspects of the report reflect the final stage of processing,

[3] Teller's phrase describes the response given by subjects in visual experiments which require both a "bite-bar" and a yes/no verbal response.

however, does not tell the whole story. To attach a characteristic to rehearsal invites a question of the form, "How does rehearsal become organized?" For the simple free-recall case, the organization for rehearsal is taken from the order of arrival at short-term memory. Thus, the left-to-right order of report reflects ordered rehearsal, and ordered rehearsal, in turn, reflects the organization implied by the order of entry into short-term memory. Similarly, the response runs reflect the unit-construction associated with the scan-parse mechanism.

Tracing forward from the scan-parse mechanism, it finds its input in the character buffer. The character buffer, in turn, collects output from the character-identification process. The latter uses basic visual data as input. The characteristics of the response reflect the collective action of all the submechanisms.

The development of evidence illustrating the separate processes and data buffers used in the free-recall task took, in historical terms, a similar response-forward form, and we shall review the work in a roughly chronological order using a response-forward organization. Before starting the review, however, we offer a mild warning: the early work illustrates the ambience of its time. In particular, it sometimes reflects a bias to design and to interpret experiments in terms of detection/threshold ideas. As a result, some theoretical alternatives received more attention than they deserved. An example concerns the familiarity effect and the idea that guessing and/or response bias might account for performance.

1. Response Bias and the Familiarity Effect

In the free-recall task, accuracy of report depends on the familiarity of the material; subjects report more letters from a fourth-order string than from a zero-order string. An account based on guessing suggests that subjects guess letters which they did not see (or do not remember, Baddeley, 1964) by filling in items on the basis of the context. Thus, they use their knowledge of English in combination with the context provided by the material available to guess missing letters. With such a guessing strategy, subjects would be able to report more from a familiar string than from a random one because the familiar material better matches the language on which they have based their guesses. For the guessing account, then, better performance on higher order pseudowords reflects a stable guessing strategy rather than a mechanism related to perception, to memory, or to report organization.

The guessing account is a doctrine of desperation: it claims that subjects will respond on the basis of partial (sometimes negligible) information (e.g., Goldiamond & Hawkins, 1958). Further, it claims that such responses are educated. The guessing (response-bias) idea has a long history: Underwood and Schulz (1960, p. 86) called a close neighbor the "spew" hypothesis; Broadbent (1967) used a variation of the idea to explain the word-frequency effect; and Newbigging (1961) applied the idea to explain word identification.

The response-bias/guessing account seems to provide a reasonable explanation for situations in which subjects are forced to guess (but see Johnston, 1978). It does not generalize, however, to other situations, i.e., it does not provide the basis for an account of the familiarity effect in a free-recall tachistoscopic trial: the problem is that it can deal with only one measure of performance, accuracy of report. To account for the free-recall trial, however, one wishes to account for behavior—the whole response—not a single description of the response, the accuracy-of-report measure.

To illustrate the point, let us apply the guessing idea to the free-recall experiment, i.e., let us suppose that subjects guess items which they did not see (or do not remember) using their experience with English as a guide. Because guesses generated from language habits are more likely to match the letters in a higher order string, one may be able to explain the increase in accuracy of report in terms of the guessing idea. But, by the nature of a guessing operator, it is hard to understand how guessing could increase the response runs or how it could increase the tendency to report from left to right. Both features of report are associated with performance on higher order pseudowords. Thus, while it may explain simple accuracy of report, an account based on guessing cannot explain the difference in accuracy of report along with both the order-of-report and the response-topology features of the trial. Similarly, it is hard to understand why some manipulations, such as masking, should have so little influence on the size of familiarity effect while others, such as letter spacing, have a large influence (Campbell & Mewhort, 1980).

The response-bias/sophisticated-guessing idea is based on an analogy to a detection/threshold calculation and provides an example of the difficulties noted in our mild warning: because of a preoccupation with one measure of performance, rather than with behavior as a whole, certain hypotheses have received more emphasis than they deserve. Even sticking with the accuracy measure, however, the guessing hypothesis fares less well than usually thought. We suggested that guessing may be able to account for differences in accuracy of report but that it cannot account for other aspects of behavior on a typical trial. In fact, it is doubtful that guessing can account for all of the difference in accuracy usually obtained in a free-recall case. Using the eight-letter pseudowords supplied by Miller et al. (1954), Mewhort (1970) printed the material on file cards, one pseudoword per card, with one letter replaced by a question mark. The subjects were required to fill in the missing letter on the basis of the context provided by the remaining seven letters, and they were given an unlimited viewing time. In effect, the task simulated the process suggested for a tachistoscopic trial by the guessing account, except that the simulation guaranteed perfect identification of all of the context items.

The results showed a small effect of context: the subjects were more likely to guess the missing letter from higher orders of approximation than from lower orders. But, their success rate was remarkably low, much lower than the rate observed in bona fide tachistoscopic tasks and, thus, much lower than the rate demanded if guessing were to serve as an account for the familiarity effect under tachistoscopic conditions. In short, although guessing can contribute to the size of the familiarity effect (and in contrast to the then-current opinion), guessing is not a potential explanation for the familiarity effect. Lefton (1973) has provided a replication and extension of the Mewhort (1970) result.

One may object to the test of guessing provided by Mewhort (1970) and by Lefton (1973) on the grounds that it is not a fair simulation of the guessing argument. In particular, their technique does not provide subjects with partial information about the missing letter. In another context, Massaro (1973) has argued strongly that subjects can make good use of such partial information. It is possible, then, that in a bona fide tachistoscopic task subjects could combine the context information with partial information about missing letters. If the combination increased their success at filling in missing items, guessing may still provide a viable account for the familiarity effect.

Mewhort (1967) provided evidence against an account based on sophisticated guessing using a different line of reasoning. He presented two rows of pseudowords and instructed the subjects, using a tone, to report one of them. The pseudowords were of either fourth- or zero-order approximation to English. Further, the two kinds of material were paired in all ways; given that the subjects reported only one row on each trial, the pairings yielded three factors: the familiarity of the row reported, the familiarity of the row not reported, and the row reported.

The familiarity of material *not reported* had a large effect on report, a result which implies that the familiarity of pseudowords is analyzed prior to output processes. The point is that any version of a guessing account requires subjects to respond. The effect of the familiarity of the material not reported, however, illustrates a familiarity effect under circumstances which deny the opportunity to report. Thus, the effect of the familiarity of material not reported cannot be explained in terms of either a guessing account or any other variation of a response-bias theory.

Butler (1974, Expt. 2) repeated the Mewhort (1967) result and extended the experiment by varying the timing of the tone indicating which of the two rows to report. When the cue was given in advance of the double-row display, there was no effect of the familiarity of the material not reported. With a postdisplay cue, however, report was better for cases with a familiar string in the row not reported than for the cases with a zero-order string in the row not reported. That is, for a postdisplay cue, there was a large effect of the familiarity of the material not reported, as in the original study.

Taken together, the Butler (1974) and Mewhort (1967) studies show that response-based theories cannot account for all of the familiarity effect. Simultaneously, they suggest an account based on operations associated with rehearsal at the short-term memory level. As we described in Section III, rehearsal at the short-term memory level is a limited capacity operation, i.e., the success of rehearsal depends on the amount of material to be maintained and on the familiarity of the material. In Butler's (1974) experiment, when subjects were given a cue after the display, they were forced, presumably, to rehearse both rows. As a result, the total load on rehearsal depended on the familiarity of the material taken together, i.e., on the familiarity of both rows. Hence, regardless of the material to be reported, rehearsal of the material was facilitated when the material not reported (but rehearsed) was familiar. The effect of the familiarity of the material not reported, then, reflects the capacity limitation of rehearsal. When the cue preceded the display, however, the subjects ignored one of the two rows and, as a result, had only one row to rehearse. Consequently, the familiarity of the row not reported did not affect rehearsal, and the effect of the familiarity of the material not reported disappeared.

In terms of the resources described in Section III, Butler's (1974) experiment suggests one of two possibilities. On the one hand, one could argue that, with the predisplay cue, subjects select one row by filtering out the other row before passing it to memory. In effect, the argument is that the scan-parse mechanism has time, with a predisplay cue, to select which of the two rows to consider. On the other hand, one could argue that the selection is associated with rehearsal itself, i.e., that selection occurs when rehearsal actively tosses out material. Both positions reduce the load on memory and, therefore, both fit the available data. In either case, the familiarity effect reflects both a contribution due to the scan-parse mechanism and a cumulative contribution of rehearsal as it is extended over the report interval.

The evidence presented so far has looked at the familiarity effect in the free-recall tachistoscopic task and has shown that the effect is not due wholly, or even to a major degree, to response-based mechanisms, such as simple guessing. Indeed, the evidence suggests a major role for

processes such as rehearsal at the short-term memory level. Nevertheless, we have interpreted the effect in terms of two main factors, rehearsal
and the scan-parse mechanism. Clearly, we need empirical support for
the separation of the two factors, i.e., support for the claim that the
input-to-memory operator (the scan-parse mechanism) and the rehearsal
operator provide separate contributions to the familiarity effect.

2. Rehearsal and Input to Short-Term Memory

To distinguish the contribution of rehearsal from an earlier mechanism,
we need a basis for comparison. Both the scan-parse mechanism and
rehearsal operations are abstractions which are defined within the model.
To complicate the issue, both contribute, at least superficially, in similar
ways to the familiarity effect. Both, for example, can create subunits,
and both use knowledge of language to assist the unit-formation process.
Nevertheless, there are also some differences.

We conceive of rehearsal as the more flexible of the two operations.
It is, for example, a general-purpose capability whereas the scan-parse
mechanism is a reading-specific skill. Miller's (1956) description of
"chunking"—an information-compression operation exemplified by the
conversion of 12 binary digits to four octal ones—is prototypic of the
general-purpose nature of rehearsal. Other examples range from organization induced by pauses (Bower & Springston, 1970; McLean &
Gregg, 1967) or inferred from pauses (Reitman & Rueter, 1980) to general
accounts of structure in memory (e.g., Buschke, 1976; Friendly, 1977).
The scan-parse mechanism, in contrast, is a relatively specialized process, a mechanism which is limited in purpose and limited in the knowledge which it uses.

In keeping with its general-purpose nature, rehearsal at the short-term
memory level is normally under strategic control. By strategic control,
we mean that instructions to select, to order, or to sort material will lead
to appropriate, if not always successful, action. The operations carried
out by the scan-parse mechanism, in contrast, are not under strategic
control. As we shall confirm later, one can arrange conditions which
lead to its use or which preclude its use, but the processing performed
by the scan-parse mechanism cannot be altered by instructions.

A second difference between rehearsal operations and those of the
scan-parse mechanism concerns the flexibility of ordering each provides.
With some exceptions reflecting overtraining—it is, for example, hard
to report the alphabet backward (cf. Bryden, 1967)—rehearsal provides
flexible ordering. The scan-parse mechanism, however, orders material
from left to right. The inflexibility reflects its origin as a reading-specific
skill.

Experimental evidence illustrating the separate role of both the scan-parse mechanism and rehearsal processes at the short-term memory level has been provided by Mewhort (1974) and by Mewhort and Cornett (1972). The two studies are linked, and, taken together, they illustrate the difference in flexibility of ordering, the difference in sensitivity to instructions, and the different contribution to the familiarity effect.

Mewhort and Cornett (1972) presented pseudowords tachistoscopically and required subjects to report material from left to right or from right to left. The instruction indicating in which direction to report was provided by means of a tone immediately after the tachistoscopic display. In general, then, their experiment was very similar to the Scheerer (1972) study. Unlike the Scheerer study, however, Mewhort and Cornett used pseudowords of first- and fourth-order approximation to English. Further, they presented the pseudowords under both normal and reversed orientation. For example, *CRYSTEMP* and *APONSTER* are fourth-order strings which become *PMETSYRC* and *RETSNOPA* when spelled backward. Parenthetically, we should add a cautionary note. Because it upsets the left-to-right sequential constraints associated with fourth-order strings, reversing a fourth-order string creates a first-order string. Occasionally, however, the reversal leaves a residual left-to-right constraint, and the reversed fourth-order strings are more familiar than intended. For example, *POLICKET* and *DICTORES* become *TEKCILOP* and *SEROTCID;* both are more familiar than a typical first-order string. The problem arises because of the position of consonants and vowels; hence it is particularly severe for fourth-order strings composed of alternating consonant and vowel sequences (or corresponding clusters and diphthongs).

Mewhort and Cornett (1972) found that subjects had some difficulty reporting from right to left. Indeed, the subjects claimed that it was hard to report "backward," i.e., against their preferred order of report. Nevertheless, the subjects complied with the instructions. Like the results at a comparable delay of the cue in Scheerer's (1972) study, accuracy of report was best on the side reported first. Overall accuracy of report was lower, however, when the subjects reported from right to left than when they reported from left to right. Further, for the material presented in normal orientation, accuracy of report showed the usual familiarity effect, regardless of the direction of report. For the material presented in reversed orientation, however, the familiarity effect was reduced dramatically for both directions of report. Finally, the reduction for reversed materials was about the same, regardless of the direction of report.

In summary, then, there were two main factors affecting performance in the experiment: the direction of report controlled both the overall level of performance and determined which side the subjects reported more accurately. The orientation of the material controlled the size of the familiarity effect, and the two factors did not interact.

In terms of the rehearsal/scan-parse distinction, the pattern of results falls nicely into place. First, consider the familiarity effect. The scan-parse mechanism, presumably, passed material to short-term memory in a left-to-right order. Its success depended on the orientation of the material. Thus, when the pseudowords were presented in normal orientation, a large familiarity effect resulted. When the pseudowords were reversed, however, the familiarity effect was reduced. In short, the scan-parse mechanism controlled the amount of material available to short-term memory. Once in short-term memory, the material was maintained by rehearsal and the subjects used the order-of-report instruction to determine the direction for rehearsal. The direction, in turn, determined the order of report, the side reported first, and, consequently, the side reported best.

That there are two factors, i.e., the scan-parse mechanism and rehearsal, is clear from the failure of the interaction between the direction of report and the orientation of the material. In particular, if one were to think in terms of a single factor—either an account considering rehearsal only, or one involving a bidirectional scanning mechanism of the sort suggested by Scheerer (1972, 1973)—the subjects should have been able to exploit the familiarity of the pseudowords when the orientation of the materials matched the direction of report, e.g., when *PMETSYRC* was reported from right to left. Instead of a clear separation of the direction-of-report and orientation manipulations, the single-factor view predicts a large familiarity effect for two of the four cells defined by their combination, i.e., for the case involving a left-to-right report of material in normal orientation and for the case involving right-to-left report of material in reversed orientation. There was a large familiarity effect in two cells, but it occurred in the cells predicted by the rehearsal/scan-parse idea, not in the cells predicted by the single-factor view.

Scheerer (1972) found that accuracy of report is better for the material reported first provided that instructions indicating the direction of report are given in time. In particular, the cue must be available within 700 milliseconds following the display. If the cue is late, accuracy is best on the left, regardless of the order of report. As indicated earlier (Section IV,A,1), his results are consistent with the idea that rehearsal is more flexible than the scan-parse mechanism and that the latter mechanism provides the basis for the default organization used when the cue is too late to influence rehearsal. By linking the use of the scan-parse mechanism to the default organization, we can interpret his experiment in the same terms used to account for the Mewhort and Cornett (1972) task.

In a related study, Scheerer (1973) presented letter strings and required subjects to report them in alphabetic order. The strings were constructed such that the order of report was independent of the position in the stimulus array. Nevertheless, accuracy of report was better for the material reported from the left side. Scheerer interpreted his results using the idea of a left-to-right scan, in much the fashion of Heron (1957). In particular, Scheerer argued against an interpretation based on an order-of-report artifact and suggested, instead, that the left-side superiority reflects a perceptual advantage for the material on the left side.

We can agree that the experiment rules out an artifact-of-report account for the left-side superiority, but several other accounts are as plausible as the account Scheerer (1973) suggested. For example, to assist in ordering their response, subjects may adopt a rehearsal scheme which imposes the left-side advantage. In particular, suppose that subjects transfer the material to memory in a left-to-right order and that rehearsal is used both to maintain it and to sort it into alphabetic order. A plausible sorting strategy can be constructed from a series of passes through the stored data. Each pass selects one item from the list; for Scheerer's task, the criterion for selecting a particular item is, of course, based on its position in the alphabet. If subjects were to run through the stored data in left-to-right order, i.e., in the order of entry to short-term memory, rehearsal would favor items from the left of the display, regardless of the order of report. Thus, Scheerer's results do not imply a perceptual advantage for material on the left side. Instead, the advantage could as easily reflect a particular rehearsal scheme.

By exploiting the loading-into-memory characteristic of the scan-parse mechanism simultaneously with rehearsal's sensitivity to order-of-report instructions, Mewhort and Cornett (1972) illustrated the separate contribution of rehearsal and the scan-parse mechanism. Mewhort (1974) illustrated the same separation using a temporal manipulation which selectively impairs the scan-parse mechanism. In his experiment, eight-letter pseudowords of either first- or fourth-order of approximation to English were presented, one letter at a time, on a horizontal row. Each letter appeared for only 5 milliseconds, and the interletter interval was varied from 0 to 100 milliseconds. As in the Mewhort and Cornett study, the pseudowords were presented in both normal and reversed orientation. Finally, the letters were written successively starting from the left or from the right side of the screen.

The letter-by-letter technique is an unusual one, and several aspects of it deserve comment before describing Mewhort's (1974) data. First, consider the phenomenal appearance of the display. When the letters are presented at the fast rate, i.e., with a zero interletter interval, they appear to be on the display simultaneously. As the rate is reduced, however, the successive nature of the presentation becomes clear phenomenally. Nevertheless, each letter remains distinct and clear. Second, as the rate of presentation is reduced, subjects lose the ability to locate the letters correctly: the latter point was clarified in an experiment reported by Hearty and Mewhort (1975). Using the letter-by-letter technique, they designated a target letter before each trial and asked their subjects to indicate its ordinal position in the row. Regardless of the speed, the subjects had no trouble finding the designated letter; furthermore, they had little difficulty locating the item at the fastest rate. Locating the letters accurately, however, became difficult as the rate of presentation was decreased. Thus, as the display loses the appearance of simultaneity, subjects lose precise location information. Finally, if the display involves words, the near-simultaneous condition is likely to be very easy: subjects are unlikely to make many mistakes with an exposure of 5 milliseconds and an interletter interval of zero. To make the task more difficult, an experimenter need only increase the exposure duration.

Mewhort (1974) examined both accuracy and order of report. We shall consider the order of report first. At the fast rates of presentation, i.e., at or near the zero interletter interval, subjects reported the pseudowords in a markedly left-to-right order. As the interletter interval was increased, however, their order of report changed: instead of a standard left-to-right order, the subjects reported in terms of time-of-arrival on the display. Thus, they reported from left to right for slow left-to-right presentations and from right to left for slow right-to-left presentations.

The order-of-report data illustrate that the successful use of the scan-parse mechanism (or, in the limiting case, the decision to use the general-purpose attentional mechanism, instead) depends on the quality of the subject's spatial resolution. Recall that at fast rates of presentation, i.e., when the display is close to simultaneous, the subjects have good spatial resolution. Hence, they use the scan-parse mechanism to load short-term memory. The use of the scan-parse mechanism provides the left-to-right organization which, in turn, provides the basis for a left-to-right report.

When the rate of presentation is decreased, subjects lose their spatial resolution, and the scan-parse mechanism is less successful in providing a left-to-right organization. In the limiting case, i.e., at the slowest rates, the scan-parse mechanism cannot be used at all. The reason reflects the loss of spatial information about the relative position of letters within a word; the scan-parse mechanism normally accepts a parallel input from the character buffer. For slow letter-by-letter displays, subjects are forced to use the general-purpose attentional mechanism to transfer material, one letter at a time, in the order of arrival on the display. Thus, at the slowest rates of presentation, they were forced to adopt an order of report which matched the direction in which successive letters were written on the display.

The accuracy-of-report data (reproduced in Fig. 3) matched the interpretation offered in connection with order of report. Thus, for the conditions which permitted the use of the scan-parse mechanism, the size of the familiarity effect depended on the orientation of the pseudowords; it was large for pseudowords presented in normal orientation but nil for those presented in reversed orientation. When the scan-parse mechanism could not function normally, the size of the familiarity effect was reduced. The extent of the reduction depended on the match between the orientation of the pseudowords and the direction of presentation. For cases in which the orientation did not match the direction of presentation, there was no effect of the familiarity of the material. For the cases which matched—the left-to-right presentation of normal material or the right-to-left presentation of reversed material—the familiarity effect was of moderate size.

Finally, for cases in which the subject reported from left to right, accuracy of report was best on the left side. Similarly, for cases in which they reported from right to left, accuracy of report was best for the material on the right side. For the intermediate cases, i.e., for the cells in which subjects sometimes reported left to right and sometimes right to left, accuracy took a symmetrical U function across the stimulus array.

The appearance of a familiarity effect of a moderate size (for the reversed material presented slowly from right to left and the normal material presented slowly from left to right) reflects rehearsal at the level of short-term memory. The effect is, of course, exactly the possibility which failed to appear in the Mewhort and Cornett (1972) study for reversed materials under instructions to report from right to left. In short, although instructions do not affect the order of input to memory, by disrupting adequate spatial clarity, one can break down the normal left-to-right entry into memory and simulate a letter-by-letter spelling situation. Such a situation yields a moderate familiarity effect reflecting rehearsal (see Merikle, 1969, for an elegant demonstration of rate-limited rehearsal in short-term memory).

A further point deserves mention. The manipulation of interletter intervals dramatically altered both order of report and the size of the familiarity effect. In particular, although performance on the fourth-order material was altered by increasing the interletter interval, the manipulation did not reduce performance on the less familiar material. Thus, the reduction in the size of the familiarity effect cannot be attributed to

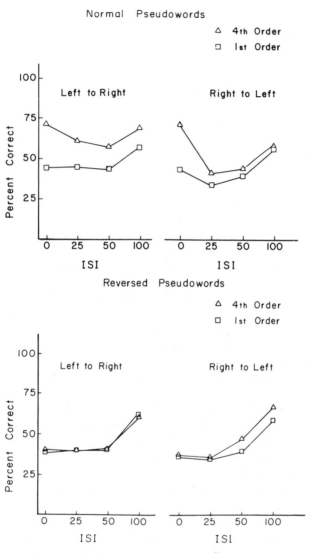

Fig. 3. Accuracy of report as a function of approximation to English, direction of presentation, orientation of the pseudowords, and interletter interval (ISI). The figure is reproduced from Mewhort (1974, Fig. 2, p. 394).

disruption of basic character-identification processes: the manipulation represents a process, not a state limitation to performance (cf. Garner, 1974, pp. 153–161).

In summary, rehearsal operations and the scan-parse mechanism offer separate and complementary functions. Rehearsal is a flexible and general purpose procedure which includes considerable opportunity for ordering material. In addition, it contributes to the familiarity effect in terms of general chunking operations. The scan-parse operator, in contrast, is a reading-specific device which provides a left-to-right organization to material passed to short-term memory. It accepts a parallel input and, therefore, depends on the availability of spatial information.

The evidence presented in this section concerns rehearsal and the scan-parse mechanism. The theory suggests that the latter mechanism uses identified materials, i.e., that it occurs after letter identification. One aspect of Mewhort's (1974) data supports the latter contention, namely the null effect of interletter interval on identification of unfamiliar strings accompanied by a large effect on familiar strings. If the manipulation affected letter identification itself, it should have affected both kinds of material in the fashion illustrated for the illuminance and exposure manipulations in Fig. 1. Thus, the large effect on familiar strings suggests that the manipulation affects a postidentification mechanism. Clearly, however, we need further empirical support for the separation of the two processes, i.e., support for the claim that the scan-parse mechanism follows letter identification.

3. Letter-Identification and the Scan-Parse Mechanism

For the free-recall task, the model postulates that the scan-parse mechanism accepts identified letters from the character buffer. The identification mechanism which fills the character buffer uses letter-frequency information during the identification operation. Thus, the model implies that two separate mechanisms contribute to the familiarity effect prior to short-term memory.

For the bar-probe task, the model suggests that processing is, to the level of the character buffer, the same as in the free-recall task. Instead of using the scan-parse mechanism to transfer the row from the character buffer to short-term memory, subjects in the bar-probe task use a general-purpose attentional mechanism to transfer individual items. The latter mechanism permits them to isolate items spatially in response to the spatial instruction.

The preceding sections have studied response-related effects and evidence separating rehearsal effects from those due to the scan-parse mechanism. The present section discusses evidence distinguishing the letter-identification and the scan-parse mechanisms and evidence supporting the idea of a character buffer.

The model separates the bar-probe and free-recall cases theoretically: the bar-probe experiment should yield a familiarity effect due to the letter-identification process. The free-recall case, in contrast, includes a contribution both from the scan-parse mechanism and from rehearsal. Thus, the model suggests that the familiarity effect in the two tasks is due to different processes. To show that the familiarity effect is due to different mechanisms, we need an experimental technique which confirms the theoretical distinctions.

A variety of experimental techniques is possible. We shall consider one modeled after a strategy popularized by Melton (1963): disputing the distinction between long- and short-term memory, he suggested a criterion for demonstrating whether or not two putative processes are, in fact, separate. To show experimentally that two processes are separate, he suggested that one needs a manipulation which yields different consequences when applied to the mechanisms separately. Thus, to show that the familiarity effect in the free-recall and the bar-probe tasks is due to different mechanisms, we need a manipulation which yields different consequences when applied to the effect in both tasks. To Melton's criterion, we shall include a stipulation: the manipulation must be of such a nature that, in principle, it does not implicate short-term memory or response-related factors. In short, we need an experimental manipulation which can serve as a lever to pry open the front end of the model.

Mewhort (1966) explored a manipulation which satisfies the latter stipulation. Using a free-recall procedure, he presented pseudowords of zero- and fourth-order approximation to English under two conditions of letter spacing. In the normal condition, the materials were prepared with spacing of the sort used in standard typing. Under the wide-spacing condition, the materials were prepared with extra space between the characters. The extra space was about the width of two characters.

Such a spacing manipulation is unlikely to affect short-term memory. Indeed, considering both the temporal nature of rehearsal and the spatial nature of the manipulation, it is hard to imagine how one could attribute any consequence of the manipulation to factors at the level of short-term memory. In contrast, given that the scan-parse mechanism accepts a spatial array, a spatial manipulation might well alter its function. For the same reason, the manipulation could affect the letter-identification mechanism. Indeed, as we have noted earlier (Section II,B,3), some have suggested that the manipulation should affect the sensory apparatus which provides the basic visual data to the latter mechanisms.

In Mewhort's (1966) study, subjects were required to report as many letters as possible without regard for order of report. Overall, subjects reported more letters for the higher order of approximation to English. In addition, the size of the familiarity effect was reduced as letter spacing increased, i.e., the spacing manipulation had little consequence for report of zero-order strings but reduced report of fourth-order strings markedly.

Campbell and Mewhort (1980) repeated Mewhort's (1966) free-recall task using a larger number of subjects and a wider range of stimulus materials. Again, increasing letter spacing markedly reduced performance on higher order approximations to English, but it had little effect on unfamiliar letter strings. Next, they used the same materials and visual details in a bar-probe partial-report task. The results for the bar-probe task showed a clear familiarity effect, but no hint of an interaction of the spacing manipulation with the familiarity variable. In short, while both tasks show a familiarity effect, the effect in the free-recall case is sensitive to letter spacing while that in the bar-probe task is not sensitive to the same manipulation. In terms of Melton's (1963) criterion, the contrast provides strong evidence that the familiarity effect reflects different underlying mechanisms in the two tasks.

In terms of the resources and processes suggested earlier (Section III), given that the scan-parse mechanism is sensitive to letter spacing, the difference in the familiarity effect for the two tasks fits the model quite well. For the bar-probe case, the familiarity effect reflects the letter-identification mechanism, whereas the effect in the free-recall case involves both the basic identification process and the scan-parse mechanism. In addition, the contrast implies the use of different transfer mechanisms connecting the character buffer to short-term memory, namely the scan-parse mechanism for the free-recall case and the attentional mechanism for the bar-probe case.

The comparison between the free-recall and the bar-probe tasks shows that the two experiments reflect different familiarity effects. Nevertheless, the free-recall case involves a multi-item report, and even though the interaction of spacing with familiarity is unlikely to reflect report processes, a skeptic may wish to compare the bar-probe example to a task with similar report characteristics. The skeptic may require, for example, a test between two partial-report tasks, one involving the scan-parse mechanism and one using the attentional mechanism. More important, because the model suggests that different mechanisms are used in the free-recall and bar-probe tasks, it should also include a means to understand why each is used in a particular situation. The skeptic may also require, then, a means to predict the assignment of resources from the processing requirements for a particular task.

In response to both of the skeptic's requests, Campbell and Mewhort

(1980) included a digit-probe task in addition to the free-recall and the bar-probe tasks. In a digit-probe task, subjects are presented a row of letters and are asked to report one item. Instead of a bar probe marking the item spatially, the cue is a digit. The digit marks the item required in terms of its ordinal position in the stimulus array. For their digit-probe task, Campbell and Mewhort included the same materials which they had used in the bar-probe task. In addition, they included the same letter-spacing conditions.

Campbell and Mewhort (1980) included the digit-probe task because it seems to meet the skeptic's requirements: like a bar-probe task, it involves a single-item report, and as in the free-recall task, subjects should use the scan-parse mechanism to carry out the experiment (Section III,C). In particular, unlike a bar-probe situation, the probe in a digit-probe task is an indirect marker, not a direct spatial indicator. Consequently, a subject cannot use the attentional mechanism to address the character buffer. Instead, the subjects must transfer the row to short-term memory and find the appropriate item by counting through the list. Counting is a temporal operation associated with short-term memory, and because the task requires them to transfer the material to short-term memory, the subjects should use the scan-parse mechanism to effect the transfer.

Consistent with their theoretical analysis of the digit-probe task, there was a large familiarity effect in the experiment, and, as in the free-recall task, the familiarity effect was reduced sharply when the letter spacing was increased. Other details of the digit-probe experiment, particularly the pattern of errors, were consistent with their theoretical analysis. Thus, when compared to the bar-probe experiment, the difference in the effect of the spacing manipulation shows that the two partial-report techniques involve different processing mechanisms. Further, the difference can be understood in terms of the resource demands each task imposes.

G. T. Campbell (1981) has corroborated the theoretical analysis using the reversed-stimulus technique exploited by Mewhort (1974) and by Mewhort and Cornett (1972). In the bar-probe case, the familiarity effect is thought to reflect the letter-identification mechanism. For the digit-probe example, however, the scan-parse mechanism is also involved. Because the two tasks require different resources, the familiarity effect in each should reflect the information used by the particular mechanisms involved in the task. The identification mechanism uses letter-frequency information, but the scan-parse mechanism uses an elaborate set of orthographic rules. Because the identification mechanism uses simple letter-frequency information, G. T. Campbell argued that reversed spelling should not change the familiarity effect in the bar-probe task. For the digit-probe case, however, she argued that reversed spelling ought to upset the left-to-right (sequential) constraints present in higher orders of approximation to English. The constraints match some of the knowledge used by the scan-parse mechanism. Thus, in contrast to the bar-probe example, reversing the material in a digit-probe case should reduce the familiarity effect. Both predictions were confirmed in her experiments: reversed spelling had little consequence in the bar-probe case but sharply reduced the familiarity effect in the digit-probe task.

The character buffer is the interface connecting letter recognition and the scan-parse mechanism. As Smith and Spoehr (1974) point out, such a buffer is a basic requirement for any account involving a grammar for parsing of the sort we urge here. It is also necessary, for example, for the BOSS (Basic Orthographic Syllabic Structure) account urged recently by Taft (1979a, 1979b). Smith and Spoehr treat the assumption as a necessary evil, i.e., as an assumption they acknowledge but would rather do without. Perhaps their reluctance to embrace the assumption reflects their apparently ad hoc endorsement of it. As Mewhort et al. (1981) document, however, the assumption is not ad hoc: direct evidence for the idea of the character buffer, i.e., for the concept of a postcategorical spatial data buffer, is provided in the bar-probe task (see also Campbell & Mewhort, 1980; Mewhort & Campbell, 1978). The evidence rests on a complicated set of interconnected relationships: in particular, the interplay among accuracy of report, errors of location, and errors of identification both across the stimulus array and across kinds of material suggest that subjects use the bar-probe to address material at a post-identification level, i.e., at the character buffer.

V. WORD IDENTIFICATION

The summary of evidence for the scan-parse model has traced the development of the account from early scanning theory to more recent work. Throughout the review, we have discussed performance in (and theories for) tasks involving displays of nonsense material. In particular, we have focused on the free-recall paradigm and on the familiarity effect associated with that task. While the focus has helped us to clarify the model, our title promises a discussion of word identification, not merely an analysis of performance in tachistoscopic paradigms. It seems appropriate, therefore, to turn the discussion of the model to problems of word identification.

Word identification is a highly overlearned skill embedded within a complex set of eye-movement controls and comprehension processes.

To reduce the difficulty of the task, we shall restrict the discussion to the problem of reading individual words. The restriction may not, however, be as severe as it seems: the control and comprehension processes appear to be independent of the processes responsible for reading individual words (Just & Carpenter, 1980).

The heart of the model is the scan-parse mechanism. It is the portion of the model which uses the most extensive part of the subject's knowledge of English orthography, and, because it converts the spatial representation to a temporal form, it is central to preparing the material for use by pronunciation- and lexical-access mechanisms. Although other parts of the system are involved to various degrees, because the use of the scan-parse mechanism is central to the model's account of a word-processing task, predictions from the model for word identification are based on the characteristics of that mechanism. Thus, to obtain predictions for a simple word-identification task, we must consider it within an experimental paradigm which exposes the scan-parse mechanism in a relatively straightforward way.

The problem is that, for a multicomponent system, one can limit performance at several levels. A masking technique could, for example, push accuracy of identification from 100 to 0%, but such a procedure would affect the letter-identification process as well as the scan-parse mechanism. To test the model, we want a relatively clean technique: although the model has been derived from an analysis of performance with nonsense materials, our claim is that it reflects reading skills and, as a result, that it predicts word identification. In particular, we claim that reading a word by itself involves the machinery which we have described—the feature- and character-buffers, the identification and scan-parse mechanisms, and the executive to establish the artificial system. If the machinery is used in reading, it follows that a word's meaning does not alter its processing up to the level of short-term memory, and, to test that claim, we need a paradigm which focuses specifically at the scan-parse mechanism.

An experimental paradigm which satisfies the requirement was illustrated by Mewhort (1974). His experiment involved a simple free-recall task using the letter-by-letter display technique. As we discussed earlier (Section IV,B,2), manipulating the interletter interval did not affect basic character identification, but it altered the size of the familiarity effect by preventing use of the scan-parse mechanism. Accordingly, to test subjects' use of the scan-parse mechanism during reading, Mewhort and Beal (1977, Expt. 1) combined the paradigm with a simple word-identification task.

To clarify the nature of the parallel that one should expect for the two experiments, we have reproduced Mewhort's (1974) pseudoword data in Fig. 3. The figure presents accuracy of report as a function of the orientation of the pseudowords (top panel for normal and bottom panel for reversed orientation), the direction of presentation across the display (left side for left-to-right presentation and right side for right-to-left presentation), the order of approximation to English, and the interstimulus, i.e., interletter, interval.

As is clear in Fig. 3, accuracy of report was greater for the pseudowords of fourth- than for those of first-order approximation to English, but the size of the effect was reduced both by reversed orientation and by increasing the interletter interval. Mewhort (1974) interpreted the results in terms of the scan-parse mechanism. Increasing the interletter interval reduces spatial clarity and, thereby, eliminates use of the scan-parse mechanism. For the material in normal orientation (top panels), the decrease in the familiarity effect reflects the mechanism directly. At the slowest rates, for the material presented from left-to-right, however, there was a residual familiarity effect reflecting rehearsal processes at the short-term memory level. The material in reversed orientation (bottom panels) illustrates the same mechanisms, including the residual rehearsal effect, but, of course, accuracy of report reflects the redundancy resulting from the reversal technique.

What outcome would one expect for a word-identification task involving the same display conditions? By a simple linear extrapolation, one might be tempted to argue that words are more familiar than pseudowords and would, as a result, behave as higher-than-fourth-order material. If so, we would predict that word-identification scores would assume shapes similar to those exhibited by the curves for fourth-order material in Fig. 3, but with a shift upward to reflect the extra familiarity. Alternately, one might argue that words have meaning, a property not shared by the nonsense material. Because of the difference, one might be tempted to suggest that little parallel could be expected, i.e., that nonsense cannot predict sense.

Because the scan-parse mechanism is central to the process, word identification should reflect use of the mechanism. In terms of Mewhort's (1974) account, the size of the familiarity effect reflects two mechanisms, the scan-parse mechanism and a residual rehearsal (chunking) factor. Both mechanisms should work in about the same way when words are used instead of pseudowords. But, because the pseudoword task includes a baseline reflecting maintenance and ordered report—even with first-order material, report never fell below two letters—and because a single word should impose little (if any) maintenance load, one must subtract the baseline to estimate the impact of chunking and of the scan-parse mechanism. Thus, word-identification scores should parallel the size of the familiarity effect—literally, the difference in letters reported correctly for fourth-order and first-order material—in corresponding conditions.

Figure 4 presents the same data shown in Fig. 3, but the data have been recast to show the size of the familiarity effect. To draw the figure, the size of the familiarity effect was calculated by subtracting the accuracy of report score for first-order material from that for the fourth-order material. Thus, the data shown in the left panel of Fig. 4 show the differences for the data in the top panels of Fig. 3, and the data in the right panel of Fig. 4 show the differences for the cells in the bottom panels of Fig. 3.

Figure 5 shows the word-identification scores obtained by Mewhort and Beal (1977, Expt. 1). As is clear from a comparison of Figs. 4 and 5, the pattern for the word-identification scores is an excellent match to the pattern obtained from the pseudoword task. In short, word identification illustrates the predictions derived with the scan-parse account from a pseudoword task.

The success of the prediction, i.e., of the link between word identi-

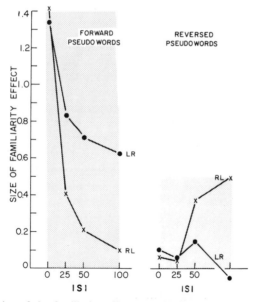

Fig. 4. The size of the familiarity effect as a function of direction of presentation, orientation of the pseudowords, and interletter interval (ISI). The figure shows the same data presented in Fig. 3 recast by subtracting performance on first-order material from that on fourth-order material. The figure is reproduced from Mewhort and Beal (1977, Fig. 3, p. 635).

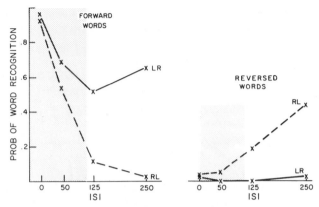

Fig. 5. Word identification as a function of direction of presentation, orientation of the words, and interletter interval (ISI). The figure is reproduced from Mewhort and Beal (1977, Fig. 1, p. 632). The shaded portion shows the range of interletter intervals used by Mewhort (1974).

fication and performance in free-recall pseudoword tasks, implies that word identification uses the same initial processing steps which are used in a pseudoword study. From the present perspective, the prediction implies that word identification uses the same processes used in a free-recall task, up to the level of short-term memory. A second implication concerns the idea that words are like superfamiliar pseudowords. The prediction is based on our ability to manipulate a mechanism used in reading, not the properties of words versus pseudowords. The super-familiarity idea refers to a property of the stimulus itself, and, as a result, it puts emphasis on the wrong aspect of the task: it is silly to manipulate properties of the stimulus without due regard for the mechanisms underlying performance.

The latter distinction is similar to a dispute offered J. J. Gibson by his critics. According to Gibson (1966), as we gain perceptual expertise, we learn to differentiate the invariants built into stimuli. His position has been very influential, and it has helped to destroy some myths about the complexity of perception. Nevertheless, the position can be carried too far: artificial invariants, such as regularities of spelling, require rules to decode them (cf. Boden, 1977, pp. 410ff), and rules imply an active decoding system rather than simple stimulus differentiation (cf. E. J. Gibson & Levin, 1975, Ch. 3 and 6).

The scan-parse model provides an account of a set of diverse word-identification experiments. Mewhort and Beal (1977, Expt. 2) presented nonoverlapping letter groups from left to right or from right to left across a display. When the letter groups formed syllables—units which permit the parser to function well—word identification was more accurate than when the groups formed nonsyllabic units of equivalent size. Accuracy of report also depended, however, on both the rate of presentation and the direction of presentation. For fast rates, i.e., rates which yield the illusion of simultaneity, the parser could act on the whole word, and there was little effect of the kind of unit or of the direction of presentation. For slower rates, however, performance reflected the degree to which chunking at the short-term memory level could make up for deficiencies in the data passed to it by the scan-parse mechanism. When the material passed to short-term memory had to be reassembled to form a word—especially if the rate of presentation "pushed" the reassembly process—word identification was reduced.

In a related experiment, Mewhort and Beal (1977, Expt. 3) presented a column of nonoverlapping letter groups. Each group, in turn, comprised a column of letters—a configuration which does not permit the parser to function. Word identification was poor regardless of the rate of presentation. Taken together, their experiments suggest that the parser cannot function if input to it is not in the form of a horizontal row. In addition, the experiments show that short-term memory operations are too slow to make up for deficiencies in the data either when the parser has not functioned properly or when the appropriate units have been passed in an inappropriate order. Mewhort and Campbell (1980) have confirmed both conclusions using an overprinting technique. With the overprinting technique, letters and/or letter groups were presented on the same retinal location, and the rate of presentation was manipulated by changing the interitem interval. Oléron (1972) has provided comparable data which also support the idea that integration at the short-term memory level is too slow to make up deficiencies produced by a failure of the parser.

Newman (1966) presented a paragraph of text (from Locke's *Treatise of Civil Government*) one line at a time. The text was presented using a motion-picture technique, and the letters appeared as if they were moving rapidly from right to left behind a stationary slit. Newman varied the width of the slit and, thereby, varied the context available to the subject. In addition, he varied the speed at which the letters appeared to move behind the slit.

In terms of the scan-parse account, Newman's (1966) technique should affect the scan-parse mechanism in a fairly straightforward way. By reducing the width of the slit, for example, he effectively reduced the spatial context on which the parser depends. The impact of the reduction, of course, should depend on the rate of presentation; at slow rates, integration at the short-term memory level may be fast enough. Newman's results were consistent with the analysis based on the scan-parse account. In his words, the "numerical results make clear what was strikingly obvious to the Ss; namely, that the lack of context radically reduces the speed at which material can be read . . . text that could be read easily . . . so long as a string of eight letters was present became almost totally unintelligible as a series of single letters" (p. 275).

The scan-parse account is an example of a "box" model within the information-processing tradition. Craik and Lockhart (1972) have objected to models expressed in such terms. Instead, they have suggested a position involving a depth-of-processing metaphor. One of the difficulties which they sought to overcome with the new metaphor concerns the apparent rigidity of an account expressed in solid boxes. A block diagram does not seem to capture the flexibility, the ambiguity, and the subtlety of a subject's behavior.

One reason for the apparent rigidity may reflect a too literal reading of the theorist's efforts. The present model, for example, is too rigid when taken too literally. To illustrate the point, suppose that a subject were shown a word in a simple bar-probe task: the model suggests that the attentional mechanism will be used to pass material from the character buffer to short-term memory. Once in short-term memory, the item is passed to a report mechanism. While it deals with word identification in other contexts, there is nothing in the account to suggest that subjects in a bar-probe task would know that the material shown was, in fact, a word. But, it is clear that subjects in such a task do know that the material is composed of words (e.g., Mewhort & Campbell, 1978, Expt. 1). Thus, taken literally, the model does not anticipate the fact that, even in a bar-probe task, subjects may identify the word. The difficulty is that the model leaves the subject deep in thought at the end of a trial.

Craik and Lockhart (1972) attempt to solve the problem by weakening the structure of box models; instead of clear processing steps, they prefer to slide on a continuum through the system. Our approach to the problem of inflexibility is to acknowledge flexibility at the level of the executive. Why should the executive stop all processing at the end of a trial? Perhaps subjects engage in extracurricular behavior between trials.

To explore the flexibility question, Mewhort and Marchetti (1980) used words as stimuli in both a bar-probe and a digit-probe task. Following the experiment, the subjects were given an unexpected recognition test requiring them to identify which words had appeared during the probe task by selecting them from an equal number of new items.

The rationale for the experiment follows: if subjects identify a word during either probe task, they do so outside the formal requirements of the task. Nevertheless, the model does suggest that subjects take the stimulus to different "depths" during the formal task. In a digit-probe task, for example, the model suggests that subjects use the scan-parse mechanism to transfer all of the stimulus to the level of short-term memory. For the bar-probe task, the model suggests that only one, or perhaps two, items need to be taken to the level of short-term memory. Inasmuch as the account leaves the data at a deeper level following the digit-probe task (and in a temporal rather than a spatial form), subjects should be more likely to identify the word after that task than after the bar-probe task. Correct recognition during the unexpected test, presumably, provides an adequate measure of the extent to which subjects have extended processing past the formal requirement of their task.

The results confirmed the prediction: subjects identified more words following a digit- than a bar-probe experiment. There was no relation between performance on the probe tasks and on subsequent identification, however. In addition, in a control experiment which required subjects to report each word aloud during both the bar- and digit-probe tasks (in addition to the letter probed), word identification improved, and the difference in identification for the two kinds of probe task was eliminated, a point confirming the incidental nature of word-identification in the original study.

The preceding interpretation suggests a method for studying the executive. Presumably, incidental word identification results because subjects have time and/or capacity between trials to explore the task beyond its formal requirement. If so, one ought to be able to reduce such activity by keeping the subject busy with a secondary task. At present, the possibility remains unexplored, however.

VI. CONCLUDING REMARKS

Our review has not been exhaustive, and there are a multitude of issues remaining. In closing, however, it is important to note that we are committed to some ideas more strongly than to others. For the present account, the important issues concern the structure, or architecture, of the model. Many of the other issues are much less important. For example, we have suggested that character identification involves an educated feature-analysis mechanism which accepts precategorical data and passes its decisions to a postcategorical memory. The important part of the suggestion concerns the levels of data storage and the access different tasks have to different kinds of data. Thus, the idea of a precategorical data store versus a postcategorical character buffer is crucial; the idea of a particular kind of feature analysis is less critical. Indeed, in a rough way, an autocorrelation model for form identification (e.g., Engel, Dougherty, & Jones, 1973) might do as well as the feature analysis we have suggested.

Similarly, while the distinction between the spatial data representation at the character buffer and the temporal representation in short-term memory is crucial, the details of the parsing system which converts data from one form to the other are less critical. We do not mean to suggest that the current parser is entirely arbitrary or subject to change on a whim but, rather, to emphasize the structural aspect of the account. While changes to the parsing scheme would alter a number of features of the model, other parsing systems deserve note. Taft (1979a, 1979b), for example, has suggested an alternate system based on semantic–orthographic rules. We have some reservations about his suggestions (see, for example, Mewhort & Campbell, 1980), but, at the same time, they are not so radically different from the present scheme (or from the scheme suggested by Smith & Spoehr, 1974) that all could not benefit from intermarriage. Although it would force a more radical change, Adams (1980) has suggested a parsing scheme based on a letter-association network, and her account has remarkable success at simulating the kind of parsing rules suggested here.

Building a model for reading when a good deal of the effort concerns work with pseudowords may seem to some readers to be an ivory-tower enterprise. Such readers may well ask whether or not such an account can offer teachers immediate advice. The answer is both yes and no. At one level, we regret the lack of concrete information to assist day-to-day decisions. At the same time, however, we fear that a premature attempt to intervene would lead more to mischief than to help. Nevertheless, a few generalizations seem appropriate.

The heart of our account is the scan-parse mechanism. It is a rule-based mechanism, and the rules, presumably, are acquired by experience with reading. If there is any merit to such an account, it follows that the beginning reader must be given as much opportunity to acquire the rules as possible. Obviously, acquisition of rules requires practice. Less obvious, however, it also requires experience with a full range of examples. It is dangerous to truncate the beginning reader's experience by even well-intentioned editing of the samples of orthography which he sees (cf. Gibson & Levin, 1975, Ch. 9); the beginning reader may discover inappropriate rules as a consequence of limited exposure to the language. A related point concerns "reforms" to English spelling. In developing a computer simulation for the parser, we have had occasion to inquire into details of English orthography. Orthographic rules in English are complicated and rich. A number of authorities seem to feel that orthography needs reform, usually to encourage greater regularity in the correspondence between spelling and pronunciation. We suggest instead, however, that most of the difficulties which they wish to reform reflect semantic properties of words, not irregularities in spelling-to-sound rules (cf. Gibson & Levin, 1975, pp. 183–187). Thus, we are not among those who seek reform based on simplistic spelling-to-sound rules; change is likely to occur at the expense of meaning.

The scan-parse mechanism developed from Heron's (1957) concept of a scanning mechanism. His ideas concerning the scanning mechanism were based, in turn, on Hebb's (1949) speculations concerning sensory–motor interaction. If there is any merit in the idea of an internalized shift of attention developed from sensory–motor integration, a beginning reader cannot help but be disadvantaged by training with odd configurations of text. How, for example, could one acquire an internal distribution-of-attention mechanism if one sees only a few words on a line of text? In the same vein, recent evidence suggests that subtle changes to the configuration of text—specifically, alterations in right-justification of typescript—alter undergraduates' reading speed, and, perhaps, their comprehension while reading (e.g., Campbell, Marchetti, & Mewhort, 1981).

ACKNOWLEDGMENTS

The preparation of this manuscript was supported by a grant from the Natural Sciences and Engineering Research Council Canada (AP 318) and from the Advisory Research Committee, School of Graduate Studies and Research, Queen's University at Kingston. We wish to thank Dr. B. E. Butler for his advice and careful reading of an earlier draft of the manuscript. In addition, we thank Dr. G. K. Humphrey, F. M. Marchetti, G. T. Campbell, R. S. McCann, and R. Woodhouse for helpful comments. Finally, we wish to acknowledge many happy discussions with Dr. Rainer von Königslöw on the problems of theory, artificial intelligence, and their relation to modern experimental psychology.

REFERENCES

Adams, M. J. What good is orthographic redundancy? In O. J. L. Tzeng & H. Singer (Eds.). *Perception of print: Reading research in experimental psychology*. Hillsdale, New Jersey: Erlbaum, 1980.

Anderson, J. R. *Language, memory, and thought*. Hillsdale, New Jersey: Erlbaum, 1976.

Anderson, J. R., & Bower, G. H. *Human associative memory*. New York: Wiley, 1974.

Averbach, E., & Coriell, A. S. Short-term memory in vision. *The Bell System Technical Journal*, 1961, **40**, 309–328.

Ayres, J. J. B. Some artifactual causes of perceptual primacy. *Journal of Experimental Psychology*, 1966, **71**, 896–901.

Ayres, J. J., & Harcum, E. R. Directional response-bias in reproducing brief visual patterns. *Perceptual and Motor Skills,* 1962, **14,** 155–165.

Baddeley, A. D. Immediate memory and the "perception" of letter sequences. *Quarterly Journal of Experimental Psychology,* 1964, **16,** 364–367.

Bjork, E. L., & Murray, J. T. On the nature of input channels in visual processing. *Psychological Review,* 1977, **84,** 472–484.

Bobrow, D. G., & Collins, A. (Eds.). *Representation and understanding: Studies in cognitive science.* New York: Academic Press, 1975.

Bobrow, D. G., & Winograd, T. An overview of KRL, a knowledge representation language. *Cognitive Science,* 1977, **1,** 3–46.

Bobrow, D. G., & Winograd, T. KRL another perspective. *Cognitive Science,* 1979, **3,** 29–42.

Boden, M. A. *Artificial intelligence and natural man.* New York: Basic Books, 1977.

Bower, G. H., & Springton, F. Pauses as recoding points in letter series. *Journal of Experimental Psychology,* 1970, **83,** 421–430.

Breitmeyer, B. G., & Ganz, L. Implications of sustained and transient channels for theories of visual pattern masking, saccadic suppression, and information processing. *Psychological Review,* 1976, **83,** 1–36.

Brewer, W. F. Is reading a letter-by-letter process? In J. F. Kavanagh & I. G. Mattingly (Eds.), *Language by ear and by eye.* Cambridge, Massachusetts: MIT Press, 1972.

Broadbent, D. E. Word-frequency effect and response bias. *Psychological Review,* 1967, **74,** 1–15.

Bruner, J. S., & Anglin, J. M. *Beyond the information given.* New York: Norton, 1973.

Bryden, M. P. Tachistoscopic recognition of non-alphabetical material. *Canadian Journal of Psychology,* 1960, **14,** 78–86.

Bryden, M. P. The role of post-exposural eye movements in tachistoscopic perception. *Canadian Journal of Psychology,* 1961, **15,** 220–225.

Bryden, M. P. Left-right differences in tachistoscopic recognition: Directional scanning or cerebral dominance? *Perceptual and Motor Skills,* 1966, **23,** 1127–1134. (a)

Bryden, M. P. Accuracy and order of report in tachistoscopic recognition. *Canadian Journal of Psychology,* 1966, **20,** 262–272. (b)

Bryden, M. P. A model for the sequential organization of behaviour. *Canadian Journal of Psychology,* 1967, **21,** 37–56.

Bryden, M. P. Symmetry of letters as a factor in tachistoscopic recognition. *American Journal of Psychology,* 1968, **81,** 513–524.

Bryden, M. P., Dick, A. O., & Mewhort, D. J. K. Tachistoscopic recognition of number sequences. *Canadian Journal of Psychology,* 1968, **22,** 52–59.

Buschke, H. Learning is organized by chunking. *Journal of Verbal Learning and Verbal Behavior,* 1976, **15,** 313–324.

Butler, B. The limits of selective attention in tachistoscopic recognition. *Canadian Journal of Psychology,* 1974, **28,** 199–213.

Butler, B. E. Selective attention and stimulus localization in visual perception. *Canadian Journal of Psychology,* 1980, **34,** 119–133. (a)

Butler, B. E. The category effect in visual search: Identification versus localization factors. *Canadian Journal of Psychology,* 1980, **34,** 238–247. (b)

Butler, B. E. Canadian studies of visual information processing: 1970–1980. *Canadian Psychology,* 1981, in press.

Campbell, A. J. *Mechanisms of letter and word identification.* Unpublished doctoral dissertation, Queen's University at Kingston, 1979.

Campbell, A. J., Marchetti, F. M., & Mewhort, D. J. K. Reading speed and text production: A note on right-justification techniques. *Ergonomics,* 1981, in press.

Campbell, A. J., & Mewhort, D. J. K. On familiarity effects in visual information processing. *Canadian Journal of Psychology,* 1980, **34,** 134–154.

Campbell, G. T. *Early visual processing: Performance without iconic memory.* Unpublished doctoral dissertation, Queen's University at Kingston, 1981, in preparation.

Cattell, J. McK. Ueber die Zeit der Erkennung und Benennung von Schriftzeichen, Bildern, und Farben. *Philosophische Studien,* 1885, **2,** 635–650. Reprinted in translation in A. T. Poffenberger (Ed.), *James McKeen Cattell: Man of science.* York, Pennsylvania: Science Press, 1947. (a)

Cattell, J. McK. The inertia of the eye and brain. *Brain,* 1885, **8,** 295–312. (b)

Chall, J. S. *Learning to read: The great debate; an inquiry into the science, art, and ideology of old and new methods of teaching children to read, 1910–1965.* New York: McGraw-Hill, 1967.

Chall, J. S. Learning and not learning to read: Current theories and trends. In F. A. Young & D. B. Lindsley (Eds.), *Early experience and visual information processing in perceptual and reading disorders.* Washington, D.C.: National Academy of Sciences, 1970.

Chastain, G. Feature analysis and the growth of a percept. *Journal of Experimental Psychology: Human Perception and Performance,* 1977, **3,** 291–298.

Cornett, S. M. *The tachistoscopic recognition of alphabetic and geometric sequences.* Unpublished M.A. thesis, Queen's University at Kingston, 1972.

Craik, F. I. M., & Lockhart, R. S. Levels of processing: A framework for memory research. *Journal of Verbal Learning and Verbal Behavior,* 1972, **11,** 671–684.

Crovitz, H. F., & Daves, W. Tendencies to eye movement and perceptual accuracy. *Journal of Experimental Psychology,* 1962, **63,** 495–498.

Davidson, M. L., Fox, M., & Dick, A. O. Effect of eye movements on backward masking and perceived location. *Perception and Psychophysics,* 1973, **14,** 110–116.

Engel, G. R., Dougherty, W. G., & Jones, G. B. Correlation and letter recognition. *Canadian Journal of Psychology,* 1973, **27,** 317–326.

Estes, W. K. Perceptual processing in letter recognition and reading. In E. C. Carterette & M. P. Friedman (Eds.), *Handbook of Perception* (Vol. 9). New York: Academic Press, 1978.

Feigenbaum, E. A., & Feldman, J. (Eds.). *Computers and thought.* New York: McGraw-Hill, 1963.

Feigenbaum, E. A., & Simon, H. A. A theory of the serial position effect. *British Journal of Psychology,* 1962, **53,** 307–320.

Fodor, J. A. *The language of thought.* Hassocks, England: Harvester Press, 1976.

Fodor, J. A. The mind-body problem. *Scientific American,* 1981, **244** (1), 114–123.

Freeburne, C. M., & Goldman, R. D. Left-right differences in tachistoscopic recognition as a function of order of report, expectancy, and training. *Journal of Experimental Psychology,* 1969, **79,** 570–572.

Friendly, M. L. In search of the m-gram: The structure of organization in free recall. *Cognitive Psychology,* 1977, **9,** 188–249.

Garner, W. R. *Uncertainty and structure as psychological concepts.* New York: Wiley, 1962.

Garner, W. R. *The processing of information and structure.* Potomac, Maryland: Erlbaum, 1974.

Gibson, E. J., & Levin, H. *The psychology of reading.* Cambridge, Massachusetts: MIT Press, 1975.

Gibson, J. J. *The senses considered as perceptual systems.* Boston, Massachusetts: Houghton, 1966.

Goldiamond, I., & Hawkins, W. F. Vexierversuch: The log relationship between word-

D. J. K. Mewhort and A. J. Campbell

frequency and recognition obtained in the absence of stimulus words. *Journal of Experimental Psychology*, 1958, **56**, 457–463.

Goldstein, I., & Papert, S. Artificial intelligence, language, and the study of knowledge. *Cognitive Science*, 1977, **1**, 84–123.

Gough, P. B. One second of reading. In J. F. Kavanagh & I. G. Mattingly (Eds.), *Language by ear and by eye*. Cambridge, Massachusetts: MIT Press, 1972.

Gough, P. B., & Cosky, M. J. One second of reading again. In N. J. Castellan, Jr., D. B. Pisoni, & G. R. Potts (Eds.), *Cognitive Theory* (Vol. 2). Hillsdale, New Jersey: Erlbaum, 1977.

Haber, R. N., & Hershenson, M. *The psychology of visual perception*. New York: Holt, 1973.

Hall, D. C. Eye movements in scanning iconic memory. *Journal of Experimental Psychology*, 1974, **103**, 825–830.

Hansen, D., & Rodgers, T. S. An exploration of psycholinguistic units in initial reading. In K. S. Goodman (Ed.), *The psycholinguistic nature of the reading process*. Detroit, Michigan: Wayne State University Press, 1973.

Hanson, A. R., Riseman, E. M., & Fisher, E. Context in word recognition. *Pattern Recognition*, 1976, **8**, 35–45.

Harcum, E. R. Effects of symmetry on the perception of tachistoscopic patterns. *American Journal of Psychology*, 1964, **77**, 600–606.

Harcum, E. R. Mnemonic organization as a determinent of error-gradients in visual pattern recognition. *Perceptual and Motor Skills*, 1966, **22**, 671–696.

Harcum, E. R. Parallel functions of serial learning and tachistoscopic pattern perception. *Psychological Review*, 1967, **74**, 51–62.

Harcum, E. R. Perceptibility gradients for tachistoscopic patterns: Sensitivity or saliency? *Psychological Review*, 1970, **77**, 332–337.

Harcum, E. R., & Dyer, D. W. Monocular and binocular reproduction of binary stimuli appearing right and left of fixation. *American Journal of Psychology*, 1962, **75**, 56–65.

Harcum, E. R., & Filion, R. D. L. Effects of stimulus reversals on lateral dominance in word recognition. *Perceptual and Motor Skills*, 1963, **17**, 779–794.

Harcum, E. R., & Finkel, M. E. Explanation of Mishkin and Forgays' result as a directional-reading conflict. *Canadian Journal of Psychology*, 1963, **17**, 224–234.

Harcum, E. R., & Friedman, S. M. Reversal reading by Israeli observers of visual patterns without intrinsic directionality. *Canadian Journal of Psychology*, 1963, **17**, 361–369.

Harcum, E. R., Hartman, R. R., & Smith, N. F. Pre- versus post-knowledge of required reproduction sequence for tachistoscopic patterns. *Canadian Journal of Psychology*, 1963, **17**, 264–273.

Harcum, E. R., & Nice, D. S. Serial processing shown by mutual masking of icons. *Perceptual and Motor Skills*, 1975, **40**, 399–408.

Hearty, P. J., & Mewhort, D. J. K. Spatial localization in sequential letter displays. *Canadian Journal of Psychology*, 1975, **29**, 348–359.

Hebb, D. O. *The organization of behavior*. New York: Wiley, 1949.

Heron, W. Perception as a function of retinal locus and attention. *American Journal of Psychology*, 1957, **70**, 38–48.

Hirata, K., & Bryden, M. P. Tables of letter sequences varying in order of approximation to English. *Psychonomic Science*, 1971, **25**, 322–324.

Huey, E. B. *The psychology and pedagogy of reading*. Cambridge, Massachusetts: MIT Press, 1968. (Originally published by Macmillan, 1908).

Hunt, E. The memory we must have. In R. C. Shank & K. M. Colby (Eds.), *Computer models of thought and language*. San Francisco, California: Freeman, 1973.

Jackson, M. D., & McClelland, J. L. Processing determinants of reading speed. *Journal of Experimental Psychology: General*, 1979, **108**, 151–181.

Johnson, N. F. On the function of letters in word identification: Some data and a preliminary model. *Journal of Verbal Learning and Verbal Behavior*, 1975, **14**, 17–29.

Johnson, N. F. A pattern-unit model of word identification. In D. LaBerge & S. J. Samuels (Eds.), *Basic processes in reading: Perception and comprehension*. Hillsdale, New Jersey: Erlbaum, 1977.

Johnston, J. C. A test of sophisticated guessing theory of word perception. *Cognitive Psychology*, 1978, **10**, 123–153.

Just, M. A., & Carpenter, P. A. A theory of reading: From eye fixations to comprehension. *Psychological Review*, 1980, **87**, 329–354.

Kaufman, L. *Sight and mind: An introduction to visual perception*. London and New York: Oxford University Press, 1974.

Kimura, D. The effect of letter position on recognition. *Canadian Journal of Psychology*, 1959, **13**, 1–10.

Kintsch, W., & Vipond, D. Reading comprehension and readability in educational practice and psychological theory. In L.-G. Nilsson (Ed.), *Perspectives on memory research*. Hillsdale, New Jersey: Erlbaum, 1979.

Kolers, P. A. Experiments in reading. *Scientific American*, 1972, **227** (1), 84–91.

Krueger, L. E. Familiarity effects in visual information processing. *Psychological Bulletin*, 1975, **82**, 949–974.

Krueger, L. E. Evidence for directional scanning with the order-of-report factor excluded. *Canadian Journal of Psychology*, 1976, **30**, 9–14.

Lefton, L. A. Guessing and the order of approximation effect. *Journal of Experimental Psychology*, 1973, **101**, 401–403.

Lefton, L. A., & Spragins, A. B. Orthographic structure and reading experience affect the transfer from iconic to short-term memory. *Journal of Experimental Psychology*, 1974, **103**, 775–781.

Lehnert, W., & Wilks, Y. A critical perspective on KRL. *Cognitive Science*, 1979, **3**, 1–28.

Mason, M. Reading ability and letter search time: Effects of orthographic structure defined by single-letter positional frequency. *Journal of Experimental Psychology: General*, 1975, **104**, 146–166.

Massa, R. J. The role of short-term visual memory in visual information processing. In W. Wathen-Dunn (Ed.), *Models for the perception of speech and visual form*. Cambridge, Massachusetts: MIT Press, 1967.

Massaro, D. W. Perception of letters, words, and nonwords. *Journal of Experimental Psychology*, 1973, **100**, 349–353.

Massaro, D. W. (Ed.). *Understanding language: An information-processing analysis of speech perception, reading, and psycholinguistics*. New York: Academic Press, 1975.

McLean, R. S., & Gregg, L. W. Effects of induced chunking on temporal aspects of serial recitation. *Journal of Experimental Psychology*, 1967, **74**, 455–459.

Melton, A. W. Implications of short-term memory for a general theory of memory. *Journal of Verbal Learning and Verbal Behavior*, 1963, **2**, 1–21.

Merikle, P. M. Presentation rate and order of approximation to English as determinants of short-term memory. *Canadian Journal of Psychology*, 1969, **23**, 196–202.

Merikle, P. M., Coltheart, M., & Lowe, D. G. On the selective effects of a patterned masking stimulus. *Canadian Journal of Psychology*, 1971, **25**, 264–279.

Merikle, P. M., Lowe, D. G., & Coltheart, M. Familiarity and method of report as determinants of tachistoscopic performance. *Canadian Journal of Psychology*, 1971, **25**, 167–174.

Mewhort, D. J. K. Sequential redundancy and letter spacing as determinants of tachistoscopic recognition. *Canadian Journal of Psychology*, 1966, **20**, 435–444.

Mewhort, D. J. K. Familiarity of letter sequences, response uncertainty, and the tachistoscopic recognition experiment. *Canadian Journal of Psychology*, 1967, **21**, 309–321.

Mewhort, D. J. K. Guessing and the order-of-approximation effect. *American Journal of
Psychology*, 1970, **83**, 439–442.

Mewhort, D. J. K. Accuracy and order of report in tachistoscopic identification. *Canadian
Journal of Psychology*, 1974, **28**, 383–398.

Mewhort, D. J. K., & Beal, A. L. Mechanisms of word identification. *Journal of Experimental Psychology: Human Perception and Performance*, 1977, **3**, 629–640.

Mewhort, D. J. K., & Campbell, A. J. *Parsing and the problem of "perceptual" units.*
Paper presented at the meeting of the Canadian Psychological Association, Vancouver, B.C., June 1977.

Mewhort, D. J. K., & Campbell, A. J. Processing spatial information and the selective-
masking effect. *Perception and Psychophysics*, 1978, **24**, 93–101.

Mewhort, D. J. K., & Campbell, A. J. The rate of word integration and the overprinting
paradigm. *Memory and Cognition*, 1980, **8**, 15–25.

Mewhort, D. J. K., Campbell, A. J., Marchetti, F. M., & Campbell, J. I. D. Identification
localization, and "iconic memory": An evaluation of the bar-probe task. *Memory
and Cognition*, 1981, **9**, 50–67.

Mewhort, D. J. K., & Cornett, S. Scanning and the familiarity effect in tachistoscopic
recognition. *Canadian Journal of Psychology*, 1972, **26**, 181–189.

Mewhort, D. J. K., & Marchetti, F. M. *Incidental learning during partial report task: An
analysis of word identification and depth of processing.* Unpublished manuscript,
1980.

Mewhort, D. J. K., Merikle, P. M., & Bryden, M. P. On the transfer from iconic to short-
term memory. *Journal of Experimental Psychology*, 1969, **81**, 89–94.

Mewhort, D. J. K., Thio, H., & Birkenmayer, A. C. Processing capacity and switching
attention in dichotic listening. *Canadian Journal of Psychology*, 1971, **25**, 111–129.

Mewhort, D. J. K., & Tulving, E. *Sequential redundancy, illumination level, and exposure
duration as determinants of tachistoscopic recognition.* Paper presented at the meeting of the Canadian Psychological Association, Halifax, N.S., June 1964.

Miller, G. A. The magical number seven, plus or minus two: Some limits on our capacity
for processing information. *Psychological Review*, 1956, **63**, 81–97.

Miller, G. A., Bruner, J. S., & Postman, L. Familiarity of letter sequences and tachistoscopic identification. *Journal of General Psychology*, 1954, **50**, 129–139.

Miller, L. Has artificial intelligence contributed to an understanding of the human mind?
A critique of arguments for and against. *Cognitive Science*, 1978, **2**, 111–127.

Mishkin, M., & Forgays, D. G. Word recognition as a function of retinal locus. *Journal
of Experimental Psychology*, 1952, **43**, 43–48.

Moray, N. Where is capacity limited? A survey and a model. *Acta Psychologica*, 1967,
27, 84–92.

Neisser, U. *Cognitive psychology.* New York: Appleton, 1967.

Newbigging, P. L. The perceptual redintegration of frequent and infrequent words. *Canadian Journal of Psychology*, 1961, **15**, 123–132.

Newell, A. You can't play 20 questions with nature and win: Projective comments on the
papers of this symposium. In W. G. Chase (Ed.), *Visual information processing.*
New York: Academic Press, 1973.

Newell, A. Physical symbol systems. *Cognitive Science*, 1980, **4**, 135–183.

Newell, A., & Simon, H. A. *Human problem solving.* New York: Prentice-Hall, 1972.

Newman, E. B. Speed of reading when the span of letters is restricted. *American Journal of Psychology*, 1966, **79**, 272–278.

Nice, D. S., & Harcum, E. R. Evidence from mutual masking for serial processing of tachistoscopic letter patterns. *Perceptual and Motor Skills*, 1976, **42**, 991–1003.

Oléron, G. Étude des conditions temporelles de l'intégration mnémonique seriélle. *L'Année Psychologique*, 1972, **72**, 301–317.

Pillsbury, W. B. A study in apperception. *American Journal of Psychology*, 1897, **8**, 315–393.

Popper, K. R. *The logic of scientific discovery* (2nd ed.). New York: Harper, 1968. (Originally published in 1935.)

Posner, M. I., & Rossman, E. Effect of size and location of informational transforms upon short-term retention. *Journal of Experimental Psychology*, 1965, **70**, 496–505.

Purcell, D. G., Stanovich, K. E., & Spector, A. Visual angle and the word superiority effect. *Memory and Cognition*, 1978, **6**, 3–8.

Raphael, B. *The thinking computer: Mind inside matter*. San Francisco, California: Freeman, 1976.

Reicher, G. M. Perceptual recognition as a function of meaningfulness of stimulus material. *Journal of Experimental Psychology*, 1969, **81**, 274–280.

Reitman, J. S., & Rueter, H. H. Organization revealed by recall orders and confirmed by pauses. *Cognitive Psychology*, 1980, **12**, 554–581.

Ryle, G. *The concept of mind*. London: Hutchinson, 1949.

Scheerer, E. Order of report and order of scanning in tachistoscopic recognition. *Canadian Journal of Psychology*, 1972, **26**, 382–390.

Scheerer, E. A further test of the scanning hypothesis in tachistoscopic recognition. *Canadian Journal of Psychology*, 1973, **27**, 95–102.

Scheerer, E. Task requirement and hemifield asymmetry in tachistoscopic partial report performance. *Acta Psychologica*, 1974, **38**, 131–147.

Shannon, C. E., & Weaver, W. *The mathematical theory of communication*. Urbana, Illinois: University of Illinois Press, 1949.

Shinghal, R., & Toussaint, G. T. A bottom-up and top-down approach to using context in text recognition. *International Journal of Man-Machine Studies*, 1979, **11**, 201–212.

Simon, H. A. *The sciences of the artificial*. Cambridge, Massachusetts: MIT Press, 1969.

Simon, H. A. *Models of thought*. New Haven, Connecticut: Yale University Press, 1979.

Simon, H. A. Cognitive science: The newest science of the artificial. *Cognitive Science*, 1980, **4**, 33–46.

Skinner, B. F. *About behaviorism*. New York: Knopf, 1974.

Smith, E. E., & Spoehr, K. T. The perception of printed English: A theoretical perspective. In B. H. Kantowitz (Ed.), *Human information processing: Tutorials in performance and cognition*. Hillsdale, New Jersey: Erlbaum, 1974.

Smith, M. C., & Ramunas, S. Elimination of visual field effects by use of a single report technique: Evidence for order-of-report artifact. *Journal of Experimental Psychology*, 1971, **87**, 23–28.

Sperling, G. A model for visual memory tasks. *Human Factors*, 1963, **5**, 19–31.

Sperling, G. Successive approximations to a model for short-term memory. *Acta Psychologica*, 1967, **27**, 285–292.

Sperling, G. Short-term memory, long-term memory, and scanning in the processing of visual information. In F. A. Young & D. B. Lindsley (Eds.), *Early experience and visual information processing in perceptual and reading disorders*. Washington, D.C.: National Academy of Sciences, 1970.

Taft, M. Lexical access via an orthographic code: The basic orthographic syllabic structure (BOSS). *Journal of Verbal Learning and Verbal Behavior*, 1979, **18**, 21–39. (a)

Taft, M. Recognition of affixed words and the word frequency effect. *Memory and Cognition*, 1979, **7**, 263–272. (b)

Teller, D. Y. Locus questions in visual science. In C. S. Harris (Ed.), *Visual coding and adaptability*. Hillsdale, New Jersey: Erlbaum, 1980.

Terrace, H. S. The effects of retinal locus and attention on the perception of words. *Journal of Experimental Psychology*, 1959, **58**, 382–385.

Toussaint, G. T. The use of context in pattern recognition. *Pattern Recognition*, 1978, **10**, 189–204.

Townsend, J. T. Issues and models concerning the processing of a finite number of inputs. In B. H. Kantowitz (Ed.), *Human information processing: Tutorials in performance and cognition*. Hillsdale, New Jersey: Erlbaum, 1974.

Tulving, E. Familiarity of letter-sequences and tachistoscopic identification. *American Journal of Psychology*, 1963, **76**, 143–146.

Underwood, B. J., & Schulz, R. W. *Meaningfulness and verbal learning*. Chicago, Illinois: Lippincott, 1960.

Venesky, R. *The structure of English orthography*. The Hague: Mouton, 1970.

von Königslöw, R. *A cognitive process model of person evaluation and impression formation based on a computer simulation of natural language processing*. Unpublished doctoral dissertation, University of Michigan, 1974.

Wheeler, D. D. Processes in word recognition. *Cognitive Psychology*, 1970, **1**, 59–85.

Winograd, T. What does it mean to understand language? *Cognitive Science*, 1980, **4**, 209–241.

Wolford, G. Perturbation model for letter identification. *Psychological Review*, 1975, **82**, 184–199.

Woodworth, R. S. *Experimental psychology*. London: Methuen, 1950. (Originally published in 1938.)

DEVELOPMENT OF VISUAL WORD RECOGNITION: A REVIEW

RODERICK W. BARRON

Department of Psychology
University of Guelph
Guelph, Ontario, Canada

I. INTRODUCTION

Although the importance of learning to recognize printed words rapidly and accurately is acknowledged in a number of models of the reading process (e.g., LaBerge & Samuels, 1974; Lesgold & Perfetti, 1978; Stanovich, 1980) and in most programs for teaching children to read, relatively little is known about how visual word recognition actually develops in children. There may be several reasons for this lack of knowledge. One, most of the research on visual word recognition during the past decade has focused upon the skills of the fluent reader; there has been comparatively little direct concern for the emerging skills of the novice (see Allport, 1979; Baron, 1978; Gibson & Levin, 1975; Henderson, 1977, 1981; Henderson & Chard, 1980; Krueger, 1975 for reviews of the literature on fluent word recognition). Two, the research that has been done with children has often not been motivated by developmental perspectives on word recognition, although there are some notable exceptions (e.g., Ehri, 1978, 1980, 1981; Gibson, 1970, 1974; Marsh, Friedman, Welch, & Desberg, this volume). Instead, many investigators have been

119

concerned with determining how well children perform in tasks designed to assess adult abilities and they have tended to interpret the children's performance with reference to models of fluent word recognition. Despite the limited amount of research specifically motivated by developmental models, the work that has been carried out on children's word recognition does provide a great deal of information about what children know about printed words, how this knowledge is expressed in reading related tasks, and how this knowledge changes with increasing age and reading experience.

The purpose of this article is to organize and evaluate the literature on four topics in the development of visual word recognition. The first topic will be concerned with the characteristics of English orthographic structure and the development of children's ability to use it. The second will deal with "units of processing" in word recognition (e.g., letters, spelling patterns, syllables, morphemes, and words) and with how the use of these units might change developmentally and with task demands. The third topic will be concerned with the development of the use of partial graphic information in word recognition, such as the initial and final letters, and the outline or envelope of a word. Beginning readers may be particularly reliant upon these types of information as "cues" for recognizing words. Finally, the fourth topic will deal with developmental changes in the use of visual and phonological information in obtaining access to word meanings. Important topics such as the development of skills for reading words aloud (e.g., Baron, 1979), the effects of different types of instruction on word learning (e.g., Barr, 1974–1975; Ehri & Roberts, 1979), and the relationships between word recognition and comprehension (e.g., Perfetti & Lesgold, 1978; West & Stanovich, 1978) will not be covered in any detail in this necessarily limited review.

The choice of development of orthography, units of processing, use of partial graphic information, and word meaning access as topics for this article was based upon several considerations. First, these topics have generated a reasonable amount of research involving children as subjects and they are of considerable interest to investigators concerned with the characteristics of fluent reading. Second, these four topics are often involved in the implicit assumptions about the nature and development of word recognition which underlie programs of instruction. For example, reading programs are often based upon unstated assumptions about the characteristics of English orthography, "basic" or "natural" units of processing in written language, the reliability of certain types of graphic information in word recognition, and the use of phonological information in accessing lexical meaning. Third, the theory and data relevant to these four topics might provide an alternative perspective on what children do and do not know about printed words than is available from conventional sources (e.g., reading tests). For example, experimental control over tasks and materials may allow more detailed analyses of the types of information children actually use in recognizing printed words under various conditions. Evidence on these four topics might be helpful in determining what children need to learn about visual word recognition, and when they should learn it.

II. USE OF ORTHOGRAPHIC STRUCTURE

Consider a nonsense letter string like *ohrdc*. It does not look much like a word, it is difficult to read aloud, and it does not have a lexical meaning. Now consider the pseudoword *dorch*. It does not have a lexical meaning either, but it is easier to read aloud and it looks more like a word. The differences between these two nonwords in pronounceability and appearance suggest that it might be easier to recognize *dorch* than *ohrdc*. This possibility was investigated in a pioneering experiment by Gibson, Pick, Osser, and Hammond (1962, experiment 2). They briefly presented either a pseudoword or a letter string in a tachistoscope and then required subjects to recognize it from among four similar alternatives. As predicted, Gibson *et al.* (1962) found that the pseudowords (e.g., *sland, clats*) were recognized more accurately than the letter strings (e.g., *ndasl, tsacl*). Differences in recognition accuracy between these two types of nonwords were also obtained in other tachistoscopic tasks in which subjects had only to recognize which one of two letters was in a displayed item (e.g., Baron & Thurston, 1973) as well as when they had to report all of the letters (e.g., Adams, 1979; Gibson *et al.*, 1962, experiment 1). In tasks measuring response latency, subjects were faster at deciding that a pair of pseudowords was visually identical (e.g., *dorch* displayed above *dorch*) than a pair of letter strings (e.g., Barron & Pittenger, 1974). They were also faster in searching for a single letter in an array of pseudowords than in an array of letter strings (Krueger, 1970).

Gibson *et al.* (1962) interpreted their original finding as indicating that subjects used the invariant correspondences between graphemes and phonemes to facilitate the recognition of pseudowords over letter strings. One implication of their interpretation is that subjects actually pronounced the words implicitly during the process of recognizing them. This possibility was questioned in a subsequent experiment as Gibson, Shurcliff, and Yonas (1970) found that deaf subjects were more accurate on pseudowords than letter strings and that the size of the difference was the same as for hearing subjects. As a result of this evidence, Gibson (1970, 1974, 1978; Gibson & Levin, 1975) has more recently argued that the pseudoword–letter string difference may arise from subjects' ability to use their knowledge of English orthographic structure without necessarily translating the items into phonological representations.[1]

Venezky and Massaro (1979) have suggested that English orthographic structure can be characterized as a rule-based system or as a probabilistic system. One difficulty with a rule-based characterization is that it would have to be comprehensive enough to deal with over 1000 years of changes in English orthography brought about by religious conversions, military conquests, scribes, printers, lexicographers, etymologists, and even accidents (e.g., Scragg, 1974; Venezky & Massaro, 1979). The products of these changes are expressed in a variety of positional and sequential constraints on letters in words. These constraints are, for example, graphotactic (e.g., *ck* does not begin a word, letters are not tripled, the letter *q* is always followed by *u*), phonotactic (e.g., stop consonants like *bp* are difficult to articulate in succession), grapheme-to-phoneme translation (e.g., a silent final *e* in a word may indicate that the preceding vowel should be lengthened), and morphemic (the *ph* consonant cluster in telephone is pronounced differently than it is in shepherd). Unfortunately, an explicit, comprehensive set of rules has not been developed for characterizing these as well as other constraints on English orthography,

---

[1] There may be an alternative interpretation of the basis of the deaf readers' performance in the Gibson *et al.* (1970) experiment. Dodd and Hermelin (1977) found that prelinguistically deaf adolescents could use the similarity in pronunciation between two homophones (e.g., *weigh/way*) to facilitate paired-associate learning. After ruling out visual (i.e., number of shared letters) and kinesthetic–articulatory similarity interpretations of their results, Dodd and Hermelin (1977) suggested that the deaf subjects may have used the similarity in the way the items looked when they were pronounced (i.e., derived from experience in lip reading) as their source of information about the phonological similarity of the homophones. This interpretation was consistent with the fact that deaf subjects found it easier to make rhyme judgments of items which had their final consonants articulated in the front (which would make them easier to lip read) than in the back. These results suggest the possibility that the deaf subjects in the Gibson *et al.* (1970) experiment may have performed better on the pseudowords, at least in part, because the pseudowords might look less complicated than the letter strings when they were pronounced; hence they might have been easier to encode. It should be noted, however, that other evidence indicates that phonological processing may not be necessary to obtain a pseudoword–letter string difference in tachistoscopic tasks. Both Baron and Thurston (1973) and Hawkins, Reicher, Rogers, and Peterson (1976) showed that fluent readers' superior performance on words (they did not use pseudowords) over letter strings was not influenced by an incorrect alternative (e.g., *roll*) response which was homophonic with the word that was presented (e.g., *role*).

although there have been several attempts (e.g., Venezky, 1970; Whorf, 1956; Wijk, 1966). Nevertheless, it does appear that pseudowords like *dorch* are, on the average, more consistent with the constraints on English orthography than letter strings like *ohrdc* even though it may not be possible to account completely for this difference in consistency with reference to a set of rules.

The probabilistic approach to describing English orthographic structure arises from the fact that letters in words are not equally likely to follow each other or to appear in the same letter positions. This redundancy can be assessed by counting the number of times a letter or letter cluster (e.g., bigram, trigram) appears within a sample of printed text. These measures capture some of the same information as the rule-based approaches since nonwords with, for example, high summed single letter and bigram frequency values are more likely to be consistent with various types of orthographic constraint than nonwords with low summed values, particularly when the position of the letter or letter cluster in the word is taken into account (e.g., Mayzner & Tresselt, 1965; Mayzner, Tresselt, & Wolin, 1965). These frequency counts are not completely adequate, however, as they often suffer from being drawn from limited samples of text and nonwords can be produced which have high summed frequency counts, but are inconsistent with some orthographic constraints. For example, Venezky and Massaro (1979) point out that an item like *sthse* has a higher summed bigram count than an item like *slevy*. Furthermore, there is evidence suggesting that some of these frequency measures of orthographic structure do not account for much of the variance in word recognition over factors such as rated pronounceability and length (e.g., Gibson, 1964; Gibson *et al.*, 1970), particularly when a narrow range of values is used (e.g., Barron & Henderson, 1977; Chambers & Forster, 1975; Manelis, 1974). Other evidence, however, suggests that subjects can use information about the frequency of positionally constrained single letters to facilitate word recognition. Mason (1975) and Massaro, Venezky, and Taylor (1979) found that subjects searched more rapidly for single letters in letter strings which had high than low summed single letter positional frequency counts and Gibson *et al.* (1970) and McCelland and Johnston (1977) found that single letter positional frequency was correlated with performance in tasks requiring report from briefly presented displays.

Despite the difficulties in adequately characterizing orthographic structure within either a rule-based or a probabilistic framework, it appears that pseudowords are generally more consistent with orthographic constraints and/or have higher positional frequency values than letter strings. Although the underlying mechanisms are still very controversial (e.g.,

Adams, 1979; Estes, 1975; Mason, 1975; Massaro *et al.*, 1979; McClelland
& Johnston, 1977; Rumelhart & Siple, 1974), fluent readers appear to
be able to use their knowledge of orthographic structure to facilitate
recognition of pseudowords over letter strings. The question of interest
for this article is how the use of this knowledge develops. For example,
when do children first show that they can use orthographic structure in
word recognition? Does this ability increase with age and reading experience? How do various tasks influence children's ability to use orthographic structure? In order to deal with these questions, the relevant
research will be organized around the tasks which have been most commonly employed in assessing children's use of orthographic structure in
word recognition: visual search, tachistoscopic presentation, judgments
of word likeness, lexical decision, and visual matching. This list of tasks
does not include those requiring reading aloud as they have the potential
of confounding visual–orthographic effects with grapheme-to-phoneme
translation and/or articulation effects.

Visual search has been a popular task for assessing the use of orthographic structure. Krueger, Keen, and Rublievich (1974), for example,
required fourth graders and adults to search through five-item lists of
words and nonwords for a single target letter. Using search time through
random letter strings as a baseline, both groups of subjects were able
to reduce their search time by about the same percentage: 2.5% (*grade
four*) and 3.1% (adult) for third order of approximation nonwords (*lep-
icart*),[2] and 10.9% (grade four) and 8.4% (adults) for common words. A
similar pattern of results was obtained by Juola, Schadler, Chabot, and
McCaughey (1978) and McCaughey, Juola, Schadler, and Ward (1980).
They had kindergarten, first, second, and fourth graders, plus college
students search for a single letter in word, pseudoword, and letter string
displays made up of single items. The search time for the kindergarten
and grade one children did not differ between the pseudowords and letter
strings indicating that they were unable to use orthographic structure to
facilitate their search. The second and fourth graders were, however,
influenced by orthographic structure as they searched more rapidly
through pseudowords than letter strings. The same pattern of results was

---

[2] Order of approximation provides an index of the sequential constraint in English
orthography. Zero-order items (e.g., *okebgihn*), for example, are strings of letters drawn
at random from the alphabet whereas first-order items (e.g., *lhsndtyu*) are made up of
letters which reflect their relative frequency of occurrence. Second-order items (e.g.,
edstheul) reflect the relative frequency of bigrams, while third-order items (e.g., *dracketw*)
reflect the relative frequency of trigrams and fourth-order items (e.g., *cultings*) reflect the
relative frequency of tetragrams. As a result, third- and fourth-order items, for example,
may more closely approximate English orthographic structure than zero-order strings.

obtained for the adult subjects, except that the difference between the pseudowords and letter strings was significant only in the McCaughey et al. (1980) experiment. Consistent with Krueger et al. (1974), they found that the use of orthographic structure reduced response time by a relatively constant percentage across grade. Using performance on letter strings as a baseline, the second graders were 2.7% faster on the pseudowords, the fourth graders 2.3% faster, and the adults 2.6% faster (2.3% for McCaughey et al., 1980). These percentage values were zero for the kindergarten and first grade children.

There are, however, several experiments in the literature which failed to show an orthographic effect in visual search tasks. Gibson, Tenney, Barron, and Zaslow (1972) found no difference in search time for a letter between pseudowords and letter strings for either grade five or adult subjects. As these investigators pointed out, however, the letter N was the target throughout the experiment, hence the subjects may have learned to use its graphic features to locate the target in the search list. Consequently, orthographic information may not have been particularly useful in facilitating visual search. Experimental design as well as task differences seem to influence whether or not an effect of orthographic structure is obtained in visual search tasks. Gibson et al. (1972) and James and Smith (1970) used a between-subjects design and failed to get an effect, whereas Krueger (1970) used a within-subjects design and did get it. Massaro et al. (1979) used a within-subjects design, but they failed to obtain large orthographic effects unless the to be searched item was presented briefly, masked, and then followed rather than preceded by the target letter (they also used accuracy rather than response time measures when they obtained large orthographic effects). Krueger et al. (1974), Juola et al. (1978), and McCaughey et al. (1980), however, presented the target letter first and measured response time when they obtained their orthographic effects; furthermore, Juola et al. (1978) and McCaughey et al. (1980) used a masking stimulus and only one item in their search list whereas Krueger et al. (1974) did not use a masking stimulus and used a five-item search list. Finally, Stanovich, West, and Pollak (1978) had grade three, six, and adult subjects search for a member of a semantic category (experiment two) or for three words (experiment three) through lists of words, pseudowords, and letter strings. Unlike searching for single letters, searching for words should be slowed as the items in the search list become more wordlike. They found that all groups of subjects searched for the targets more rapidly through letter strings than pseudowords, and through pseudowords than words. However, the difference between the pseudowords and letter strings was small and not significant (except for the sixth graders in experiment two, the third graders in experiment three, and third grade poor readers in a separate study by Stanovich & West, 1979). The Stanovich et al. (1978) results suggest that lexical rather than orthographic information may have had the major influence upon the subjects' performance in this search task, possibly because of the requirement to process the target at the lexical–semantic level. In summary, some of these visual search results suggest that, by the second grade, children can use orthographic structure to facilitate word recognition and that the accompanying percentage reduction in response time does not change very much with increases in age and reading experience. However, conflicting results arising from differences in the tasks, experimental designs, and measures used indicate that these conclusions should be regarded as being tentative.

Tachistoscopic tasks differ from visual search tasks as the items are displayed very briefly and response accuracy rather than response latency is typically measured. In an early tachistoscopic study, Hoffmann (1927, cited in Woodworth, 1938, p. 738) found that German children could report more letters from familiar words than from letter strings by grade two. Furthermore, the difference between the words and letter strings appeared to increase across grade. Unfortunately, Hoffmann's results are difficult to interpret without also having a pseudoword condition because lexical as well as orthographic factors could account for the increasing word–letter string difference across grade. More recently, however, Gibson, Osser, and Pick (1963) presented tachistoscopically pseudowords, as well as words and letter strings, to grade one and grade three pupils. The children were instructed to read the items aloud and then report the letters. Both the first and the third graders were more accurate on the words than the pseudowords, and on the pseudowords than the letter strings (the third grade girls were an exception to this finding as they were highly accurate on all three types of items). Only the third graders, however, were more accurate on the pseudowords than the letter strings when the items were four and five letters long. Thomas (1968) excluded the potentially confounding factor of requiring the children to read the words aloud before reporting the letters. Consistent with Gibson et al. (1963), he found that grade one, two, and three children were more accurate on words than pseudowords, and on pseudowords (at least those with consonant (C) vowel (V) consonant (C) structure) than letter strings. Gibson and Guinet (1971) also obtained results consistent with Gibson et al. (1963) as grade three, five, and adult subjects were more accurate in reporting words than pseudowords, and pseudowords than letter strings. Using performance on the letter strings as a baseline, the third graders were 76.2%, the fifth graders 49.8%, and the adults 32.8% more accurate on the pseudowords, suggesting a decrease in the relative facilitation due to orthographic structure across grade.

Strings of letters eight items in length were used by Lefton and Spragins (1974) in a tachistoscopic task. One-half of the items were first- and the other half fourth-order approximations to English and they were briefly presented for durations ranging from 50 to 300 milliseconds. Lefton and Spragins (1974) found that the first graders were no more accurate on the fourth- than the first-order items, whereas the third graders, fifth graders, and adults were more accurate on the fourth-order items. When performance on the first-order items was used as a baseline, the percentage improvement in accuracy on the fourth-order items varied across grade: 8.4% for grade one, 22.2% for grade three, 15.2% for grade five, and 24.7% for adults. A somewhat similar pattern of results was obtained by Lefton, Spragins, and Byrnes (1973) in a task in which subjects were required to guess the missing letter in letter strings. They found that the third and fifth graders were more accurate at guessing letters in fourth- than first-order strings, particularly on the right side of the display (where there was more sequential constraint). The first graders, on the other hand, showed no difference in guessing accuracy between the two types of strings.

Bishop (1976) also employed tachistoscopic presentation, but she used a probe task in which subjects were required to decide which one of two letters appeared in an item (e.g., Reicher, 1969) in addition to a task in which they just reported what they saw. The advantage of the probe over the report task is that it reduces the contribution of memory and guessing factors to the accuracy of item recognition. In the report task, both the grade three and six subjects were more accurate on pseudowords than letter strings, but with the probe procedure, only the grade six subjects were significantly more accurate on the pseudowords than the letter strings. Again using letter string performance as a baseline, the relative increase in percentage accuracy on the pseudowords declined across grade in the report task (72.5% for grade three, 58.0% for grade six) and increased across grade in the probe task (5.2% for grade three, 8.1% for grade six).

Taken together, the experiments by Gibson *et al.* (1963), Thomas (1968), Gibson and Guinet (1971), Lefton and Spragins (1974), Lefton *et al.* (1973), and Bishop (1976) suggest that between the second and fourth grades children begin to be able to use orthographic structure to facilitate word recognition in tachistoscopic tasks. Evidence that first grade or younger children can use orthographic structure seems to be confined to short items (three letters) with CVC structures. Contrary to some of the visual search results, the tachistoscopic evidence suggests that the percentage increase in accuracy due to orthographic structure varies across grade. Although some of this variability might be attributed to differences in tasks and materials, it may also reflect floor or ceiling effects upon performance at various grade levels. One possible way of diminishing these effects would be to establish the same criterion of baseline performance on the letter strings at all grades (e.g., 60% correct), and then determine the percentage increase in accuracy at each grade when the pseudowords are presented.

Tasks in which subjects have to decide how closely an item approximates a word have also been used to assess the development of the use of orthographic information. Rosinski and Wheeler (1972), for example, had children in grades one, three, and five point out the member of a pair of words that was "more like a word." The stimuli were selected randomly from those used by Gibson et al. (1962, 1963) and a pseudoword was paired with a letter string. The first grade children were very close to chance (50%) in their judgment accuracy, whereas the third and fifth graders were well above chance (69 to 80%) in picking a pseudoword over a letter string. There was no effect of number of letters in the words. Golinkoff (1974) used different pseudowords and letter strings than Rosinski and Wheeler (1972), but found essentially the same thing as her first graders were again very close to chance performance, while her second graders were above chance (83%) in the accuracy of their judgments. In addition, she found that the first graders' performance was increased to 72% when they both heard and saw the items (they were read aloud by a linguist). Finally, Allington (1978), Bishop (1976), and Pick, Unze, Brownell, Drozdal, and Hopmann (1978) have also shown that by about grades two or three children begin to show that they can use consistently orthographic structure in making judgments of word likeness.

Henderson and Chard (1980) used response time as a dependent variable in a lexical decision task in which subjects were required to decide whether or not an item was a word. In this task, the absence of orthographic structure would allow subjects to decide more rapidly that an item is not a word. Using grade two and four subjects and six letter words and nonwords, they varied the single letter positional frequency values of nonwords independently of whether or not they contained vowels. Both groups of readers made faster nonword decisions on the items when they were low (e.g., *kugafp*) than high (e.g., *turild*) in positional frequency and when vowels were absent (e.g., *sprnth*) rather than present (e.g., *juwfac*). In addition, vowels did not have any effect on the response times of the fourth grade subjects to the low positional frequency nonwords, but did influence both the high and low positional frequency nonword decisions of the second graders. These results are also consistent with the findings that subjects as young as grade two are sensitive to the characteristics of orthographic structure. They also suggest a developmental shift whereby the older subjects may be able to reject items with low positional frequency very early in the lexical search process, possibly on the basis of initial or final bigrams. Apparently, they are able to do this without the necessity of resorting to vowel analysis (which usually involves attending to the middle as well as the initial and final letters) and/or deeper lexical processing.

Visual matching tasks have been used to investigate the role of orthographic structure in word recognition (e.g., Barron & Pittenger, 1974) and Doehring (1976) has employed one type of matching task in an extensive developmental study. He used a matching-to-sample task in which subjects were required to indicate which one of three alternative items was identical to a sample item. Using three letter items, he showed that subjects were faster on pseudowords (CVC structure) than letter strings from the second through the eleventh grades, considering every grade in between. Doehring's (1976, p. 15) data can be used to assess how facilitation in word recognition due to orthographic structure changes across grade. Using letter strings as a baseline, second graders (based on an average of children in the last half of the first grade and the first half of the second grade) were 28.6% faster on the pseudowords. This value was 23.5% in the third grade (average of the last half of the second grade and the first half of the third grade) and remained relatively constant through the eleventh grade (20.0%). The range of values across grade was from 15.8 to 27.6%.

Considered together, the results from visual search, tachistoscopic, word likeness, lexical decision, and visual matching tasks provide a reasonably consistent picture of the development of the use of visual–orthographic structure. Despite the difficulties with the visual search task and in defining adequately orthographic structure, they indicate that sometime between the second and the fourth grade children seem to be able to use some of the gross characteristics of orthographic structure in visual word recognition. Apparently, younger children can use orthographic structure, but it appears to be critically dependent on using three-letter items with CVC structures. Finally, once orthographic effects begin to appear, their relative size does not seem to change very much across grade in visual search and visual matching tasks. In the tachistoscopic tasks, however, the change in the relative size of the orthographic effect appeared to be more variable, although some of this variability may be due to floor and ceiling effects on performance at different grades.

III. UNITS OF PROCESSING

The fact that readers possess skills for capitalizing upon various levels of linguistic structure to facilitate word recognition has led to several interpretations of how that structure is used. One of the most commonly accepted is that the linguistic structure allows items to be processed in chunks or units which are larger than the units available in unstructured strings of letters. Presumably, processing items in large, multiple letter units allows word recognition to be faster and more accurate than if, for example, the items were processed serially, letter-by-letter because fewer units are involved. Cattell (1886) was one of the first to argue that letters are not the fundamental units of processing in word recognition. He based his argument, in part, on his finding that the time required to recognize a word was only slightly longer than for a letter. More recently Reicher (1969) and Wheeler (1970) have shown that a single letter (e.g., *k*) is recognized more accurately in the context of a word (e.g., *work*) than alone when subjects are required to choose between two letters which both spell a word (e.g., *d* and *k*). This effect is even obtained when the set of possible letters is small and known in advance to the subject as long as the size of the display is less than one degree of visual angle (Purcell, Stanovich, & Spector, 1978). Cattell (1886) interpreted his results as indicating that individual letters are not perceived separately during word recognition; instead, the word is perceived as a whole unit. This idea has several contemporary advocates (e.g., Smith, 1971; Johnson, 1975, 1977), while others have suggested that morphemes (e.g., Gibson & Guinet, 1971; Murrell & Morton, 1974), syllables (e.g., Spoehr and Smith, 1973), and spelling patterns (e.g., Gibson, 1965; Santa, Santa & Smith, 1977) function as units intermediate between letters and words.

Henderson (1980, 1981) has argued that wholistic (holistic), or the more modern units of processing interpretations of word recognition, suffer from some theoretical ambiguity. He points out that there are actually several types of wholism represented in theories of word recognition; for example, wholism in visual feature analysis and attentional wholism. Wholism at the feature analysis level can refer to the use of word outline (i.e., envelope, shape) information or to the idea that there are feature analyzers which extract information across letter boundaries (transgraphemic features). This wholistic information is argued to be sufficient to specify higher order units (e.g., letter clusters or words), but not individual letters. Featural wholism can also refer to matching operations in which a common set of elementary features is compared to property lists or pattern descriptions in memory which correspond to units larger than a single letter. Attentional wholism, on the other hand, refers to the idea that some units (e.g., words) might be more accessible to conscious attention than other units (e.g., letters, syllables). It is important to analyze wholistic or units of processing theories as the development of visual word recognition is often characterized as involving the acquisition of increasingly larger units (e.g., Gibson & Levin, 1975; LaBerge & Samuels, 1974).

Henderson (1980, 1981) argues that theories which advocate wholism at the feature analysis level are vulnerable to several criticisms. He points out that Cattell (1886), for example, proposed a variant of feature analysis wholism by suggesting that the outline of a word was sufficient information for word recognition. Although some words can be distinguished by their outlines when they are printed in lower case type (e.g., *dog* versus *pad*), others cannot (e.g., *cat* versus *eel*). Furthermore, printing words in upper case type removes the distinctive outline information of lower case type without noticeably altering recognition accuracy (e.g., McClelland, 1976, found no difference between upper and lower case stimuli in the size of his word–pseudoword effects). These arguments and evidence suggest that word outline may not be sufficient information for word recognition. Nevertheless, word outline, particularly when combined with word length information, may be used in some circumstances by providing an additional, global source of information for word recognition (e.g., Broadbent & Broadbent, 1977; Estes, 1977; McClelland, 1977). See Section IV for further discussion of the use of word outline information.

The idea that there are feature analyzers which extract transgraphemic feature information (e.g., Wheeler, 1970) is also vulnerable to criticism according to Henderson (1980, 1981). McClelland (1976) has shown that the size of the difference between words and pseudowords is not reduced when the items are presented in alternating type case (e.g., *wOrD* versus *dOrD*), which breaks up transgraphemic feature information. Adams (1979) obtained the same result using a combination of case and type style alternation; unlike McClelland (1976), however, this manipulation did not diminish the difference between pseudowords and letter strings (e.g., *dOrD* versus *oRwD*). McClelland (1976) and Adams (1979) used tachistoscopic tasks in which exposure duration was limited and response accuracy emphasized. In tasks using relatively long exposure durations and emphasizing response latency, there is some evidence indicating that case alternation reduces the size of the word–pseudoword difference. However, the evidence is not consistent as Taylor, Miller, and Juola (1977) found that the reduction was slight and the difference remained significant whereas Bruder (1978) found that the reduction was substantial and the difference nonsignificant. More consistent results have been obtained with letter strings as several investigators (e.g., Bruder, 1978; Pollatsek, Well, & Schindler, 1975; Taylor *et al.*, 1977) showed that case alternation does not influence response times to letter strings as much as to words and pseudowords. These results suggest that transgraphemic units common to words and pseudowords (e.g., based on spelling patterns) may be disrupted by case alternation. These findings are consistent with McClelland (1976), but not Adams (1979).

In the one developmental study manipulating case alternation, Stanovich, Purcell, and West (1979) used a visual search task and found that case alternation reduced the difference between words and letter strings so much for grade three and adult subjects that it was no longer significant (the word–letter string difference was not significant with normal or alternated type case for their grade one and kindergarten subjects). However, Stanovich *et al.* (1979) also found that overall subjects were faster in the case alternation condition than in the conditions in which the items appeared in all upper case or all lower case type. This result suggests that subjects may have ignored transgraphemic information and focused exclusively upon the graphic features of individual letters, particularly as the target letters appeared in only one type case in the case alternation condition. In order to examine this possibility, Stanovich *et al.* (1979) repeated the case alternation condition with adult subjects, but had them search for target letters which could occur in either upper or lower case. Again, the word–letter string difference was not significant. Although subjects were slower overall in the repeated case alternation condition than in the upper and lower case conditions of the original study, this result could have arisen from the increased complexity of the subjects' task in the repeated case alternation condition rather than from case alternation disrupting transgraphemic feature processing.

Another variant of featural wholism which encounters some difficulties involves theories in which the products of elementary feature extraction are matched with lists of stored features which correspond to units larger than single letters. Smith (1971), for example, argued that the constraints on printed English allow a word to be identified by a smaller set of features than would be necessary for identifying independently each of its component letters. Suppose that all of the features characterizing the word *horse* had been matched with their corresponding representations in memory, except for those in the fourth letter position. According to Smith's (1971) theory, the critical feature tests for this position would be constrained to those distinguishing the letters *d* and *s* (assuming the item was known to be a word). The contextual information provided by the results of the feature tests in other letter positions reduced the necessity of carrying out additional tests in position four to distinguish the remaining letters of the alphabet. Although Smith's (1971) theory appears to eliminate the necessity of letter-mediated word identification, there are several problems with it. First, contrary to expectations from Smith's (1971) theory, Johnston (1978) found that subjects were not any more accurate in deciding which one of two letters appeared in a briefly exposed word when the constraint provided by the letter context was high (*g* or *b* in _*oat* context) rather than low (*m* or *t* in an _*ill* context). Second, Smith's (1971) theory requires that each word, as well as each form in which it appears (e.g., upper case, lower case, handwriting), be represented in memory by a unique set of criterial features. The problem with this requirement is that readers must memorize a very large number of criterial feature sets even to be able to read material in one typeface, and they cannot easily transfer their knowledge to other typefaces. Finally, Smith's (1971) theory would appear to have difficulty accounting for the fact that the word–pseudoword difference often survives case alternation or that pseudowords are recognized more accurately than letter strings. As Rozin and Gleitman (1977, p. 27) have commented, Smith's (1971) theory seems to involve a great deal of effort just "to avoid noticing 26 inoffensive little squiggles."

In summary, the evidence suggests that units of processing theories which are based upon wholism at the feature level do not provide a very adequate account of how words are recognized, particularly when the unit involved is a word. Although the evidence against a wholistic feature account of the recognition of intermediate sized units of processing (e.g., spelling patterns) does not appear to be as strong as it is for words, there are other reasons for thinking that theories based on featural wholism may be inadequate. One of the reasons is that it may be possible to account for the same phenomena as wholistic feature analysis theories by assuming that individual letters are processed in parallel. For example, advocates of parallel letter processing theories have proposed several different interpretations of why words and pseudowords are recognized more accurately than letter strings. These interpretations include the possibility that orthographic effects arise from the interfacilitation among letters that have appeared together previously (e.g., Adams, 1979; Adams & Collins, 1979; Smith & Kleiman, 1979); from the construction of abstract phonological representations (e.g., McClelland & Johnston, 1977); and from using orthography as an independent source of information about letter identities (e.g., Estes, 1975; Massaro, 1979) and letter position (e.g., Estes, 1975). Although none of these parallel processing based interpretations may be completely adequate, they may be less vulnerable to the criticisms which have been levelled against theories

based upon featural wholism. In addition, parallel processing-based interpretations can be used to provide an alternative account of results which
suggests that the development of word recognition involves the acquisition of increasingly larger units of processing, such as those of Samuels,
LaBerge, and Bremer (1978). These investigators required grade two,
four, six, and adult subjects to make semantic category decisions (animal,
nonanimal) about words which varied in length (three to six letters).
They obtained a developmental change whereby response time increased
quite a bit with the number of letters in a word for the second graders,
did not increase as much for the fourth and sixth graders, and did not
increase at all for the adult subjects. Although these results might be
interpreted as indicating that there was a development shift toward processing the words as wholistic feature patterns, it is also possible that
the developmental shift involved an increasing ability to process individual letters in parallel, a possibility acknowledged by Samuels *et al.*
(1978).

Attentional wholism, a second type of wholism represented in theories
of word recognition according to Henderson (1980, 1981), deals with the
relative accessibility of various linguistically specified units (e.g., letters,
spelling patterns, syllables, morphemes, words, phrases) to conscious
attention. This type of wholism is relevant to the development of word
recognition as reading fluency is often characterized by the ability to
read for a number of different purposes (Gibson, 1972), including scanning the financial page of a newspaper for specific words, letter groups,
and numbers, reading a poem, or skimming a novel. These activities
appear to involve the ability to attend to different units in printed language
and it is possible that beginning readers are less able than fluent readers
to attend to certain types of units and/or several units simultaneously.

The development of the ability to attend to units of printed language
has been examined by several investigators using variations of the visual
search task. Drewnowski and Healy (1977) and Healy (1976), for example, have shown that subjects make a disproportionate number of
errors in detecting single letters (e.g., *t, n*) in highly frequent function
words like *the* and *and* while simultaneously reading passages for meaning. These errors can be reduced by scrambling the passage, presenting
the words in alternating type case, or altering the spatial organization
of the text by presenting the words in a list. These effects were not
obtained for the control word *ant*. Drewnowski and Healy (1976) proposed that during normal reading, subjects attempt to process text at the
highest level of unit available to them (e.g., a word or a phrase) and that
higher level unit processing can begin before lower level unit (e.g., letters)
processing is completed. Note that the assumption that different units

are processed in parallel does not require that the units be defined as wholistic feature complexes. Detection errors in the words *and* and *the* were argued to arise from a failure to complete lower level letter identification processes when higher level processing was facilitated by highly frequent words or syntactically and semantically familiar phrases. Experimental manipulations which force the subjects to process the text at a lower level (e.g., scrambling the word order, presenting the words in a list, typing letters in alternating type cases) increase the likelihood that lower level processing will be completed and the target letters detected.

Drewnowski (1978) used the above letter detection task with children in grades one through five and adults in order to evaluate developmental changes in units of processing. The children were required to detect every instance of the letter *t* by circling it in prose passages, scrambled letter passages, and lists of words. He argued that subjects' ability to process higher order units of text (e.g., phrases) should be reflected in differences in the percentage of detection errors made on the word *the* in the different types of passages. Drewnowski (1978) measured the conditional percentage of detection (omission) errors by dividing the total number of detection errors (errors on the word *the* plus errors on *t-h-e* letter patterns in words, such as in *lather*) into the detection errors on the word *the*. He found that all groups of subjects were at chance (33%) or below in errors on *t* in the word *the* for word list and scrambled letter passages (the letter *t* in the scrambled letter passages appeared in positions which corresponded to positions in the word lists for *the* or *t-h-e* letter patterns). On the other hand, all of the subjects were above chance in the percentage of detection errors they made on the word *the* in prose passages (see also Mohan, 1978), except for children reading at the grade one level. Only the grade four, five, and adult subjects made a higher percentage of detection errors on *the* while reading prose passages than scrambled word passages, although it is not clear why the errors tended to decrease rather than increase across grade on these passages. These results suggest that not until grade four are subjects able to use the syntactic and semantic constraints on printed language to process efficiently the text at the level of prose units. Younger subjects, who are reading at grade two and above, appear to be able to process the text at the level of individual words in this task. Only the children who are reading at the grade one level appear to rely on letter-by-letter processing when they have the opportunity to use higher order word and prose units.

Rather than have subjects search for one type of target through different linguistic backgrounds, Friedrich, Schadler, and Juola (1979) had subjects detect different types of targets in the same linguistic background. These investigators required grade two, four, and adult subjects to detect target items as they read through sentences for comprehension. The targets were individual letters, syllables, words, and members of a semantic category. Overall, subjects were fastest at detecting words followed by category members, syllables, and letters, respectively. This ordering of response times may reflect the decreasing compatibility between the words making up the sentences and the target items (e.g., McNeill & Lindig, 1973; Marmurek, 1977). Considering the within-grade results, the grade two subjects were significantly faster on words than category members, and on category members than syllables, but were not significantly faster on syllables than individual letters. Category detection time decreased substantially by grade four so that it did not differ from word detection time. In addition, grade four subjects were significantly faster on syllables than letters. Although the adult subjects showed the same ordering of response times as the younger subjects, they were only significantly faster on the words than the letters. These results suggest that grade two subjects may have some difficulty with rapid retrieval of semantic category information and in detecting syllables relative to the older subjects.

Santa (1976–1977) also examined subjects' ability to detect different targets in a constant linguistic background, but her linguistic background was a word rather than a sentence. Using a procedure developed by Santa *et al.* (1977), she required subjects to decide whether or not a letter or group of letters (i.e., spelling patterns) appeared in a word. Second graders and adults were as fast in deciding that a single letter (e.g., *s*) was in a word (e.g., *blast*) as they were in deciding that the first two letters (e.g., *bl*) were in the word. Poor grade two readers, however, were slower on the first two letters than a single letter. This appears to be consistent with Drewnowski's (1978) evidence for letter-by-letter processing by children reading at the grade one level. In addition, both groups of second graders were slowest at matching a word (*blast*) with a word (*blast*), but the adult subjects were as fast or faster in matching words than groups of letters, except for the first two letters or a single letter.

Finally, Gibson and Guinet (1971) used a tachistoscopic task to investigate the development of the role of morphemes as units of processing in word recognition. They presented grade three, five, and adult subjects with words, pseudowords, and letter strings which either did or did not have the morphemic inflections *s, ed,* and *ing* added to them. Overall, the three groups of subjects did not recognize items with inflections more accurately than items of equivalent length which did not have inflections.

They did find, however, that the younger subjects tended to make fewer errors on the *ing* of inflected items than on the last three letters of noninflected items of equivalent length. Unfortunately, this result was limited to the letter strings and may reflect the relative familiarity of the groups of letters making up the endings rather than any effect of morphology per se. There was, however, a greater tendency (though not significant) for the younger subjects to substitute one ending for another (e.g., *ed* for *ing*) on the inflected than the noninflected words. These results suggest the possibility that the morphological characteristics of the endings, rather than their frequency, were influencing the subjects' recognition accuracy.

Considered together, these results suggest that children develop the ability to attend to different linguistic units in printed information. However, the accessibility of these units to conscious attention appears to be influenced substantially by the characteristics of the subject's task. These influences include whether or not the linguistic background through which the subject searches is varied and the targets held constant (Drewnowski, 1978), or vice versa (Friedrich *et al.*, 1979; Santa, 1976–1977), the type of response measure emphasized (i.e., latency or accuracy), and the degree of compatibility between the search list and the target item (i.e., searching for words in a list of words is more compatible than searching for a letter in a list of words). Possibly as a result of these and other task factors, there does not appear to be much evidence for the emergence of a single basic or natural unit of processing during development in the sense that one unit is substantially more accessible to conscious attention than other units across task parameters. Although children in some grade levels appear to be more adept in attending to words or letters than to other units (e.g., spelling patterns, syllables, morphemes, phrases), this ability varies with the task and it may reflect, at least in part, the greater ease with which words and letters can be isolated visually. The results do not appear to be consistent with the notion that the development of word recognition proceeds from the ability to attend to lower order units to the ability to attend to higher order units, or vice versa. Although Drewnowski's (1978) results, for example, suggest that subjects attended to words as units before they were able to attend to phrases as units, the results of Friedrich *et al.* (1979) suggest a reversal in the progression from lower to higher order units in development as their younger subjects attended to words as units before they could attend to syllables as units. Instead, the available evidence suggests the possibility that children develop the ability to attend to several different units of processing (e.g., spelling patterns, syllables, some morphemes) about the same time (grades two to four) and that this ability coincides with the development of the use of orthographic structure (see Section II). Attending to phrases as units may emerge somewhat later (e.g., Drewnowski, 1978), though not in all tasks (e.g., Doehring, 1976), while even first graders seem to be able to attend to letter information (e.g., Doehring, 1976; Drewnowski, 1978) and probably some simple words.

IV. USE OF PARTIAL GRAPHIC INFORMATION

Printed words are very complex visual patterns and not all of the information they contain can be used to specify uniquely the identity of a single item. Certainly one of the goals of reading instruction is to teach children to attend to the information that is most reliable for distinguishing one word from another. Despite considerable efforts in instruction, there is evidence indicating that children may use partial graphic information which is not sufficient for word recognition, such as the initial and final letters of a word and its outline (i.e., envelope, shape). These types of information may be very salient for the beginning reader, particularly as he or she may have difficulty using effectively more reliable information about the orthographic structure of words.

Some of the early research on the development of word recognition (Hill, 1936) suggests that children learn very quickly to attend to the initial letters of a word. More recent research (e.g., Dunn-Rankin, 1978; Marchbanks & Levin, 1965; Williams, Blumberg, & Williams, 1970) suggests that beginning readers tend to devote most of their attention to the first letter, followed by the last and then the middle letters. There was not, however, much evidence that they tend to use word outline information. The results of these studies were based upon tasks in which subjects were required to make judgments about the visual similarity of printed items. In the Marchbanks and Levin (1965) and Williams et al. (1970) experiments, for example, subjects were presented with a target nonword (e.g., cug). After a delay, four nonwords were presented which were similar to the target item in a particular way: same first letter (che), same middle letter (tuk), same final letter (ilg), and same outline (arp). The subjects' task was to pick the response alternative which was most similar to the target item.

Rayner and Hagelberg (1975) have argued that the construction of the alternatives in this task might bias the subjects against choosing the same outline alternative over the other alternatives because the alternatives with the same outline as the targets tended to share fewer letters in common with the target items. In order to remedy this problem, they altered the task so that all of the response alternatives (six for a three-letter target item) shared one letter with the target item (one corresponding to each letter position), but only one-half of them shared the same outline. The target item *cug,* for example, had three same outline alternatives (*cwq, ouq, owg*) and three different outline alternatives (*cqn, jun, jqg*). Using this design, with both three- and five-letter items, Rayner and Hagelberg (1975) found that first grade subjects based their similarity judgments of three-letter items upon both word outline and the initial letter, whereas they used only the initial letter with five-letter items. Adult subjects used information about outline and the first two letters with both three- and five-letter items. The letter in the final position did not seem to be used more often than the middle letters in three or five-letter items by either children or adults. In a subsequent and more extensive developmental study (kindergarten through grade six, plus adults), Rayner (1976) found that the tendency to base similarity judgments on the first letter increased until grade two and then decreased thereafter, while the tendency to use outline information increased steadily across grade (from 55 to almost 90% of the choices). Rayner's (1976) results conflict with those obtained by other investigators who showed that the use of outline information declined with an increase in grade (Fisher & Price, 1970) or the use of the first letter increased with grade (Dunn-Rankin, 1978). However, Dunn-Rankin (1978) and Fisher and Price (1970) did not hold constant the number of shared letters between the target and the alternatives when they varied word outline similarity, hence it is difficult to interpret their results.

It is somewhat surprising to find that children use word outline in their similarity judgments as Groff (1975) has shown that it provides a unique specification for only about 20% of the highest frequency words available in children's books. Furthermore, word outline information does not appear to be sufficient for word recognition (see Section III) and it is not available when words are printed in upper case type. Even more surprising is Rayner's (1976) finding that subjects tend to prefer word outline over initial letter information with increasing age and reading experience. Although it is possible that fluent readers use word outline as an additional, global source of information in word recognition in some circumstances (see Section III), Rayner's (1976) developmental results may be specific to the particular characteristics of the task he used and will fail to generalize to tasks in which subjects are not required to make similarity judgments about the items, but only to recognize them. It should be noted, however, that Rayner and Hagelberg (1975) and Rayner (1976) specifically pointed out that the outline of a word is difficult to separate from the distinctive features of the letters making it up. In fact, they constructed their alternative items out of letters chosen from confusion matrices of lower case letters (e.g., Bouma, 1971). Alternatives that had the same outline as the target item were made up of letters which were more likely to be confused with letters in corresponding letter positions in the target item (suggesting more shared features) than alternatives which had different outlines. As Rayner (1976) suggested, it is possible that his results may be accounted for by subjects' tendency to base their judgments on the featural similarity between the letters in the target and the alternative items with increasing age and reading experience. Word outline information per se may have made a relatively minimal contribution to their judgments.

In order to explore further the use of letter and word outline information, Posnansky and Rayner (1977) employed a picture–word interference task, first used by Rosinski, Golinkoff, and Kukish (1975), which produces effects similar to that produced by the Stroop (1935) color–word interference task. Subjects in the picture–word task were required to name pictures of familiar objects as fast as possible. In one condition, the label (i.e., name) of the depicted object (e.g., the word *apple*) was printed in the center of the picture (i.e., of an apple), while in the other conditions the print varied in its relationship to the label of the picture; for example, the print might be a nonword (e.g., *dorch*) or a word that does not label the picture (e.g., *peach*). Subjects were faster at picture naming when the print labeled the picture than when the picture was presented alone (Ehri, 1976; Posnansky & Rayner, 1977, experiment two) or when the print was a nonword. They were slowest when the printed word did not label the picture. In general, the magnitude of the interference effect produced by the mismatch between the printed word and the picture label tended not to change developmentally (grade two through university). Furthermore, interference effects can be obtained when the subjects are required to classify rather than name pictures with words printed on them (Guttentag & Haith, 1979). Posnansky and Rayner (1977) reasoned that if subjects use word outline as well as initial letter information in word recognition, rather than just in similarity judgments, then the response time for labeling the picture should vary with the relationship between the actual label for the picture and the initial and final letters and the outline of the printed items. There were six conditions in their experiment: (1) the print (e.g., the word *apple*) labeled the picture (i.e., of an apple), (2) the print preserved the overall outline (again defined with reference to feature similarity) of the label and had the same initial and final letters (*aqqte*), (3) the print preserved only the initial and final letters (*azzme*) of the label, (4) the print preserved only the overall outline of the label (*oqqtc*), (5) the print preserved neither letters nor outline information (*kzzmf*), (6) the print is a word which is unrelated to the label of the picture (e.g., *house*). Children in the first, third, and sixth grades were presented with picture–word pairs individually in a tachistoscope for 100 milliseconds (followed by a pattern masking stimulus) and were required to name the pictures as quickly as possible. As with Rosinski *et al.* (1975), the picture–word pairs were also arranged on sheets of paper and subjects naming latencies for the pictures in conditions one, two, five, and six were recorded.

Consistent with Rosinski *et al.* (1975), subjects were fastest with both tachistoscopic and nontachistoscopic presentation when the picture label and the printed word matched (condition one) and slowest when they did not (condition six). The nonword conditions (two through five) were in between the two word conditions and differed among each other only in the tachistoscopic condition. It is possible that the brief tachistoscopic exposure of the materials increased the likelihood of subjects using the featural similarity between the print and the information activated by the picture name. Subjects were faster in the tachistoscopic condition when the print preserved both the outline and the initial and final letters of the label (condition two) than when it preserved just the initial and final letters (condition three) or just the outline (condition four). Furthermore, these two latter conditions did not differ from each other, but did differ from the condition (five) in which neither outline nor letters were preserved. These results suggest that subjects can use both word outline and initial–final letter information in word recognition, but that one type of information is not preferred over the other. An examination of the data for each grade suggested that the first graders may not have differentiated among the four nonword conditions, whereas the other three groups of subjects seemed to show the pattern of results described above. Contrary to Rayner (1976), there was not any evidence of a developmental trend whereby outline information was used over initial or final letter information; in fact, the two types of information seemed to show similar developmental trends.

To summarize, the results of these studies indicate that children as well as adults use partial graphic information about initial and final letters and outline in recognizing words. Although these two sources of information are not sufficient for word recognition, they may be useful in some circumstances. The initial and final letters often provide more information about the identity of a word than the middle letters (e.g., Broerse & Zwaan, 1966), possibly because of the orthographic, phonological, and morphological constraints on printed English. For example, only certain letters can begin and end words; knowledge of the first letter of a word is often more useful than the subsequent letters in producing a pronunciation (Eriksen & Eriksen, 1974); morphological information in the form of prefixes and suffixes is located in the initial and final positions of words. The initial and final letters are also less subject to lateral masking effects as they are not completely surrounded by other letters. These are probably only incomplete accounts of why initial and final letters are used, however, as Rayner and Hagelberg (1975) found that initial letters were chosen even with orthographically irregular (e.g., *cqn*) nonsense words and that adult subjects used the second letter of a word as often as the first. Word outline appears to be less useful in word recognition than the initial and final letters as it provides little linguistic information. If, however, word length is included in the definition of word outline, then it may, for example, provide some gross, global information about pronunciation and syntactic category (e.g., functors tend to be short words). It is possible, however, that there was only minimal use of word outline information in the experiments by Rayner and his co-workers. As with the experiments on similarity judgments (Rayner, 1976; Rayner & Hagelberg, 1975), subjects in the Posnansky and Rayner (1977) word–picture experiments may have been influenced by the features of the letters making up the printed items. Items which share initial and final letters and their outline with the picture label (condition two) have more letter features in common with the label than items which share only their initial and final letters (condition three), only outline information (condition four), or neither type of information (condition five). Accordingly, the faster response time in condition two than in three, four, and five, and in conditions three and four than in five may indicate the effects of letter feature similarity rather than word outline. Finally, this letter feature similarity interpretation is inconsistent with some theories of word recognition based on wholism at the feature level as it suggests that word outline information may not exist independently of features of component letters.

V. ACCESS TO WORD MEANINGS

There is now evidence from a variety of tasks indicating that it is not necessary for subjects to use phonological information in order to obtain access to the meanings of printed words (e.g., Kleiman, 1975; Meyer & Ruddy, 1973). Instead, it appears that subjects can use both visual and phonological information in accessing word meanings (Baron, 1973; see Barron, 1978a, for a review), although they may differ in the efficiency with which they can use one or the other type of information (e.g., Barron, 1978b, 1980; Boder, 1973; Marshall & Newcombe, 1973;

Patterson & Marcel, 1977). It is possible, however, that the use of both visual and phonological information in lexical access is a developmental phenomenon and that children begin to acquire reading skill by relying exclusively on one or the other type of information and then, with increasing reading experience, shift to using both types of information.

Most of the experimental work on the development of word meaning access has been concerned with whether or not there is a developmental shift from relying exclusively on phonological information to using both visual and phonological information. The possibility that children might begin to learn the meanings of printed words by obtaining access to them through sound has several indirect arguments in its favor. Children frequently have established a relationship between the phonological representation of a word and its meaning before they learn to read. Accordingly, they could access the meanings of many printed words by learning how to translate them into their corresponding sounds. This translation process may involve using spelling-to-sound correspondence "rules" and/or other mechanisms (e.g., Baron, 1977; Brooks, 1977, 1978; Glushko, 1979) and can provide children with powerful procedures for learning to read words they have not previously encountered in print. There is, in fact, considerable evidence suggesting that the ability to translate printed words into sound is very important in learning to read fluently (e.g., Firth, 1972; Perfetti & Hogaboam, 1975) and that reading programs which encourage children to learn relatively analytic print-to-sound translation procedures (i.e., involving letters and letter groups rather than whole words), such as phonics based programs, appear to be the most successful with beginning readers (Chall, 1967).

There are several studies which have been designed to test the phonological to visual–phonological developmental shift hypothesis. Rader (1975), required grade two, four, and six children and adults to decide whether or not pairs of auditorily and visually presented words rhymed (e.g., *pie, buy*) or belonged to the same semantic category (e.g., *dog, cat*). She hypothesized that if phonological access to meaning drops out with an increase in subjects' age, then there should be a greater decrease in response time across age in the difference between the category and the rhyme judgments with visual than auditory presentation. There are two rationales for this prediction. First, the use of phonological information is obligatory with auditory presentation, hence the difference between the rhyme and the category tasks (the category was slower) can be used as a baseline against which to evaluate performance with visual presentation. Second, the use of phonological information is obligatory in the rhyming task, but not in the category task with visual presentation as the rhyming pairs did not share corresponding spelling patterns. Accordingly, a smaller rhyme-category difference with visual than auditory presentation would suggest that phonological information was not being used in the category condition as it is the only condition in which the use of phonological information is optional. Contrary to the phonological to visual–phonological developmental shift hypothesis, Rader (1975) found that the rhyme-category difference was smaller with visual than auditory presentation for all age groups, although the effect was confined to the yes responses for the second graders. These results suggest that even grade two children do not require phonological access to meaning.

Barron and Baron (1977) took a different approach to testing the hypothesis that meaning access involves a developmental shift from phonological to visual and phonological access. They required children in grades one, two, four, six, and eight to decide whether or not picture–word pairs rhymed (e.g., the picture of a horn paired with the word *corn*) or went together in meaning (e.g., the picture of a pair of pants paired with the word *shirt*). In order to determine whether or not phonological mediation was involved in accessing word meanings, subjects were required to repeat the word *double* aloud at the same time that they made the rhyme and meaning decisions. Since this concurrent vocalization appears to tie up subjects' auditory and articulatory mechanisms, this activity was expected to interfere with the rhyme and meaning decisions to the extent that the decisions involved the use of these mechanisms. Although subjects in all five grades made more errors on the rhyming task when they were concurrently vocalizing than when they were not, concurrent vocalization did not have any effect on the meaning task at any grade level, including grade one. Consistent with Rader (1975), these results do not support the phonological to visual–phonological developmental shift hypothesis. It should be noted, however, that the word phonological has been used as a general term in this article for a variety of sound-based processes which may be involved in accessing word meanings, including articulation, auditory imagery, and abstract phonological coding. It is possible that the concurrent articulation task ties up only auditory and/or articulatory mechanisms and leaves the abstract phonological mechanism intact. Accordingly, the Barron and Baron (1977) experiment should probably be restricted to the interpretation that auditory and/or articulatory information is not necessary in accessing word meanings for beginning readers. This restricted interpretation may not, however, necessarily apply to Rader's (1975) experiment or to an experiment by Condry, McMahon-Rideout, and Levy (1979) which will be discussed next.

Condry *et al.* (1979) presented grade two, five, and university students with a target word and two choice words. The subjects were required to decide which one of the choice words was similar to the target word in a specific way: graphically, phonologically, and semantically. The distractor or incorrect choice words were varied systematically so that in the semantic condition, for example, subjects might have a distractor (e.g., *wait*) which rhymed with the target (e.g., *plate*); the correct choice word (e.g., *dish*) was semantically similar to the target. Condry *et al.* (1979) predicted that if subjects shift developmentally from using phonological coding to using both visual and phonological coding, then rhyming distractors in the semantic task should have a decreasing influence on subjects' performance across age. This prediction was not confirmed; in fact, the influence of the rhyming distractors tended to increase rather than decrease across age.

Although Barron and Baron (1977), Rader (1975), and Condry *et al.* (1979) used different tasks, their results are similar as they are all inconsistent with the phonological to visual–phonological developmental shift hypothesis of word meaning access. Instead, they suggest that phonological coding is not necessary for accessing word meanings from grade one through adulthood. Furthermore, there is some indication, particularly from the Condry *et al.* (1979) study, that beginning readers may be somewhat more efficient at using visual than phonological information in word meaning access, whereas more mature readers may be more likely to use both visual and phonological information.

There are several sources of indirect evidence which suggest the possibility of a visual to visual–phonological developmental shift. First, apparently children often enter school knowing the meanings of a small group of printed words, yet have only very rudimentary knowledge of how to read words aloud except by associating whole words with their corresponding pronunciations, or perhaps by using a limited number of large unit analogies (e.g., Baron, 1979). Second, learning to read words aloud is often difficult and very time consuming. Children who are having trouble acquiring reading skill seem to be specifically deficient in their use of print-to-sound translation procedures (e.g., Barron, 1978b, 1980; Boder, 1973; Firth, 1972; Perfetti & Hogaboam, 1975), hence they may be particularly reliant on visual information for word recognition. Third, the results of some experiments using the picture–word interference task described in Section IV suggest that beginning readers can access easily the meanings of familiar words. The question is whether they rely solely upon visual information, or whether they use both visual and phonological information in these tasks.

The fact that there is greater interference in picture–word experiments when the picture (e.g., of an apple) and the label printed on the picture are semantically incongruous (e.g., *peach*) than when the printed label is a nonword (e.g., *dorch*) has been interpreted as indicating that the interference is semantically based (Rosinski *et al.*, 1975) and that word meaning access is not phonologically mediated (Golinkoff & Rosinski, 1976). There are, however, problems with these two conclusions. There may be less interference on nonwords only because subjects have had less experience in reading them aloud than words, hence they may be less likely to interfere with the articulatory response for the picture label than the words. Ehri (1977), however, has shown that highly familiar function words (e.g., conjunctions, prepositions, auxiliary verbs) produce no more interference than nonsense words for grade three and six children, whereas adjectives and particularly nouns produced more interference. These results were obtained even though the function words were read aloud as rapidly as the nouns and adjectives. Furthermore, Rosinski (1977) has shown that words belonging to the same semantic category as the picture label produce more interference than those which do not for children in grades two, four, and six, and adults. These results suggest that the picture–word interference effect involves the use of semantic information and does not occur solely because of competing articulatory responses.

Guttentag and Haith (1978) found that although children tested late in the first grade showed more interference on semantically similar than dissimilar picture–word pairs, these children did not show any more interference on pictures with easy to pronounce (e.g., *lart*) than difficult to pronounce (e.g., *lbch*) nonwords printed on them. Differences in ease of pronunciation produced differences in amount of interference only for good grade three (marginally) and adult readers. It might be tempting to interpret these results as being consistent with the visual to visual–phonological developmental shift hypothesis as they suggest that beginning readers can access semantic information without being able to use effectively phonological information. The problem with this interpretation is that the ability to use a print-to-sound translation strategy cannot be distinguished from the ability to use visual–orthographic structure in Guttentag and Haith's (1978) experiment as the difficult to pronounce nonwords were also less consistent with orthographic constraints than the easy to pronounce nonwords. In addition, Posnansky and Rayner (1977, experiments three and four) found that even beginning readers (grade one) were able to use the phonological characteristics of print in their picture–word task. For example, subjects were faster in conditions in which the print (e.g., *leef, lefe*) preserved the sound of the label (*leaf*) than in conditions which it did not (e.g., *loef, lofe*). Subjects were also faster, however, in conditions in which the print preserved the initial and final letters and outline of the label (i.e., *loef*) than in conditions in which this information was not preserved (i.e., *lofe*). Posnansky and Rayner's (1977) results suggest that beginning readers may be able to use both visual and phonological information in accessing word meanings in picture–word interference tasks.

The evidence on the development of word meaning access provides very little support for the hypothesis that there is a developmental shift from sole reliance on phonological information to the use of both visual and phonological information. Although there was some evidence (e.g., Condry *et al.*, 1979) which was consistent with the opposite hypothesis that development proceeds from sole reliance upon visual information to reliance upon both visual and phonological information, the most plausible hypothesis suggests that beginning, as well as fluent, readers can use both visual and phonological information in word meaning access. Beginning readers may, however, be more reliant on visual than phonological information when they are required to read familiar words and they have not received much instruction in analytic print-to-sound translation strategies such as phonics. Once they learn how to translate print into sound rapidly and accurately, they might be able to use effectively phonological processing in word meaning access, particularly with unfamiliar words.

VI. CONCLUSIONS AND IMPLICATIONS

The material surveyed in this review suggests several conclusions about the development of visual word recognition. First, sometime between grades two and four children are able to use the gross characteristics of orthographic structure to facilitate word recognition in a wide variety of tasks. The relative size of this facilitating effect does not appear to change very much with development in tasks measuring response latency. However, in tasks using brief, tachistoscopic exposures and measuring response accuracy, the relative size of the orthographic effect is considerably more variable across age. Some of this variability may be attributed to floor or ceiling effects upon performance at various grade levels. Second, there appears to be evidence challenging the adequacy of theories of word recognition which are based upon wholism at the feature level, particularly when the unit of processing is a word. Foremost among this evidence is the fact that manipulations which disrupt wholistic feature information (e.g., case alternation) do not diminish substantially the size of the difference between words and pseudowords in several different tasks. Furthermore, parallel letter processing models appear to offer alternative accounts of results in which intermediate sized units (e.g., spelling patterns) are interpreted as being processed wholistically at the feature level. Children seem to be able to attend to several different units of processing (e.g., spelling patterns, syllables, some morphemes) at about the same time in development (grades two through four), but the evidence appears to be highly dependent upon the subjects' task. Third, both children and adults appear to use the initial and final letters and the outline of a word as partial graphic information in word recognition. Although these sources of information are not sufficient for word recognition, they may be useful in some circumstances. However, several experiments were interpreted as suggesting that word outline information may be indistinguishable from the features of the letters making up the word. Fourth, there does not seem to be much evidence that beginning readers rely exclusively on phonological information in accessing word meanings and then later shift to using both visual and phonological information. Rather, the available evidence suggests that beginning readers may be able to use both sources of information in lexical access.

There are several possible theoretical and practical implications of these conclusions. Although the current evidence suggests that theories based on wholism at the feature level may provide an inadequate account of fluent word recognition, there is actually little available evidence for evaluating how well feature wholistic theories account for performance during initial word learning. It is possible, for example, that beginning readers use a feature wholistic strategy in recognizing the small set of words they may learn informally, prior to receiving formal instruction in school. In fact, young children may treat some of these early acquired "sight" words almost as if they were logographs; consequently, the recognition of these items might be easily disrupted by case alternation and/or spatial transformations of the relationships among the letters. Formal instruction in word recognition may encourage children to abandon feature wholistic strategies, if in fact they are used, for more analytic strategies emphasizing the component letters of individual words.

The results discussed in Section II (orthographic structure) indicated that children learned to use orthographic structure to facilitate word recognition in several different tasks and at about the same time in development despite the possibility of being taught by a variety of different methods. This finding raises some questions about the relationships between methods of teaching and what children learn about printed words. Programs which emphasize analytic spelling-to-sound translation strategies (e.g., phonics) seem to be the most successful in teaching word recognition to the widest variety of children (Chall, 1967). On the other hand, attempts to teach children the visual structural regularities of words without emphasizing their corresponding sounds have not been very successful, at least in laboratory learning experiments (e.g., Gibson, 1974). This lack of success might be viewed as surprising given the evidence reviewed in Section V indicating that beginning readers do not have to use phonological information in accessing word meanings. Perhaps, as Gibson (1974) has suggested, abstracting the visual structural regularities in printed words and transferring that knowledge to new words involves a long process of perceptual learning which cannot be simulated in relatively short-term (e.g., 1 week) learning experiments. It is also possible, however, that learning phonics provides readers with much more than a mechanism for accessing the phonological representations of words they have not previously encountered in print. Phonics-based instruction may encourage children to attend to the visual–orthographic constraints (sequential and positional) on letters in printed words rather than to less reliable initial and final letter and word outline information (e.g., Venezky & Massaro, 1979). There is some evidence suggesting that sight word methods may be less effective in this regard (e.g., Barr, 1974–1975, 1975). Phonics might also be very useful in relating or amalgamating (e.g., Ehri, 1979, 1980, 1981; Ehri & Wilce, 1979) information about the visual-orthographic structure of words to phonological information already represented in the internal lexicon. A visual–orthographic entry for a word in the lexicon would be very useful for spelling as well as for reading (e.g., Barron, 1980). Finally, there may be some disadvantages to overemphasizing phonics-based instruction, at least insofar as children are encouraged to concentrate on visual–orthographic and phonological information at the expense of semantic and syntactic information. Ehri and Roberts (1979), for example, have shown that children acquired more information about semantic and syntactic information in printed words when they learned to recognize them in the context of sentences, whereas they acquired more orthographic information about words when they learned to recognize them in isolation.

There may be some additional implications of the conclusions drawn in this article for teaching reading. First, there does not appear to be much evidence which suggests that programs for reading instruction should necessarily emphasize one unit of processing over another or introduce units of processing in a particular order, at least insofar as the units are spelling patterns, syllables, and morphemes. Second, children seem to have little difficulty learning to use partial graphic information such as outline and initial and final letter information in printed words. Nevertheless, this information has limited utility when they are required to transfer their knowledge to recognizing new words. As a result, children might be helped if the opportunity for them to learn about initial and final letters, and particularly about word outline, is reduced by presenting children with sets of words in which this information cannot be used systematically (e.g., Barr, 1975). Third, phonological information should be considered as an alternative to visual information in accessing word meanings, rather than being obligatory. One implication of this conclusion is that successful reading programs may be those which emphasize learning about the visual–orthographic characteristics of words as well as about procedures for translating print into phonological representations. These programs may help children to use both visual and phonological strategies in accessing word meanings. As aforementioned, one of the reasons that phonics-based programs may be relatively successful is that they may help children to learn about the visual–orthographic structure of words as well as how they are related to sound.

Although not discussed in the previous sections, it is important to note that children became progressively faster in responding to printed words over the age range involved in schooling. This decrease occurred in every study discussed in this article which used response time as a dependent variable. Furthermore, subjects continued to get faster even though their error rates tended to be fairly low. It is not clear how to interpret this decrease in response time over age. On one hand, it is possible to attribute some of the effect to fundamental changes in the efficiency of "central processing" capabilities (e.g., Wickens, 1974). On the other hand, this effect may also reflect age-related changes in cognitive control processes, attention, motivation, and practice, particularly where central processing factors are defined as fundamental processes such as comparison (e.g., Chi, 1977). As far as visual word recognition is concerned, it does not appear that the ability to use orthographic structure accounts for much of the increase in recognition speed across age because the percentage by which orthography facilitated word recognition remained relatively constant after about the second to the fourth grade. It is possible, however, that across age children may become increasingly faster at activating individual letter identities and they may also increase the number of letter identities they can activate simultaneously. These possibilities are consistent with the fact that letter recognition speed increases across grade in a variety of tasks (e.g., Biemiller, 1977–1978; Henderson, 1974; McFarland, Frey, & Landreth, 1978; Reitsma, 1978; Staller & Sekuler, 1975) and that the effect of word length on word categorization time decreases across grade (Samuels et al., 1978). However, these results may have other interpretations, hence it is not yet possible to specify the bases for the increase in the speed of word recognition across grade.

Regardless of why word recognition speed increases developmentally, it is clear that rapid word recognition is important in acquiring reading fluency because the grade two to four readers who, for example, could use orthographic structure to facilitate word recognition were far from being fluent readers. Apparently, years of reading practice is necessary in order to bridge the gap between being able to use orthographic structure to facilitate word recognition and being fluent in word recognition. Several recent models of the reading process (e.g., LaBerge & Samuels, 1974; Lesgold & Perfetti, 1978; Perfetti & Lesgold, 1978, 1979) have strongly emphasized the role of rapid word recognition in achieving fluency in reading comprehension. Consistent with this emphasis, Stanovich (1980) has argued that readers who are slow in recognizing words when sentence and other context is not available, may compensate by relying very heavily on such context when it is available. This reliance may be purchased at some cost, however, as they may have fewer cognitive resources available for higher order comprehension operations.

ACKNOWLEDGMENTS

Portions of this article were written while I was on sabbatical leave at the Department of Experimental Psychology, University of Oxford. I wish to thank the department for the use of their facilities and the leave fellowship program of the Social Sciences and Humanities Research Council of Canada for financial support. I gratefully acknowledge the comments of L. Henderson, P. Bryant, G. Kleiman, T. Carr, K. Rayner, K. Stanovich, G. Marsh, C. Hulme, E. Dalrymple-Alford, and M. Schadler on an earlier version of this article.

REFERENCES

Adams, M. J. Models of word recognition. *Cognitive Psychology,* 1979, **11,** 133–176.
Adams, M. J., & Collins, A. A schema-theoretic view of reading. In R. O. Freedle (Ed.), *New directions in discourse processing* (Vol. 2). Norwood, New Jersey: Ablex, 1979.
Allington, R. L. Sensitivity to orthographic structure as a function of grade and reading ability. *Journal of Reading Behavior,* 1978, **10,** 437–439.
Allport, D. A. Word recognition in reading: A tutorial review. In P. A. Kolers, M. E. Wrolstad, & H. Bouma (Eds.), *Processing of visible language I.* New York: Plenum, 1979.
Baron, J. Phonemic stage not necessary for reading. *Quarterly Journal of Experimental Psychology,* 1973, **25,** 241–246.
Baron, J. What we might know about orthographic rules. In S. Dornic (Ed.), *Attention and performance VI.* Hillsdale, New Jersey: Erlbaum, 1977.
Baron, J. The word superiority effect: Perceptual learning from reading. In W. K. Estes (Ed.), *Handbook of learning and cognitive processes* (Vol. 6). Hillsdale, New Jersey: Erlbaum, 1978.
Baron, J. Orthographic and word specific mechanisms in children's reading of words. *Child Development,* 1979, **50,** 60–72.

Baron, J., & Thurston, I. An analysis of the word superiority effect. *Cognitive Psychology,* 1973, **4,** 207–228.

Barr, R. The effect of instruction on pupil reading strategies. *Reading Research Quarterly,* 1974–1975, **10,** 555–582.

Barr, R. Influence of reading materials on response to printed words. *Journal of Reading Behavior,* 1975, **8,** 123–135.

Barron, R. W. Access to the meanings of printed words: Some implication for reading and learning to read. In F. B. Murray (Ed.), *The recognition of words: I R A series on the development of the reading process.* Newark, Delaware: International Reading Association, 1978. (a)

Barron, R. W. Reading skill and phonological coding in lexical access. In M. M. Gruneberg, R. N. Sykes, & P. E. Morris (Eds.), *Practical aspects of memory.* New York: Academic Press, 1978. (b)

Barron, R. W. Visual and phonological strategies in reading and spelling. In U. Frith (Ed.), *Cognitive processes in spelling.* New York: Academic Press, 1980.

Barron, R. W., & Baron, J. How children get meaning from printed words. *Child Development,* 1977, **48,** 587–594.

Barron, R. W., & Henderson, L. The effects of lexical and semantic information on same-different visual comparison of words. *Memory and Cognition,* 1977, **5,** 566–579.

Barron, R. W., & Pittenger, J. B. The effect of orthographic structure and lexical meaning on same-different judgments. *Quarterly Journal of Experimental Psychology,* 1974, **26,** 566–581.

Biemiller, A. Relationship between oral reading rates for letters, words and simple text in the development of reading achievement. *Reading Research Quarterly,* 1977–1978, **13,** 223–253.

Bishop, C. H. Orthographic structure, word recognition and reading. Unpublished doctoral dissertation, Cornell University, 1976.

Boder, E. Developmental dyslexia: A diagnostic approach based on three atypical reading-spelling patterns. *Developmental Medicine and Child Neurology,* 1973, **15,** 663–687.

Bouma, H. Visual recognition of isolated lower case letters. *Vision Research,* 1971, **11,** 459–474.

Broadbent, D. E., & Broadbent, M. General shape and local detail in word perception. In S. Dornic (Ed.), *Attention and performance VI.* Hillsdale, New Jersey: Erlbaum, 1977.

Broerse, A. C., & Zwaan, E. J. The information value of initial letters in the identification of words. *Journal of Verbal Learning and Verbal Behavior,* 1966, **5,** 441–446.

Brooks, L. Visual pattern in fluent word identification. In A. S. Reber and D. L. Scarborough (Eds.), *Toward a psychology of reading.* Hillsdale, New Jersey: Erlbaum, 1977.

Brooks, L. Non-analytic correspondences and pattern in word pronunciation. In J. Requin (Ed.), *Attention and performance VII.* Hillsdale, New Jersey: Erlbaum, 1978.

Bruder, G. A. The role of visual familiarity in the word superiority effects obtained with the simultaneous-matching task. *Journal of Experimental Psychology: Human Perception and Performance,* 1978, **4,** 88–100.

Cattell, J. M. The time taken up by cerebral operations. *Mind,* 1886, **11,** 220–242. Reprinted in A. T. Poffenberger (Ed.), *James McKeen Cattell: Man of science.* Lancaster, Pennsylvania: The Science Press, 1947.

Chall, J. *Learning to read: The great debate.* New York: McGraw-Hill, 1967.

Chambers, S. M., & Forster, K. I. Evidence for lexical access in a simultaneous matching task. *Memory and Cognition,* 1975, **3,** 549–559.

Chi, M. T. Age differences in speed of processing: A critique. *Developmental Psychology,* 1977, **13,** 543–544.

Condry, S. M., McMahon-Rideout, M., & Levy, A. A. A developmental investigation of selective attention to graphic, phonetic and semantic information in words. *Perception and Psychophysics,* 1979, **25,** 88–94.

Dodd, B., & Hermelin, B. Phonological coding by the prelinguistically deaf. *Perception and Psychophysics,* 1977, **21,** 413–417.

Doehring, D. G. Acquisition of rapid reading responses. *Monograph of the Society for Research in Child Development,* 1976, **41** (2, Serial No. 165).

Drewnowski, A. Detection errors on the word *the:* Evidence for the acquisition of reading levels. *Memory and Cognition,* 1978, **6,** 403–409.

Drewnowski, A., & Healy, A. F. Detection errors on *the* and *and:* Evidence for reading units larger than a word. *Memory and Cognition,* 1977, **5,** 636–647.

Dunn-Rankin, P. The visual characteristics of words. *Scientific American,* 1978, **238,** 122–130.

Ehri, L. C. Do words really interfere in naming pictures? *Child Development,* 1976, **47,** 502–505.

Ehri, L. C. Do adjectives and functors interfere as much as nouns in naming pictures? *Child Development,* 1977, **48,** 697–701.

Ehri, L. C. Beginning reading from a psycholinguistic perspective: Amalgamation of word identities. In F. B. Murray (Ed.), *The recognition of words: I R A series on the development of the reading process.* Newark, Delaware: International Reading Association, 1978.

Ehri, L. C. Reading and spelling in beginners: The development of orthographic images as word symbols in lexical memory. In U. Frith (Ed.), *Cognitive processes in spelling.* New York: Academic Press, 1980.

Ehri, L. C. The role of orthographic images in learning printed words. In R. L. Venezky & J. F. Kavanagh (Eds.), *Orthography, reading and dyslexia.* Baltimore, Maryland: University Park Press, 1981.

Ehri, L. C., & Roberts, K. T. Do beginners learn printed words better in contexts or in isolation? *Child Development,* 1979, **50,** 675–685.

Ehri, L. C., & Wilce, L. S. The mnemonic value of orthography among beginning readers. *Journal of Educational Psychology,* 1979, **71,** 26–40.

Eriksen, B. A., & Eriksen, C. W. The importance of being first: A tachistoscopic study of the contribution of each letter to the recognition of four letter words. *Perception and Psychophysics,* 1974, **15,** 66–72.

Estes, W. K. The locus of inferential and perceptual processes in letter identification. *Journal of Experimental Psychology: General,* 1975, **104,** 122–145.

Estes, W. K. On the interaction of perception and memory in reading. In D. LaBerge & S. J. Samuels (Eds.), *Basic processes in reading: Perception and comprehension.* Hillsdale, New Jersey: Erlbaum, 1977.

Firth, I. *Components of reading disability.* Unpublished doctoral dissertation, University of New South Wales, 1972.

Fisher, V. L., & Price, J. H. Cues to word similarity used by children and adults. *Perceptual and Motor Skills,* 1970, **31,** 849–850.

Friedrich, F. J., Schadler, M., & Juola, J. F. Developmental changes in units of processing in reading. *Journal of Experimental Child Psychology,* 1979, **28,** 344–358.

Gibson, E. J. On the perception of words. *American Journal of Psychology,* 1964, **77,** 667–669.

Gibson, E. J. Learning to read. *Science,* 1965, **148,** 1066–1072.

Gibson, E. J. The ontogeny of reading. *American Psychologist*, 1970, **25**, 136–143.

Gibson, E. J. Reading to some purpose. In J. P. Kavanagh & I. G. Mattingly (Eds.), *Language by ear and by eye*. Cambridge, Massachusetts: MIT Press, 1972.

Gibson, E. J. Trends in perceptual development: Implications for the reading process. In A. D. Pick (Ed.), *Minnesota symposium on child psychology* (Vol. 8). Minneapolis: University of Minnesota Press, 1974.

Gibson, E. J. Perceptual aspects of the reading process and its development. In R. Held, H. W. Leibowitz, & H. L. Teuber (Eds.), *Handbook of sensory physiology* (Vol. 8). Berlin and New York: Springer-Verlag, 1978.

Gibson, E. J., & Guinet, L. Perception of inflections in brief visual presentations of words. *Journal of Verbal Learning and Verbal Behavior*, 1971, **10**, 182–189.

Gibson, E. J., & Levin, H. *The psychology of reading*. Cambridge, Massachusetts: MIT Press, 1975.

Gibson, E. J., Osser, H., & Pick, A. D. A study of the development of grapheme-phoneme correspondences. *Journal of Verbal Learning and Verbal Behavior*, 1963, **2**, 142–146.

Gibson, E. J., Pick, A. D., Osser, H. T., & Hammond, M. The role of grapheme-phoneme correspondences in the perception of words. *American Journal of Psychology*, 1962, **75**, 554–570.

Gibson, E. J., Shurcliff, A., & Yonas, A. Utilization of spelling patterns by deaf and hearing subjects. In H. Levin & J. P. Williams (Eds.), *Basic studies on reading*. New York: Basic Books, 1970.

Gibson, E. J., Tenney, Y. J., Barron, R. W., & Zaslow, M. The effect of orthographic structure on letter search. *Perception and Psychophysics*, 1972, **11**, 183–186.

Glushko, R. J. The organization and activation of orthographic knowledge in reading aloud. *Journal of Experimental Psychology: Human Perception and Performance*, 1979, **5**, 674–691.

Golinkoff, R. M. *Children's discrimination of English spelling patterns with redundant auditory information*. Paper presented at the meeting of the American Educational Research Association, Chicago, April 1974.

Golinkoff, R. M., & Rosinski, R. R. Decoding, semantic processing, and reading comprehension skill. *Child Development*, 1976, **47**, 252–258.

Groff, P. Shapes as cues to word recognition. *Visible Language*, 1975, **9**, 67–71.

Guttentag, R. E., & Haith, M. M. Automatic processing as a function of age and reading ability. *Child Development*, 1978, **49**, 707–716.

Guttentag, R. E., and Haith, M. M. A developmental study of automatic word processing in a picture classification task. *Child Development*, 1979, **50**, 894–896.

Hawkins, H. L., Reicher, G., Rogers, M., & Peterson, L. Flexible coding in word recognition. *Journal of Experimental Psychology: Human Perception and Performance*, 1976, **2**, 380–385.

Healy, A. F. Detection errors on the word *the*: Evidence for reading units larger than letters. *Journal of Experimental Psychology: Human Perception and Performance*, 1976, **2**, 235–242.

Henderson, L. Word recognition. In N. S. Sutherland (Ed.), *Tutorial essays in psychology*, (Vol. 1). Hillsdale, New Jersey: Erlbaum, 1977.

Henderson, L. Wholistic models of feature analysis in word perception: A critical examination. In P. A. Kolers (Ed.), *Processing of visible language II*. New York: Plenum, 1980.

Henderson, L. *Orthography in word recognition and reading*. New York: Academic Press, 1981 (in press).

Henderson, L., and Chard, J. The readers' implicit knowledge of orthographic structure. In U. Frith (Ed.), *Cognitive processes in spelling*. New York: Academic Press, 1980.

Henderson, S. E. Speed of letter cancellation on the basis of visual and name identity in children. *Journal of Experimental Child Psychology*, 1974, **17**, 347–352.

Hill, M. B. A study of the process of word discrimination in individuals learning to read. *Journal of Educational Research*, 1936, **29**, 487–500.

James, C. T., & Smith, D. E. Sequential dependencies in letter search. *Journal of Experimental Psychology*, 1970, **85**, 56–60.

Johnson, N. F. On the function of letters in word identification: Some data and a preliminary model. *Journal of Verbal Learning qnd Verbal Behavior*, 1975, **14**, 17–29.

Johnson, N. F. A pattern-unit model of word identification. In D. LaBerge & S. J. Samuels (Eds.), *Basic processes in reading: Perception and comprehension*. Hillsdale, New Jersey: Erlbaum, 1977.

Johnston, J. C. A test of the sophisticated guessing theory of word perception. *Cognitive Psychology*, 1978, **10**, 123–153.

Juola, J. F., Schadler, M., Chabot, R. J., & McCaughey, M. W. The development of visual information processing skills related to reading. *Journal of Experimental Child Psychology*, 1978, **25**, 459–476.

Kleiman, G. M. Speech recoding and reading. *Journal of Verbal Learning and Verbal Behavior*, 1975, **14**, 323–339.

Krueger, L. E. Search time in a redundant visual display. *Journal of Experimental Psychology*, 1970, **83**, 391–399.

Krueger, L. E. Familiarity effects in visual information processing. *Psychological Bulletin*, 1975, **82**, 949–974.

Krueger, L. E. Features versus redundancy: Comments on Massaro, Venezky and Taylor's orthographic regularity, positional frequency and visual processing of letter strings. *Journal of Experimental Psychology: General*, 1979, **108**, 125–130.

Krueger, L. E., Keen, R. H., & Rublevich, B. Letter search through words and nonwords by adults and fourth grade children. *Journal of Experimental Psychology*, 1974, **102**, 845–849.

LaBerge, D., & Samuels, S. J. Towards a theory of automatic information processing in reading. *Cognitive Psychology*, 1974, **6**, 293–323.

Lefton, L. A., & Spragins, A. B. Orthographic structure and reading experience affect the transfer from iconic to short-term memory. *Journal of Experimental Psychology*, 1974, **103**, 775–781.

Lefton, L. A., Spragins, A. B., & Byrnes, J. English orthography: Relation to reading experience. *Bulletin of the Psychonomic Society*, 1973, **2**, 281–282.

Lesgold, A. M., & Perfetti, C. A. Interactive processes in reading comprehension. *Discourse Processes*, 1978, **1**, 323–336.

McCaughey, M. W., Juola, J. F., Schadler, M., & Ward, N. J. Whole-word units are used before orthographic knowledge in perceptual development. *Journal of Experimental Child Psychology*, 1980, **30**, 411–421.

McClelland, J. L. Preliminary letter identification in the perception of words and nonwords. *Journal of Experimental Psychology: Human Perception and Performance*, 1976, **2**, 80–91.

McClelland, J. L. Letter and configuration information in word identification. *Journal of Verbal Learning and Verbal Behavior*, 1977, **16**, 137–150.

McClelland, J. L., & Johnston, J. C. The role of familiar units in the perception of words and nonwords. *Perception and Psychophysics*, 1977, **22**, 249–261.

McFarland, C. E., Jr., Frey, T. J., & Landreth, J. M. The acquisition of abstract letter codes. *Journal of Experimental Child Psychology*, 1978, **25**, 437–446.

McNeill, D., & Lindig, L. The perceptual reality of phonemes, syllables, words and sentences. *Journal of Verbal Learning and Verbal Behavior*, 1973, **12**, 419–430.

Manelis, L. The effect of meaningfulness on tachistoscopic word perception. *Perception and Psychophysics*, 1974, **16**, 182–192.

Marchbanks, G., & Levin, H. Cues by which children recognize words. *Journal of Educational Psychology*, 1965, **56**, 57–61.

Marmurek, H. H. C. Processing letters in words at different levels. *Memory and Cognition*, 1977, **5**, 67–72.

Marshall, J. C., & Newcombe, F. Patterns of paralexia: A psycholinguistic approach. *Journal of Psycholinguistic Research*, 1973, **2**, 175–199.

Mason, M. Reading ability and letter search time: Effects of orthographic structure defined by single letter positional frequency. *Journal of Experimental Psychology: General*, 1975, **104**, 146–166.

Massaro, D. W. Letter information and orthographic context in word perception. *Journal of Experimental Psychology: Human Perception and Performance*, 1979, **5**, 595–609.

Massaro, D. W., Venezky, R. L., & Taylor, G. A. Orthographic regularity, positional frequency and visual processing of letter strings. *Journal of Experimental Psychology: General*, 1979, **108**, 107–124.

Mayzner, M. S., & Tresselt, M. E. Tables of single-letter and digram frequency counts for various word length and letter position combinations. *Psychonomic Science Monograph Supplement*, 1965, **1**, 13–32.

Mayzner, M. S., Tresselt, M. E., & Wolin, B. R. Tables of trigram frequency counts for various word length and position combinations. *Psychonomic Science Monograph Supplement*, 1965, **1**, 33–78.

Meyer, D. E., & Ruddy, M. *Lexical memory retrieval based on graphemic and phonemic representations of words*. Paper presented at the meeting of the Psychonomic Society, St. Louis, 1973.

Mohan, P. J. Acoustic factors in letter cancellation: Developmental considerations. *Developmental Psychology*, 1978, **14**, 117–118.

Murrell, G. A., & Morton, J. Word recognition and morphemic structure. *Journal of Experimental Psychology*, 1974, **102**, 963–968.

Patterson, K. E., & Marcel, A. J. Aphasia, dyslexia and the phonological coding of written words. *Quarterly Journal of Experimental Psychology*, 1977, **29**, 307–318.

Perfetti, C. A., & Hogaboam, T. The relationship between single word decoding and reading comprehension skill. *Journal of Educational Psychology*, 1975, **67**, 461–469.

Perfetti, C. A., & Lesgold, A. M. Discourse comprehension and sources of individual differences. In P. A. Carpenter and M. Just (Eds.), *Cognitive processes in comprehension*. Hillsdale, New Jersey: Erlbaum, 1978.

Perfetti, C. A., & Lesgold, A. M. Coding and comprehension in skilled reading and implications for instruction. In L. B. Resnick & P. Weaver (Eds.), *Theory and practice of early reading* (Vol. 1). Hillsdale, New Jersey: Erlbaum, 1979.

Pick, A. D., Unze, M., Brownell, C. A., Drozdal, J. G., Jr., & Hopmann, M. R. Young children's knowledge of word structure. *Child Development*, 1978, **49**, 669–680.

Pollatsek, A., Well, A. D., & Schindler, R. M. Familiarity affects visual processing of words. *Journal of Experimental Psychology: Human Perception and Performance*, 1975, **1**, 328–338.

Posnansky, C. J., & Rayner, K. Visual-feature and response components in a picture-word interference task with beginning and skilled readers. *Journal of Experimental Child Psychology,* 1977, **24,** 440–460.

Purcell, D. G., Stanovich, K. E., & Spector, A. Visual angle and the word superiority effect. *Memory and Cognition,* 1978, **6,** 3–8.

Rader, N. *From written words to meaning: A developmental study.* Unpublished doctoral dissertation, Cornell University, 1975.

Rayner, K. Developmental changes in word recognition strategies. *Journal of Educational Psychology,* 1976, **68,** 323–329.

Rayner, K., & Hagelberg, H. Word recognition cues for beginning and skilled readers. *Journal of Educational Psychology,* 1975, **20,** 444–455.

Reicher, G. M. Perceptual recognition as a function of meaningfulness of stimulus material. *Journal of Experimental Psychology,* 1969, **81,** 275–280.

Reitsma, P. Changes in letter processing in beginning readers. *Journal of Experimental Child Psychology,* 1978, **25,** 315–325.

Rosinski, R. R. Picture-word interference is semantically based. *Child Development,* 1977, **48,** 643–647.

Rosinski, R. R., Golinkoff, R. M., & Kukish, K. S. Automatic semantic processing in a picture-word interference task. *Child Development,* 1975, **46,** 247–253.

Rosinski, R. R., & Wheeler, K. E. Children's use of orthographic structure in word discrimination. *Psychonomic Science,* 1972, **26,** 97–98.

Rozin, P., & Gleitman, L. R. The structure and acquisition of reading II: The reading process and the acquisition of the alphabetic principle. In A. S. Reber & D. L. Scarborough (Eds.), *Toward a psychology of reading.* Hillsdale, New Jersey: Erlbaum, 1977.

Rumelhart, D. E., & Siple, P. Process of recognizing tachistoscopically presented words. *Psychological Review,* 1974, **81,** 99–118.

Samuels, S. J., LaBerge, D., & Bremer, C. D. Units of word recognition: Evidence for developmental changes. *Journal of Verbal Learning and Verbal Behavior,* 1978, **17,** 715–720.

Santa, C. M. Spelling patterns and the development of flexible word recognition strategies. *Reading Research Quarterly,* 1976–1977, **7,** 125–144.

Santa, J. L., Santa, C. M., & Smith, E. E. Units of word recognition: Evidence for the use of multiple units. *Perception and Psychophysics,* 1977, **22,** 585–591.

Scragg, D. G. *A history of English spelling.* New York: Barnes & Noble, 1974.

Smith, E. E., & Kleiman, G. M. Word recognition: Theoretical issues and instructional hints. In L. B. Resnick & P. A. Weaver (Eds.), *Theory and practice of early reading* (Vol. 2). Hillsdale, New Jersey: Erlbaum, 1979.

Smith, F. *Understanding reading.* New York: Holt, 1971.

Spoehr, K. T., & Smith, E. E. The role of syllables in perceptual processing. *Cognitive Psychology,* 1973, **5,** 71–89.

Staller, J., & Sekuler, R. Children read normal and reversed letters: A simple test of reading skill. *Quarterly Journal of Experimental Psychology,* 1975, **27,** 539–550.

Stanovich, K. E. Toward an interactive-compensatory model of individual differences in reading fluency. *Reading Research Quarterly,* 1980, **16,** 32–71.

Stanovich, K. E., Purcell, D. G., & West, R. F. The development of word recognition mechanisms: Inference versus unitization. *Bulletin of the Psychonomics Society,* 1979, **13,** 71–74.

Stanovich, K. E., & West, R. F. The effect of orthographic structure on the word search performance of good and poor readers. *Journal of Experimental Child Psychology,* 1979, **28,** 258–267.

Stanovich, K. E., West, R. F., & Pollak, D. The effect of orthographic structure on word recognition in visual search. *Journal of Experimental Child Psychology*, 1978, **26**, 137–146.

Stroop, J. R. Studies of interference in serial verbal reactions. *Journal of Experimental Psychology*, 1935, **18**, 643–661.

Taylor, J. A., Miller, T. J., & Juola, J. F. Isolating visual units in the perception of words and nonwords. *Perception and Psychophysics*, 1977, **21**, 377–386.

Thomas, H. Children's tachistoscopic recognition of words and pseudowords varying in pronounceability and consonant vowel sequence. *Journal of Experimental Psychology*, 1968, **77**, 511–513.

Venezky, R. L. *The structure of English orthography*. The Hague: Mouton, 1970.

Venezky, R. L., & Massaro, D. W. The role of orthographic regularity in word recognition. In L. B. Resnick & P. A. Weaver (Eds.), *Theory and practice of early reading* (Vol. 1). Hillsdale, New Jersey: Erlbaum, 1979.

West, R. F., & Stanovich, K. E. Automatic contextual facilitation in readers of three ages. *Child Development*, 1978, **49**, 717–727.

Wheeler, D. D. Processes in word recognition. *Cognitive Psychology*, 1970, **1**, 59–85.

Whorf, B. L. Linguistics as an exact science. *Technology Review*, 1940, **43**, 61–63, 80–83. Reprinted in B. L. Whorf, *Language, thought and reality*. Cambridge, Massachusetts: MIT Press, 1956.

Wickens, C. D. Temporal limits of human information processing: A developmental study. *Psychological Bulletin*, 1974, **81**, 739–755.

Wijk, A. *Rules of pronunciation for the English language*. London and New York: Oxford University Press, 1966.

Williams, J. P., Blumberg, E. L., & Williams, D. V. Cues used in visual word perception. *Journal of Educational Psychology*, 1970, **61**, 310–315.

Woodworth, R. S. *Experimental psychology*. New York: Holt, 1938.

SEGMENTAL ANALYSIS ABILITY: DEVELOPMENT AND RELATION TO READING ABILITY

REBECCA TREIMAN[1] AND JONATHAN BARON

Department of Psychology
University of Pennsylvania
Philadelphia, Pennsylvania

I. INTRODUCTION

A. Overview

To most adults, it is obvious that spoken words consist of smaller units. We know that the spoken word *something* has two syllables, the first of which is identical to the first syllable of *summer*. We know that *bat* and *pat* are alike in the two final phonemes and different in the first. To young children, however, these insights do not come easily. Children

---

[1] Present address: Department of Psychology, Indiana University, Bloomington, Indiana.

159

typically have trouble on tasks that demand a sensitivity to the number of segments in a spoken word, such as judging that *motorcycle* is longer than *mow* (Rozin, Bressman, & Taft, 1974) or that *bat* contains three segments and *at* only two (Elkonin, 1973; Liberman, Shankweiler, Fischer, & Carter, 1974). Questions about whether given words share a segment in a specified position also tend to baffle young children. Children cannot reliably judge whether *pat* and *bat* rhyme, or whether *bat* and *boy* start with the same sound (Calfee, Chapman, & Venezky, 1972; Savin, 1972). Hardest, perhaps, are tasks that require children to rearrange the segments of a word or to delete a specified segment. Even 8-year-olds have trouble with questions such as "If I took away the *s* sound from *nest*, what word would be left?" (Bruce, 1964; Rosner & Simon, 1971).

Roughly speaking, all the tests described above require the knowledge that spoken words consist of smaller units, units that can be disassembled and rearranged to form yet other words. It is this knowledge that young children appear to lack. The missing quantity has been called by many names in the literature—"linguistic awareness" (Mattingly, 1972), "segmentation ability" (Liberman *et al.*, 1974), and "auditory analysis" (Rosner & Simon, 1971). Our label for the construct will be "segmental analysis." By segmental analysis ability we mean the ability to represent spoken words mentally in terms of smaller segments, whether these segments be syllables ("syllabic analysis") or phonemes ("phonemic analysis"). One of the goals of the present article is to characterize segmental analysis ability more precisely.

We shall ask about the linguistic variables that affect segmental analysis ability. According to some views of segmental analysis (e.g., Gleitman & Rozin, 1977; Liberman *et al.*, 1974), children ought to be more aware of vowels than of consonants, and more aware of fricative consonants than of stop consonants. We test these predictions in the experiments reported here. We shall also consider the development of segmental analysis ability in the broader context of perceptual development. Some recent views of perceptual development (e.g., Shepp, 1978; Smith & Kemler, 1977) propose that young children perceive multidimensional stimuli *integrally,* as undifferentiated wholes. They gradually come to perceive them *separably,* in terms of their constituent dimensions. We shall suggest that the development of segmental analysis ability can be seen in these terms. Specifically, phonemes in a syllable may be integral for young children and become more separable with development. We test some implications of this proposal in Experiments Two and Three.

One of our major concerns in this article is the relationship between segmental analysis ability and reading ability. There are many reports that children's performance on tests of segmental analysis correlates with reading skill (e.g., Calfee, Lindamood, & Lindamood, 1973; Firth, 1972; Fox & Routh, 1975; Liberman, Shankweiler, Liberman, Fowler, & Fischer, 1977; Rosner & Simon, 1971). But these correlations leave two major questions unanswered. First, reading is a complex skill that involves a number of components. With which of these component processes is segmental analysis most closely related? We propose that ability to analyze spoken words into phonemes is most closely tied to ability to use spelling-sound rules to "decode" printed words. We do not expect such a high correlation between phonemic analysis and ability to read words as "sight words," by means of memorized associations specific to each word. In the experiments reported here, we provide evidence to support these claims. A second important question is that of cause and effect. Do children who are good at using spelling–sound rules do well on segmental analysis tests *because* they are good readers, or did their superior analytical abilities allow them to become good readers in the first place? The experiments reported here do not allow us to answer this question, but we shall discuss how it might be addressed.

B. Some Questions about Segmental Analysis

If preliterate children do not easily recognize that spoken words are composed of smaller units, why not? What makes the idea difficult for them to understand? One way to find out is to look for variables that affect performance on segmental analysis tasks. The results of such studies may lend insight into the nature of the difficulty. One variable that might affect ease of analysis is the acoustic representation of the segment involved (Gleitman & Rozin, 1977; Liberman et al., 1974). Phonemic analysis may be hard, in part, because phonemes do not correspond to discrete and invariant pieces of sound (see Liberman, Cooper, Shankweiler, & Studdert-Kennedy, 1967). The spoken word *bat* consists of three phonemes, but its acoustic representation does not contain three separate units of sound. We consider the initial phoneme of *boy* to be identical to the initial phoneme of *bat*, but the acoustic representations of the two words do not begin in exactly the same way. Rather, the acoustic form of the initial *b* is influenced by the other phonemes in the syllable. These facts—that the acoustic representation of a phoneme differs as a function of its context, and that the cues for nearby phonemes are blended together in the speech stream—may account for the difficulty of phonemic awareness. Since these facts do not hold as strongly for syllables as for phonemes, one might expect syllabic analysis to be easier than phonemic analysis. And indeed, there is empirical evidence to this effect (Fox & Routh, 1975; Liberman *et al.*, 1974). One might also expect differences among classes of phonemes in ease of analysis. It has been claimed that the acoustic representations of vowels are more invariant than those of consonants, and that within the class of consonants the fricatives (e.g., *f*, *z*) are more invariant than the stops (e.g., *b*, *t*) (Liberman *et al.*, 1967). If so, awareness of vowels ought to be easier than awareness of consonants, and awareness of fricatives easier than awareness of stops. We test these predictions in the experiments reported here.

It is also possible that children's poor segmental analysis ability is a manifestation of a general tendency to perceive stimuli wholistically. Young children may be prone to consider complex stimuli as unitary wholes, and it may be difficult for them to perceive the parts or attributes that make up the wholes. In the visual realm, for example, a child might perceive a form like ⊞ as a whole, and thus fail to see that the simpler form ☐ is embedded within it (see Vurpillot, 1976). An adult is more likely to analyze the form into its subparts. Similarly, a child might represent the sound of a word as a unitary whole, and only later develop the ability to represent the parts. We shall have more to say about this notion in Section III.

C. Some Questions about Reading Ability and Its Relation to Segmental Analysis

The term "reading ability" suggests that a single underlying ability determines how well one reads. If one child has a certain amount of the ability and a second child has more, the latter will be a better reader. This simple conception is probably incorrect. As many authors have pointed out, the reading process includes a number of different components or subprocesses (Baron, 1977; Gibson & Levin, 1975). We need to know what these components are, and we need to develop measures of ability on each component.

The processes involved in reading can be divided into those involved in the reading of single words and those involved in the comprehension of sentences and texts. We shall concern ourselves with the first set of processes for two reasons. First, any relation between segmental analysis ability and reading would be expected to occur at this level. Second, the reading of individual words seems to be the major hurdle in the early grades. While some children can pronounce every word of a story but do not seem to understand what they are reading, most comprehension failures are due to failures to recognize the words. This is shown by high correlations between ability to read single words and ability to comprehend passages (e.g., Shankweiler & Liberman, 1972).

We can divide the processes involved in the reading of single words into those that are based on spelling–sound rules and those that depend upon word-specific associations. By processes based on rules we mean processes that take advantage of the more-or-less regular correspondences between spellings and sounds that exist in English. For present purposes, it is unimportant *how* readers make use of these regularities. They may use correspondences between single letters and single sounds, correspondences between groups of letters and groups of sounds, or analogies. (Most likely, they use all of these methods; see Baron, 1979.) These processes allow readers to look at words they have never seen before and pronounce them in a way that is consistent with the rules of English. By processes based on word-specific associations we mean processes that require previous exposure to the words in question. Two sorts of associations could be formed by such exposure: associations between the printed words and their pronunciations or associations between the printed words and their meanings. To count as word-specific, an association must be learned by rote memory. A person who pronounces a word using only a specific association from print to sound has no idea *why* the word is pronounced as it is.

We are suggesting, then, that there are two kinds of processes by which words can be read—processes based on rules and processes based on word-specific associations. A person who used only the former could pronounce any word that conformed to the rules but would err on exception words. For example, he would pronounce the *w* in *answer*. This person could read words he had never encountered before; in fact, he would read *every* word, familiar or not, as if he had never seen it before. Let us call this person a "Phoenician" (after the Phoenicians, who are said to have invented the alphabet). A person who relied entirely on word-specific associations, on the other hand, would have no associations involving unfamiliar words and hence would be unable to read them. He could read familiar words, whether they followed the rules or not. This person will be called a "Chinese" reader (in honor of the Chinese, whose writing system has few regular correspondences between written words and their sounds).

Neither description, that of the extreme Phoenician nor the extreme Chinese, matches our picture of the normal reader. But certain patients whose reading ability has been altered by brain injury fit these characterizations rather exactly. One patient (described by Luria, 1960) seems the archetypal Phoenician. Before his injury he read French and Russian fluently. Afterwards he read Russian well, since Russian has very regular correspondences between spellings and sounds, but he had trouble with French words for which the relation between spelling and sound was not so exact. He easily read words written in a mixture of Roman and Cyrillic letters—words he had surely never seen before. Often he did not notice that anything was unusual about these words. A second patient (Saffran & Marin, 1977) seems the archetypal Chinese. She could derive meaning from a large number of written words—16,500 by one estimate—but could not read the simplest nonsense word. Given a familiar word like *soap* she could point to the appropriate picture, but given an unfamiliar but phonetically plausible spelling like *sope* she was lost. She made errors in which she substituted a semantically related word for the target word (e.g., *crocus* for *tulip*); these errors seem to indicate that she used a direct pathway from print to meaning, at least in part.

Most readers are somewhere between these two extremes. But normal individuals seem to differ in where along the continuum they fall. Some are nearer to the Chinese end, in that they rely heavily on word-specific associations and very little on rules. Others are close to the Phoenician extreme, since they rely primarily on rules and little on word-specific associations. Such individual differences have been studied both in adults (Baron & Strawson, 1976; Baron, Treiman, Wilf, & Kellman, 1980) and in children (Baron, 1979; Baron & Treiman, 1980a; Boder, 1973).

We propose that Phoenicians are better at segmental analysis than Chinese. That is, segmental analysis ability is more closely related to ability to read by rules than to ability to read by word-specific associations. Causal links between segmental analysis and use of spelling–sound rules could run in either direction (or in both directions). It might be the case that in order to benefit from the regular relationships between letters and phonemes or between groups of letters and syllables one has to represent spoken words in terms of phonemes and syllables. Thus, children who are good at segmental analysis would be good at learning spelling–sound rules. A causal link in the reverse direction is also plausible. Children who know spelling–sound rules may do well on segmental analysis tests because they can imagine the spellings of the words. In a phoneme counting test, for example, a child who counted the number of letters in the spelling of a word rather than the number of phonemes in the spoken word would usually get the right answer. On the other hand, there is no reason to suppose that segmental analysis ability would influence ability to learn word-specific associations, or that formation of such associations would promote segmental analysis. We therefore predict a closer relationship between use of rules and segmental analysis than between use of word-specific associations and segmental analysis.

To state the hypothesis in another way, Phoenicians should perform better on segmental analysis tasks than Chinese.

To test the hypothesis that segmental analysis is most closely related to ability to read by rules, we use a method that we have recommended elsewhere, one that involves looking for differences between correlation coefficients (Baron & Treiman, 1980b). We design two reading tests, one that taps ability to use rules and one that taps primarily ability to use word-specific associations. We give a group of children both reading tests, along with a test of segmental analysis. Each reading test will presumably be affected by intelligence, schooling, motivation, and so on, and thus the two reading tests will correlate with each other. The segmental analysis test will probably be affected by some of these same factors, and so will correlate with each of the reading tests. But suppose that the segmental analysis test correlates *more* highly with the test of ability to read by rules than with the test of ability to read using word-specific associations. The difference in correlation coefficients cannot be due to the general factors that affect performance on both reading tests. Rather, there must be a particular relationship between segmental analysis ability and use of rules. (Note that in order to compare correlation coefficients in this way, one must statistically take into account the correlation between the two reading tests. Methods for doing this are cited in Baron and Treiman (1980b). Also, as discussed in that paper, one must show that the two reading tests are equally reliable.) This method is superior to the usual alternative, the attempt to "partial out" extraneous variables such as intelligence and exposure to reading instruction. Extraneous variables of this sort cannot be measured with complete validity or reliability, so their influence cannot be completely removed. Thus, a demonstration that segmental analysis correlates with rule use when IQ (or ability to use specific associations, for that matter) is held constant cannot fully remove the effect of the extraneous variable.

II. EXPERIMENT ONE: CHILDREN'S ABILITY TO COUNT PHONEMES, SYLLABLES, AND NONSPEECH SOUNDS

The aspect of segmental analysis examined in the first experiment is ability to judge the number of units—both syllables and phonemes—in spoken words. This skill has been previously investigated by Elkonin (1973) and by I. Y. Liberman and her associates (Liberman *et al.*, 1974). Liberman *et al.* (1974) used a tapping task: Children were to tap a dowel once for each segment in a spoken word. In the syllable counting test they might hear *butterfly* and would have to tap three times; in the phoneme counting test they might hear *at* and would have to tap twice. At each grade level—nursery school, kindergarten, and first grade—one group of children counted syllables and another group counted phonemes. The results were clear: performance on both tasks increased with grade level, but at all levels performance on the phoneme task was inferior to that on the syllable task. Several months later, some of the children who had participated in the study were given the word reading section of the Wide Range Achievement Test. Those children who had done well on the phoneme counting test tended to be the better readers. Poor performance on the phoneme counting test was associated with reading difficulty (Liberman *et al.*, 1977).

The studies described above, while suggestive, lack an important control. In order for a child to pass the phoneme and syllable counting tests, it is not enough for him to represent the word he hears in terms of the proper units. He must also tap the dowel once for each unit. Some children may have failed the test because they failed to do this correctly. To assess this possibility, we gave all children a control test that differed from the phoneme and syllable counting tests in that the stimuli were nonspeech sounds containing one, two, or three discrete units. The control test thus measures many of the abilities that are necessary for success in the phoneme and syllable counting tests. It does *not* measure the ability we wish to study: the ability to represent spoken words in terms of phonemes or syllables.[2] We should point out that control tests of this sort are useful whenever a test designed to measure a certain ability necessarily requires other abilities than the one of interest (see Baron & Treiman, 1980b).

A minor quibble with the procedure of Liberman *et al.* (1974) is that the use of a tapping response could conceivably have accounted for the relative ease of the syllable counting task. The rhythmic motor response of tapping a dowel may be intrisically more compatible with counting syllables than with counting phonemes. This may occur because each syllable typically corresponds to a pulse of air, while phonemes have no such obvious motor correlates. We chose a more neutral response, one in which children put down the number of checkers equal to the number of segments in the stimulus (after Elkonin, 1973).

Our stimuli were nonsense words rather than real words as in previous studies. We had two reasons for this choice. First, children may be so used to thinking about the meanings of familiar words that they have trouble thinking about their sounds. It may be easier to think about

---

[2] There is another ability that is required by the phoneme and syllable counting tests but not by the control tests: the ability to remember spoken nonsense words.

sounds when the words have no meaning at all. (See McNeil & Stone, 1965, for some empirical evidence to this effect.) Second, we could systematically vary the structure of the nonsense words in an effort to determine how the nature of the stimulus affects performance.

We gave our subjects two reading tests. One (designed by us) tested ability to read nonsense words. The other (the Wide Range Achievement Test or WRAT; Jastak, Bijou, & Jastak, 1965) tested ability to read real words. The WRAT contains a selection of words from children's readers, both words that are commonly taught as sight words and words that are not. The former test serves as a measure of ability to use spelling–sound rules. The latter test is more sensitive to the use of word-specific associations. If the segmental analysis tests correlate more highly with the nonsense word reading test than with the WRAT, we may be able to conclude that segmental analysis correlates with ability to read by rules.

Our subjects were inner-city children, in contrast to the suburban children tested by Liberman's group. Pilot work showed that most kindergarteners in this population had great difficulty with the tasks; we therefore tested first and second graders.

A. Method

The subjects were 31 children from one first grade and one second grade class of a New Haven public school. There were 17 first graders (mean age at start of testing 6 years, 6 months) and 14 second graders (mean age 7 years, 11 months). All the children had learned English as their native language. Three of the first graders were unavailable for the nonsense word reading test; the analyses involving this test are thus based on 14 first grade and 14 second grade subjects.

Each first grader was seen four times. Sessions one, two, and three (in January and February of the school year) consisted of the WRAT, the phoneme counting test, and the nonspeech sound and syllable counting tests, respectively. The nonsense word reading test was given in a fourth session in April. The second graders were seen three times each. The first session included the WRAT, the second session the nonspeech sound counting test and the phoneme counting test, and the third session the nonsense word reading test. Sessions one and two were held in January and February; session three in April. (Unfortunately, time constraints did not permit us to give the syllable counting test to the second graders.)

The nonspeech sound counting test, the syllable counting test, and the phoneme counting test were identical in procedure and instructions. They differed only in the nature of the stimuli. For all tests, three checkers were made available. The child had to put down one, two, or three checkers depending on the number of units in the stimulus. There were three sets of training trials, each set containing three items. The experimenter demonstrated the first two training sets in order of increasing length, from one to three units. The child then tried these items himself, with help from the experimenter. Next, the child attempted the third training set on his own, with the experimenter correcting him if necessary. Finally, the test items were given. The experimenter pronounced each stimulus, and the child put down one, two, or three checkers. No feedback was given.

The stimuli in the nonspeech sound counting test (the control test) were made up of voiced flaps of the tongue, similar to the flap *d* in *ladder*. The flap was followed by a very brief neutral vowel. Each stimulus consisted of one, two, or three such flaps, pronounced at a rapid rate. The test given to the first graders contained 21 stimuli, 7 of each length; the test given to the second graders contained 15 items.

The stimuli for the syllable counting test were nonsense words containing one, two, or three CV (consonant–vowel) syllables. The test had 21 stimuli, 7 of each length. The stimuli are listed, using the phonetic transcription of Webster's dictionary, in Table I. (This transcription will be used throughout this article.)

The stimuli for the phoneme counting test were 30 nonsense syllables. Six contained one phoneme, 12 contained two phonemes, and 12 contained three phonemes. All one-phoneme stimuli were vowels. Half the two-phoneme stimuli were CV syllables and half were VC syllables; within each structure half the syllables contained a stop consonant and half a fricative consonant. All the three-phoneme syllables were CVCs. In half both consonants were stops and in half both consonants were fricatives. The stimuli are shown in Table I.

The nonsense word reading test contained 29 items: 9 VC, 10 CVC, and 10 CVCe. They are shown in Table II. In half the words the consonants were chosen from *p, b, t, d* (stop consonants); in the other half

TABLE I

Counting Tests Used in Experiment One

Syllable counting test

fi, supoofe, zätē, boosä, te, vēdäbō, voo, pudoo, pō, fēzita, datu, zibesō, pudavoo, bivä, sa, bu, foovadu, zitoo, po, sube, vapēti

Phoneme counting test

voos, ōz, uf, sōs, i, ood, pa, tet, ō, e, fäz, si, tä, tēb, bōd, ab, zef, boo, poob, zē, ä, fiv, vaz, ēs, däp, pud, oo, ōp, u, ve

TABLE II

Nonsense Word Reading Test
Used in Experiment One

1. *ip*	16. *iz*
2. *saf*	17. *et*
3. *tope*	18. *vaz*
4. *zef*	19. *dute*
5. *dap*	20. *vuse*
6. *suze*	21. *uf*
7. *teb*	22. *bup*
8. *zive*	23. *ov*
9. *ut*	24. *ab*
10. *fiv*	25. *vos*
11. *pube*	26. *bode*
12. *vafe*	27. *uz*
13. *bot*	28. *pid*
14. *fuve*	29. *ez*
15. *dabe*	

the letters *f, v, s, z* (fricatives) were used. Each consonant occurred approximately the same number of times in each position. The words were hand printed in large letters and children were asked to read them as best they could. A relatively lenient scoring system was adopted: if a letter was pronounced as it is in some real word that a child is likely to know, it was counted as correct. (We tried a stricter scoring criterion also; the pattern of results was the same.)

B. Results and Discussion

We shall discuss, first, the results of the sound, syllable, and phoneme counting tests. We shall then consider the results of the reading tests and, finally, the correlations among the various measures.

Table III shows the results of the nonspeech sound, syllable, and phoneme counting tests. The sound counting test appears to be easiest, the syllable counting test intermediate, and the phoneme counting test hardest. Statistical analyses confirmed this impression. For the first graders, a one-way analysis of variance revealed a significant effect due to test [$F(2,32) = 30.86, p < .01$]. Post hoc comparisons showed that the phoneme counting test differed significantly from the other two tests ($p < .01$ for both comparisons by Tukey tests). The difference between the sound test and the syllable test was nearly significant ($p = .06$ by a Tukey test). Individual children's patterns confirmed the ordering of difficulty. We considered that a child had "passed" a test if he attained

TABLE III

Results of the Sound, Syllable, and Phoneme Counting Tests

	Nonspeech sound counting test	Syllable counting test	Phoneme counting test
First graders ($N = 17$)			
Proportion correct			
Mean	.82	.69	.42
Standard deviation	.20	.31	.16
Proportion of subjects			
who passed the test[a]	.88	.65	.35
Second graders ($N = 14$)			
Proportion correct			
Mean	.92	—	.58
Standard deviation	.11		.22
Proportion of subjects			
who passed the test[a]	1.00	—	.57

[a] A subject was considered to have passed a test if he obtained a score that would be produced by random guessing less than 5% of the time.

a score that could be attained by random guessing less than 5% of the time. Using this criterion, two first graders passed no tests, four passed the sound counting test only, five passed the sound test and the syllable test, and six passed all three tests. No child passed a harder test while failing an easier one. These results show that the order of difficulty found by Liberman *et al.* (1974) holds within individual children. It seems to be harder for children to represent spoken words in terms of phonemes than in terms of syllables.

To look at changes in performance from first to second grade, we performed a two-way analysis of variance with grade as the between-subjects factor and task (sound counting vs phoneme counting) as the within-subjects factor. The analysis revealed a main effect for task [$F(1,29) = 118.43$, $p < .01$], a main effect for grade [$F(1,29) = 5.76$, $p < .05$], and no interaction [$F(1,29) = 0.70$]. These results show that in second graders, as in first graders, the phoneme counting test was harder than the sound test. Somewhat surprising is our failure to find an interaction between grade and task. Phoneme counting performance did increase with grade level, but the increase was statistically indistinguishable from the increase in ability to perform the mechanical aspects of the task, as measured by the sound test. Thus, second graders may have counted phonemes more accurately than first graders not because they were more aware of phonemes but because they were able to count more accurately or with less effort. In this group of children, at least, there is no evidence that phonemic awareness per se improved from first to second grade. If we had not included the sound counting test as a control, the observed increase in phoneme counting performance would probably have led us to a different conclusion. These results underline the need to use control tests to find out *which* aspects of performance improve with age.

We now consider the pattern of results on the phoneme counting test itself. We are interested here in the linguistic factors (structure of syllable, type of phoneme) that may affect performance. For these analyses, we included only those 14 subjects—6 first graders and 8 second graders—who passed the test. (The patterns are the same, but "noisier," when all 29 subjects who passed the control test are included.) We found that three-phoneme syllables containing fricatives were easier than three-phoneme syllables containing stops (69% correct as compared to 52% correct). This effect was significant both across stimuli [$t(10)$ = 2.05, $p < .05$ one tailed] and across subjects [$t(13)$ = 2.46, $p < .025$ one tailed]. However, two-phoneme syllables containing fricatives and stops did not differ (on both, average was 67% correct). VC syllables were easier than CV syllables (77 and 56%, respectively). For the two-phoneme syllables, a two-way analysis of variance, with one factor type of consonant (fricative vs stop) and one factor structure of syllable (CV vs VC) confirmed that there was a main effect of syllable type [$F'(1,14)$ = 8.26, $p < .05$], but no effect of consonant type. We suspect, however, that the superiority of VC syllables came about for an uninteresting reason. Probably the experimenter tended to release the final consonant of the VC syllables (e.g., *ō-puh* instead of *ōp*), making its presence more obvious.

Recall that there was reason to believe that fricatives might lead to better performance than stops. Our evidence on this point is mixed: CVC syllables in which both consonants were fricatives were easier than CVC syllables in which both consonants were stops, but CV and VC syllables containing fricatives did not differ from those containing stops. If we take these results at face value, we might explain them by supposing that children count phonemes in different ways with different sorts of syllables. With longer syllables, they may try to say the individual phonemes to themselves. This strategy would work better with fricatives, which can be pronounced in isolation, than with stops, which cannot. With shorter syllables, children may not need to use this procedure. Another possibility is that children can more easily represent syllables in terms of phonemes when the phonemes are fricatives than when they are stops, but that the effect is small. Thus a difference may appear only with the three-phoneme syllables, which contain either *two* fricatives or *two* stops. (We shall later have reason to favor the first explanation—see Section IV.)

Turning now to the results of the reading tests, we find that the first graders averaged 29 on the WRAT, a grade-level equivalent of 1.4. The second graders scored at the 2.2 level, with a mean of 42. Thus, the children were slightly below grade level. The results of the nonsense word reading test are interesting, for they allow us to examine the linguistic variables (type of segment, position in word) that affect reading performance. For these analyses, we considered only those subjects who read at least one word correctly. Five first graders were thus eliminated, leaving 23 subjects. For the CVC and CVCe stimuli, the initial consonant was correct an average of 86% of the time, the medial vowel 57%, and the final consonant 70%. (Since the *e* should affect the pronunciation of the medial vowel, we considered it together with the vowel.) A one-way analysis of variance confirmed that there was a significant effect of letter position [$F(2,28) = 23.03$, $p < .01$]. Post hoc comparisons, via Tukey tests, showed that vowels were read less accurately than either initial consonants ($p < .01$) or final consonants ($p < .05$), while final consonants were less often correct than initial ones ($p < .01$). For the two-letter stimuli (all of which were VCs), vowels were less often correct than consonants. The means were 74 and 84%, respectively. However, the difference did not reach significance across stimuli [$t(8) = 1.49$, $p < .1$, one tailed]. These patterns of results were shown at both grade levels.

The ordering of difficulty that we found for nonsense words—vowels hardest, final consonants intermediate, and initial consonants easiest—agrees with previous results for real words (Fowler, Liberman, & Shankweiler, 1977; Shankweiler & Liberman, 1972). The concordance suggests that children use some of the same strategies in reading real words that they use in reading nonsense words. Interestingly, young readers of Serbo-Croatian also make more errors on final consonants than initial ones (Lukatela & Turvey, 1980). In Serbo-Croatian, however, vowels are not harder than consonants. Each letter in Serbo-Croatian is always pronounced the same way; the poor performance on vowels in English may stem in large part from their inconsistent pronunciations.

We examined in more detail the substitution errors on consonants. When the correct response was a stop consonant, 94% of the errors were also stops; when the correct response was a fricative, 76% of the errors were fricatives. The association between phonetic category of the correct response and phonetic category of the error was highly reliable [$\chi^2(1) = 94.8$, $p < .005$]. Furthermore, when we considered the phonetic features (place of articulation, manner of articulation, and voicing) that distinguished the error from the correct response, we found that 68%

of the errors differed from the target in a single feature. Our results accord closely with those of Fowler *et al.* (1977) for real words—further evidence that children's procedures for reading real words and nonsense words have much in common. In both cases, a child who misreads a consonant generally produces one that sounds similar to the correct one. These results suggest that an important source of difficulty in early reading is learning associations between letters and their sounds, as distinct from learning to distinguish printed letters from one another. In the latter case, one would expect to find confusions between letters that look similar.

We now consider the correlations among the various measures. The correlation matrix for the first graders appears in Table IV and that for the second graders in Table V. Note first that the two reading tests, one measuring ability to read real words and one measuring ability to read nonsense words, were highly correlated. The counting tests tended to correlate with each other, and certain of the counting tests correlated with certain of the reading tests. To understand the pattern of correlations, we look for differences between correlation coefficients. In particular, we want to know whether the phoneme and syllable counting tests correlate more highly with the reading tests than does the control

TABLE IV

Correlation Matrix for First Graders[a]

	WRAT	Nonsense word reading	Nonspeech sound counting	Syllable counting	Phoneme counting
WRAT (raw score)	—	.83***	.40	.62**	.37
Nonsense word reading (number correct)		—	.50*	.76***	.66**
Nonspeech sound counting (proportion correct)			—	.77***	.58*
Syllable counting (proportion correct)				—	.66**
Phoneme counting (proportion correct)					—
Mean	28.8	7.9	.80	.65	.42
SD	9.8	8.9	.22	.33	.17

[a] $N = 14$.
* $p < .05$, one tailed.
** $p < .01$, one tailed.
*** $p < .005$, one tailed.

TABLE V

Correlation Matrix for Second Graders[a]

	WRAT	Nonsense word reading	Nonspeech sound counting	Phoneme counting
WRAT	—	.71***	.48*	.39
Nonsense word reading		—	.42	.53*
Nonspeech sound counting			—	.45
Phoneme counting				—
Mean	41.6	13.2	.92	.58
SD	6.7	9.3	.11	.22

[a] $N = 14$.
* $p < .05$, one tailed.
*** $p < .005$, one tailed.

test. If so (and if the three counting tests are equally reliable) we could conclude that the ability measured by the phoneme and syllable tests and not by the control test—the ability to represent spoken words in terms of phonemes and syllables—correlates with reading ability. Second, we want to determine whether the phoneme and syllable tests correlate more highly with the nonsense word reading test than with the WRAT. Such a result would suggest that the ability measured by these tests relates to the ability to read by rules.

In the first grade subjects, the correlation between the syllable counting test and the nonsense word reading test is significantly higher than the correlation between the sound counting test and the nonsense word reading test [$t(11) = 2.00$, $p < .05$, one tailed]. This result suggests that the ability to represent spoken words in terms of syllables correlates with rule using ability. However, the variance of the syllable counting test is larger than that of the control test, and this fact could also explain the difference in correlations. The phoneme counting test correlates more highly with the nonsense word reading test than does the sound counting test, but the difference in correlations is not significant [$t(11) = .79$]. The phoneme counting test does correlate more highly with the nonsense word reading test than with the WRAT [$t(11) = 2.42$, $p < .025$], even though the WRAT has the larger variance. This result suggests that the ability to count phonemes relates not just to reading ability in general, but to the ability to use spelling–sound rules. The pattern of results in the second grade is the same: ability to count phonemes correlates par-

ticularly highly with ability to read nonsense words, while ability to read
real words is actually predicted slightly better by the control test than
by the phoneme counting test. The tests for differences between correlations do not reach significance, however.

We did a further analysis to determine which of the counting tests
correlates most highly with the *difference* between the nonsense word
reading test and the WRAT. If ability to use spelling–sound rules is
related to phonemic analysis ability, we would expect the difference
score to correlate more highly with the phoneme counting test than with
the sound counting test. We calculated each subject's z score on the
nonsense word reading test and on the WRAT and took the difference,
z(Nons) − z(WRAT). The correlations between this difference score and
the various counting tests are shown in Table VI. In the first graders,
the phoneme counting test seems to correlate more highly with the difference score than does the control test. [The difference does not reach
significance, however; $t(11) = 1.27$.] The correlation of the syllable
counting test with the difference score is almost as low as the correlation
of the control test with the difference score. If we take these patterns
seriously, they suggest that phonemic analysis is more important than
syllabic analysis for ability to use spelling–sound rules.

Taken together, the correlational results suggest that the phoneme
counting test and perhaps to a lesser extent the syllable counting test
measure an ability that is related to reading—the ability to represent
spoken words in terms of smaller units. So far, our conclusions are
identical to those of previous studies. But our data allow us to go beyond
previous results and to suggest that segmental analysis relates not to
reading ability in general but to a particular component of reading. That
component seems to be the use of spelling–sound rules. We shall test
this hypothesis further in Experiment Three.

TABLE VI

Correlation of Counting Tests with Difference between
Nonsense Word Reading and WRAT

		Nonspeech sound counting	Syllable counting	Phoneme counting
First graders				
($N = 14$)	z(Nons) − z(WRAT)	.13	.17	.44
Second graders				
($N = 14$)	z(Nons) − z(WRAT)	− .09	—[a]	.17

[a] Note that the syllable counting test was not given to the second graders.

III. SEGMENTAL ANALYSIS IN THE BROADER CONTEXT OF
PERCEPTUAL DEVELOPMENT

The children in our first experiment had some difficulty counting non-verbal sounds, but they had even more difficulty counting syllables and phonemes. This result, along with others in the literature, suggests that preliterate children do not naturally conceive of spoken words as made up of smaller units. Even when the units are marked acoustically, as in the case of syllables, the difficulty remains. Acoustic factors, then, probably cannot provide a complete account of the segmental analysis problem. Is there a more general explanation for children's poor performance in analyzing spoken words into syllables and phonemes? In looking for an explanation, we noticed a parallel between children's difficulty in analyzing spoken words into syllables and phonemes and their difficulty in analyzing visual percepts into smaller units. Just as children have trouble hearing that the phoneme *b* is embedded in the word *bat,* so they have trouble seeing that a simpler visual figure is embedded within a complex one. Children may gradually come to analyze complex visual percepts in much the same way that they come to analyze spoken words. We are thus led to ask whether theories of perceptual development that have been proposed to account for results from the realm of visual perception might apply to the realm of speech perception as well.

According to one view of perceptual development (e.g., Gibson, 1969), young children are wholistic perceivers. They tend to see a stimulus as an unanalyzable whole. Only gradually do they become able to break it down into its parts. As Vurpillot (1976) states:

> The primary perceptual structures which make up the visual world of children three and four years of age . . . appear to be rigid, indivisible, unanalysable and undifferentiated. For the child of six to eight years the perceptual structures have lost much of their rigidity; the child of this age can break these structures down into parts, abstract certain of their characteristics and attend to one part whilst disregarding the others.

The view of perceptual development described above can be considered in light of a theoretical framework proposed by Shepard (1964), Lockhead (1972), and Garner (1974, 1976). We shall describe this framework in its original context and then show how it can be extended to the study of perceptual development and to the development of speech perception. The authors cited above stress that the way in which a person perceives relations among stimuli depends on the dimensions along which the stimuli differ. Some pairs of dimensions, such as saturation and brightness of color patches, are said to be *integral*. Roughly speaking, integral dimensions are those that are hard for the observer to "pull apart." The brightness of a color and its saturation, for example, seem to be perceived as part of the same indissoluble whole. A pair of color patches that are identical in saturation and not too different in brightness appear to be similar in color, but the fact that they are *identical* in one dimension (saturation) is not at all obvious. Other pairs of dimensions, such as size and brightness of squares, are said to be *separable*. The observer is able to consider the size of a square independently of its brightness. He can readily appreciate that two squares are identical in size, even if they are different in brightness.

The distinction between integral and separable dimensions is important for our purposes because it affects the way in which people judge the relations among stimuli in a set. With sets of stimuli that vary along integral dimensions, observers tend to base their judgments on the *overall similarity* of the stimuli in question. That is, they take distances on both dimensions into account, perhaps without knowing whether the stimuli in fact differ on one or two dimensions. With sets of stimuli that vary along separable dimensions, people generally focus on whether the stimuli are *identical* on a single dimension. An example should make this distinction clear. Consider a set of three stimuli that vary along two dimensions, dimension X and dimension Y. The stimuli are represented in Fig. 1. Stimulus 1 and Stimulus 2 have close but not identical values on both dimensions. Stimulus 1 and Stimulus 3 have the same value on dimension X but very different values on dimension Y. A subject is shown all three stimuli and is told to put together the two that seem to "go together the best." (This procedure is known as *free classification*.) If the dimensions are saturation and brightness—integral dimensions— the subject will generally put together Stimulus 1 and Stimulus 2, the two that are close in both dimensions but the same in neither. With integral dimensions, identity on a single dimension seems to carry little weight; what counts is the overall closeness of the stimuli in the space. If the dimensions are size and brightness—separable dimensions—the adult subject will tend to put together Stimulus 1 and Stimulus 3. These are the stimuli that have the same value on one dimension but widely different values on the other dimension. With separable dimensions, the criterion for classification seems to be identity on a dimension: As long as the stimuli share a value on one dimension the fact that they differ drastically on the other dimension is unimportant.

The notion that young children perceive many stimuli as undifferentiated wholes and only gradually gain the ability to analyze them into parts can be restated in terms of the theoretical framework introduced above. The hypothesis then becomes: Pairs of dimensions that are separable for adults tend to be integral for young children (Shepp, 1978;

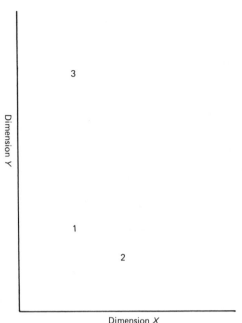

Fig. 1.

Smith & Kemler, 1977). Support for this hypothesis comes from experiments using visual dimensions such as size and brightness. Given a set
of stimuli that vary along the dimensions of size and brightness, kindergarteners' free classifications tend to be based on overall similarity,
while older children's judgments seem to be based on shared values on
a dimension (Smith & Kemler, 1977). Parallel results have been found
with other visual dimensions (Ward, 1980).

We suggest that there may be an analogous developmental trend in
the case of speech perception. In particular, we make an analogy between
identity on a dimension (for visual stimuli) and identity in a phoneme
(for words or syllables). Young children may judge relations among words
or syllables on the basis of overall similarity. They would thus consider
two syllables to be similar only if the syllables were similar as wholes.
If one phoneme were alike, but the others were very different, children
would not consider the syllables to be closely related. Adults, on the
other hand, may judge relations among syllables on the basis of identity
of a single phoneme. Thus, adults would feel that two syllables that
shared a phoneme were very close, even if the other phonemes were
quite different.

Experiment Two was designed to test this hypothesis. It used a free classification paradigm like that described above. Kindergarteners, first graders, and college students were the subjects. We set up triads of syllables in which classification based on overall similarity would give one answer and classification based on a common phoneme would give another answer. For example, in the triad *bi, ve, bō,* the first and second syllables are similar overall (in a way defined below). The first and third syllables have a phoneme in common, *b.* Classification of *bi* and *ve* together is thus called a similarity classification, while grouping of *bi* and *bō* is called a common phoneme classification. We asked whether children would make more similarity classifications and adults more common phoneme classifications. Such a result would suggest that children perceive relations among syllables differently than adults—children in a way that suggests that they consider the syllables as unanalyzed wholes, adults in a way that suggests that they consider the syllables as composed of potentially separate units.

A. Experiment Two: Free Classification

1. Method

The subjects in Experiment Two were kindergarteners, first graders, and college students. The children were members of two kindergarten and two first-grade classes at a Philadelphia public school. All had learned English as their native language. Data from 9 kindergarteners (mean age 5 years, 8 months), 19 first graders (mean age 6 years, 6 months), and 21 University of Pennsylvania undergraduates were used. (These subjects were culled from a somewhat larger group. Some of the subjects who were originally tested appeared not to understand the task, and their data were therefore not counted, as described below.)

The stimuli were triads of syllables. There were 16 training triads and 18 test triads. In the training triads, the syllables that shared a phoneme were also most similar overall. Thus we could tell subjects that these two syllables went together without biasing them toward either common phoneme or similarity classifications. (The shared phoneme was a vowel for half the training triads and a consonant for the other half.) The test triads were designed so that classification on the basis of shared phonemes and classification on the basis of overall similarity would give different results. We could thus determine whether the classification strategies of children and adults were different. Test triads contained either VC or CV syllables, and the shared phoneme was either a consonant or a vowel. This design allowed effects of syllable structure and type of phoneme to be assessed.

In order to construct the triads, we needed a measure of the overall similarity of pairs of syllables. For this purpose, we used similarity ratings of vowels (collected by Singh & Woods, 1971) and consonants (Singh, Woods, & Becker, 1972). These ratings were obtained by asking adults to rate the similarity of pairs of vowels or pairs of consonants followed by *ä* on a 7-point scale, with 1 being most similar and 7 least similar. We estimated the overall similarity of a pair of syllables to be the sum of the rated similarities of the pairs of corresponding phonemes. For example, the similarity of the syllables *bi* and *ve* is 2.8 (rated similarity of *b* and *v*) plus 2.2 (rated similarity of *i* and *e*), or 5.0. The similarity of the syllables *bi* and *bō* is 0 (since the two *b*'s are identical) plus 5.6 (rated similarity of *i* and *ō*) or 5.6.[3] Note that *bi* and *bō* have identical initial consonants but vowels that are rated as quite dissimilar; they are therefore less similar overall than *bi* and *ve*, which have no phonemes in common. The triad of syllables *bi*, *ve*, *bō* is thus one in which classification on the basis of shared phonemes gives one result (*bi* and *bō* classed together), while classification on the basis of overall similarity gives another result (*bi* and *ve* classed together). The classification *ve* and *bō* is called the anomalous classification, since it is apparently based neither on shared phonemes nor on overall similarity.

We constructed 18 test triads like the above example in which classification on the basis of shared phonemes and classification on the basis of overall similarity give different answers. There were 4 sets of test triads, each containing 4 types of triads: (1) triads of CV syllables in which the shared phoneme was a consonant (type CV:C); (2) triads of CV syllables in which the shared phoneme was a vowel (CV:V); (3) triads of VC syllables in which a consonant was shared (VC:C); and (4) triads of VC syllables in which a vowel was shared (VC:C). There were also two additional VC:V triads.[4] The triad *bi*, *ve*, *bō* is an example of a CV:C triad. The classification *bi* and *bō* is the common phoneme classification, the classification *bi* and *ve* is the similarity classification, and the classification *ve* and *bō* is the anomalous classification. The CV:V triad of the same set is *bi*, *ve*, *si*. The similarity classification is

---

[3] This procedure is based on a number of assumptions, but it does instantiate our notion that overall similarity depends on properties of whole syllables—that two syllables are similar overall if pairs of corresponding phonemes are similar. If our assumptions are incorrect, the common phoneme classification would most likely be made by all subjects. Thus, differences between age groups cannot be explained in terms of such an inadequacy.

[4] The tape contained an additional 10 triads that were not considered in the analysis due to their poor intelligibility. Intelligibility was checked by having 8 children repeat the syllables and 17 adults spell them; for the 18 triads used, intelligibility averaged 95% for the children and 87% for the adults.

again *bi* and *ve,* while the common phoneme classification is *bi* and *si*. The syllable *si* was picked because it was the response most frequently given by 19 undergraduates who were asked to generate a syllable ending in *i* that was as far away from *bi* as *bō* was. In this way we sought to ensure that the syllables that shared a consonant in the CV:C triads and the syllables that shared a vowel in the CV:V triads were equally distant. [Note that these ratings were used only to equate CV:C triads and CV:V triads. Our estimates of similarity were checked against the data of Singh and Woods (1971) and Singh *et al.* (1972).] The VC:C and VC:V triads were constructed according to the same procedures. For a complete list of stimuli, see Table VII.

The syllables were recorded on tape. The training triads were arranged in increasing level of difficulty, starting with one-phoneme syllables and progressing to two-phoneme syllables. The order of the test triads was randomized. The speaker articulated each syllable slowly and clearly, with approximately a 1 second gap between the syllables of a triad. Each triad was repeated twice.

Each child was tested individually over a period of two sessions. Testing was carried out during the early spring of the school year. The child was shown three identical pictures of people or animals arranged

TABLE VII

Triads Used in Experiment Two

Training triads							
1. *ch*	*m*	*ch*		9. *m*	*che*	*chi*	
2. *ä*	*ä*	*ōo*		10. *ze*	*lō*	*se*	
3. *l*	*z*	*z*		11. *ib*	*ip*	*ōk*	
4. *e*	*ō*	*e*		12. *eg*	*un*	*ag*	
5. *ch*	*zh*	*m*		13. *tōo*	*shā*	*dōo*	
6. *ä*	*ōo*	*ī*		14. *is*	*äk*	*äg*	
7. *z*	*l*	*s*		15. *ap*	*ōos*	*ep*	
8. *ā*	*a*	*ō*		16. *na*	*sōo*	*nä*	

Test trials							
1. *bi*	*ve*	*bō*		10. *mi*	*te*	*pi*	
2. *si*	*ve*	*bi*		11. *ev*	*ōb*	*āb*	
3. *āb*	*ām*	*ev*		12. *te*	*pō*	*pi*	
4. *bā*	*ve*	*she*		13. *ve*	*bā*	*kā*	
5. *ōb*	*ib*	*ev*		14. *āb*	*āsh*	*ev*	
6. *boi*	*bā*	*ve*		15. *mi*	*the*	*fi*	
7. *bō*	*bā*	*ve*		16. *ib*	*ev*	*id*	
8. *et*	*ip*	*ōp*		17. *āb*	*oib*	*ev*	
9. *ith*	*eb*	*es*		18. *et*	*ip*	*il*	

as if at the vertices of an equilateral triangle. The experimenter explained that the syllables were the creatures' names, and that the two whose names "sound alike" were friends. She pointed to the pictures while the tape said the syllables, and the child responded by pointing to the two he thought were friends. Feedback was given on the training triads but not on the test triads. The first session consisted of the training trials and half the test trials. The second session, 1 to 3 weeks later, included the training trials and the remaining test trials. Order of the test trials was balanced across subjects.

The adults were tested in groups. They were given answer sheets with the letters A, B, and C printed next to the number corresponding to each triad, and were told to circle the letters corresponding to the two syllables that "go together on the basis of sound." They were told to classify the syllables on the basis of their sounds, not on the basis of possible spellings or meanings. Training and test trials were given in a single session, with order of the test trials balanced across subjects. Feedback was given for the training trials but not for the test trials.

2. Results and Discussion

Some of the subjects originally tested, particularly certain kindergarteners, seemed not to understand the task, and their data were therefore not analyzed. Failure to understand the task was ascertained either by random performance on the training trials (i.e., one-third or fewer correct responses—the data for 2 kindergarteners and 2 first graders were dropped for this reason) or by random performance on the test trials (i.e., one-third or more anomalous responses—data from 5 kindergarteners, 2 first graders, and 1 adult were thus dropped). Data from 9 kindergarteners, 19 first graders, and 21 adults were used.

A preliminary analysis showed no effect of order of administration of test trials, so data from all subjects at each level were pooled. The results are shown in Table VIII, which gives the mean number of common phoneme, similarity, and anomalous classifications for each group of subjects. To test the hypothesis that common phoneme classifications increase and similarity classifications decrease with age, one-tailed t tests were done across subjects. As shown in Table VIII, older subjects made significantly more · common phoneme classifications and significantly fewer similarity classifications than did younger subjects.

Since younger subjects made more anomalous classifications, the age differences might be due to the fact that younger subjects guessed more often. To assess this possibility, each subject's number of common phoneme classifications was adjusted by using three times his number of

TABLE VIII

Means and Standard Deviations of Numbers of Common Phoneme, Similarity,
and Anomalous Classifications in Experiment Two (18 Classifications Possible),
and Results of t Tests for Differences between Groups

	Common phoneme	Similarity	Anomalous
Kindergarteners	6.67	7.33	4.00
(N = 9)	(2.50)	(2.18)	(1.12)
First graders	9.79	5.84	2.37
(N = 19)	(1.99)	(1.98)	(1.74)
Adults	12.86	4.52	.62
(N = 21)	(3.10)	(2.69)	(.80)
Kindergarten vs	3.57***	1.80*	2.56**
first graders			
(26 df)			
First graders vs	3.68***	1.75*	4.15***
adults			
(38 df)			
Kindergarteners vs	5.28***	2.76**	9.39***
adults			
(28 df)			

$*p < .05$, one tailed.
$**p < .01$, one tailed.
$***p < .005$, one tailed.

anomalous classifications as an estimate of his rate of guessing.[5] This
corrected measure of common phoneme classifications showed significant
differences between kindergarteners and first graders [$t(26) = 2.96$, $p
< .005$, one tailed] and between kindergarteners and adults [$t(28) =
3.44$, $p < .005$], although the difference between first graders and adults
was not significant [$t(38) = .36$]. Thus, the age trend seems not to be
an artifact of the children's higher guessing rate. (An analysis of similarity
classifications with a correction for guessing was not done since it would
be redundant with the analysis of common phoneme classifications. The
correction, in essence, assumes that all responses that are not guesses
are either similarity or common phoneme classifications.)

If the tendency to make common phoneme classifications is affected

[5] The correction for guessing is based on the model that a subject guesses with a certain
probability, in which case he is equally likely to make any of the three possible responses.
Thus, $C' = 18(C - A)/(18 - 3A)$ where C' is number of common phoneme responses
corrected for guessing, C is number of common phoneme responses, and A is number of
anomalous responses.

by the extent to which the common phoneme can be isolated acoustically, as discussed earlier, we ought to find more common phoneme classifications and fewer similarity classifications when a vowel is shared than when a consonant is shared. To test these hypotheses for children, we compared results within pairs of triads. Recall that there were 8 triads in which the common phoneme was a vowel and 8 matched triads in which it was a consonant. With shared consonants children made 45% common phoneme classifications and 37% similarity classifications; with shared vowels they made 54% common phoneme and 31% similarity classifications. The differences are in the predicted direction, but do not reach significance [$t(7)$ = 1.62 for common phoneme classifications, p = .08, one tailed, across stimulus pairs; $t(7)$ = 1.42 for similarity classifications, p = .10, one tailed]. Children did show evidence of a position effect: in 7 of 8 cases, they made more common phoneme classifications when the shared phoneme was in the initial position of the syllable than when it was in the final position ($p < .05$ by a sign test).

The results of Experiment Two support our hypothesis that the tendency to classify syllables on the basis of shared phonemes as opposed to overall similarity increases with age. Kindergarteners are likely to take whole syllables into account, putting together the two syllables that are most similar overall. Adults tend to base their classifications on the identity of a single attribute, i.e., a shared phoneme. Phonemes in a syllable seem to behave like relatively integral dimensions for young children and like relatively separable dimensions for adults. Phonemes as parts or "dimensions" of syllables may be important for beginning readers because it is just these parts that tend to be associated with letters. Failure to perceive these parts as separable could be a source of difficulty in learning to read.

Although syllables are less separable for children than for adults, they seem not to be totally integral for the youngest children tested here. Even the kindergarteners made a goodly number of common phoneme classifications. It is possible that children of this age have already acquired some ability to analyze syllables into phonemes, and that even younger children would make a greater proportion of similarity classifications. It is also possible that phonemes are totally integral for kindergarteners, but that they sometimes pick the second-best similarity classification—the common phoneme classification—instead of the best.

For adults, phonemes in a syllable are relatively separable—certainly more separable than they are for children. Adults can analyze syllables into phonemes, and they tend to judge relations among syllables in terms of shared phonemes. In other respects, however, syllables do not fulfill the criteria for separability that have been outlined by Garner (1974).

According to Garner (1974), separable dimensions lead to free classification by common attributes and also to no interference in speeded
classification tasks. However, this latter result is *not* found for phonemes
in a syllable. Specifically, in speeded tasks in which they must classify
syllables on the basis of a single phoneme, adults are slowed down if
other, irrelevant phonemes vary (Shand, 1976; Wood & Day, 1975).
Syllables may be only partially separable for adults, in that it takes a
certain amount of time or energy to analyze syllables into phonemes.
Consequently, a slight cost of analysis can be detected on tasks in which
speed is at a premium.

The developmental trend found in this experiment can be interpreted
in two different ways, which are not mutually exclusive. It may reflect
an increase in the ability to perceive that two syllables share a phoneme.
Children may be poor at this skill, and thus make relatively few common
phoneme classifications. A second possibility is that what increases with
development is the preference for making common phoneme classifications rather than the ability to do so. Children may be able to make
both common phoneme and similarity classifications, but prefer to make
the latter (Baron, 1978). Adults, it seems, are able to make both common
phoneme and similarity classifications. In an experiment done to test this
idea, adults were given five triads (*kud toob kāl, plä bra slē, weth viz
wōm, chen jing chōp, swō frū twā*) with the second and third syllables
of each presented in random order. When 10 subjects were asked (in
balanced order) to say which of the last two syllables was "most like
the first overall," and which was "like the first in some way," the second
instruction led to more common phoneme classifications for all five triads
and for all but two subjects (who were equal). This result suggests that
adults can choose between different strategies. If children can also choose
in this way, the observed differences between children and adults in
Experiment Two may be due to preference rather than ability. We shall
address this issue in Experiment Three.

B. Experiment Three: Constrained Classification

Our third experiment has three goals. The first is to find out whether
the age differences found in Experiment Two are due to changes in
preference or changes in ability. As discussed above, it is possible that
children are as able as adults to make common phoneme classifications,
but that they prefer to make similarity classifications when given a choice.
With age, this preference, rather than any ability, may change. Alter-
natively, children may lack the ability to make common phoneme classifications. To address this issue, we changed the free classification task

of Experiment Two. Instead of letting the children choose freely, we now told them that the common phoneme classification was correct. We shall call this new task the *constrained classification* task. Performance here should reflect ability to make common phoneme classifications rather than preference for doing so.

Second, we wish to raise again the question of whether phonemic analysis is easier with certain classes of phonemes than with others. Such differences between phoneme classes could support the view that the difficulty of phonemic analysis is in part the result of the acoustic nondistinctiveness of phonemes. Recall that in Experiment One children counted phonemes more accurately in fricative–vowel–fricative syllables than in stop–vowel–stop syllables. In Experiment Two, there was also a nonsignificant trend for vowels to lead to more common phoneme classifications than consonants. If it is indeed easier to analyze syllables into phonemes when those phonemes are fricatives rather than stops, we would expect to find similar effects in the constrained classification task. In particular, children should perform better when the shared phonemes are fricatives than when they are stops. Thus, in the third experiment one group of children was trained to make common phoneme classifications with stop consonants while another group was trained with fricative consonants. Both groups then received transfer trials with the other type of phoneme. We could thus compare the two groups in both initial learning and transfer.

Our third goal is to study the relationship between performance on the constrained classification test and reading ability. We expect performance on this segmental analysis test to correlate with reading ability, and in particular with ability to use spelling–sound rules. Recall that we tested the same hypothesis in Experiment One, using the phoneme and syllable counting tests as measures of segmental analysis ability. There we found encouraging results. The phoneme counting test correlated more highly with a measure of ability to use rules (the nonsense word reading test) than with a reading test for which specific associations are more important (the WRAT). We use the same experimental strategy here. This time, however, we use a different measure of phonemic analysis—the constrained classification test. We also use new and more elegant measures of ability to read by rules and word-specific associations.

The reading test we use here was designed and validated by Baron (1979). It contains three lists of words: regular words (such as *cut*), exception words (such as *put*), and nonsense words (such as *lut*). Use of rules will to some extent impair performance on the exception list relative to the other lists. A child who depends on rules (i.e., a Phoenician) may pronounce *put* to rhyme with *cut*, while a child who relies on word-specific associations (i.e., a Chinese) should not make this error. On the other hand, use of rules will improve performance on the nonsense list relative to the other lists. Nonsense words must be read by rules: the child has not seen them before and has not formed any associations between them and their pronunciations. One measure of rule use, then, is performance on nonsense words relative to exception words. (Note that exception words may be read correctly by means of word-specific associations, while nonsense words cannot be read in this way. Thus, use of word-specific associations has effects that are opposite to the effects of rules.) Another measure of rule use involves the type of errors that the child makes. A Phoenician child should make mistakes that stem from overapplication of the rules, such as pronouncing *put* to rhyme with *cut*. These errors are called sound-preserving errors. A Chinese child, to the extent that he uses associations between written words and their meanings, should make errors that are semantically related to the correct words (e.g., *sit* for *seat*). Such errors may be called meaning-preserving errors. The two measures of rule use—performance on nonsense words relative to exception words and number of sound-preserving errors relative to meaning-preserving errors—do correlate with each other, as they should (Baron, 1979). We hope to find that each of these measures, in turn, correlates with performance on the classification test. Such a result would indicate that ability to use spelling–sound rules correlates with ability to make common phoneme classifications—that Phoenicians are more able to make common phoneme classifications than Chinese.

1. Method

The subjects for Experiment Three were a diverse group of 22 children. They ranged from just having completed pre-kindergarten to just having completed second grade. Data from 21 of these subjects were used.

Each subject received two tests, the constrained classification test and the reading test. The stimuli for the classification test were triads of syllables like those used in Experiment Two. As in that experiment, test triads were designed so that classification on the basis of overall similarity and classification on the basis of a common phoneme would give different answers. There were four sets of test triads, each containing one triad in which the shared phoneme was a consonant (type CV:C) and one triad in which the shared phoneme was a vowel (type CV:V). In two sets (the stop sets) the shared consonants were stops, and in two sets (the fricative sets) the shared consonants were fricatives. The stop sets and the fricative sets were matched with respect to the vowels used in the syllables and the distances between pairs of syllables (according to the ratings of Singh *et al.*, 1972). Thus any performance differences must stem from the differences between the two types of consonants. In addition, there were 12 training triads in which classification on the basis of overall similarity and classification on the basis of shared phonemes gave the same result. Six were made up of syllables from the stop sets, and six of syllables from the fricative sets.

Children were assigned to one of the two groups for the classification test. There were approximately the same number of children of each age and grade level in each group. During the initial phase of the test, one group (the stop group) was trained on triads from the stop sets, and the other group (the fricative group) was trained on triads from the fricative sets. During the final phase of the test, both groups received triads from both sets.

The initial phase of the test consisted of 14 trials: the 6 training triads for the group followed by 2 occurrences of each of the test triads appropriate to the group. The final phase of the test consisted of 16 trials: two occurrences of each of the test triads. The triads were recorded on tape as in Experiment Two. They are shown in Table IX.

The procedure differed from that of Experiment Two in two respects. First, the child was asked to repeat each syllable after the tape. Correct repetition ensured that the child had at least heard the syllables, and we could discard from the analysis trials on which the repetition was faulty. Second, the common phoneme classification was counted as correct. During the initial phase, feedback was given on all trials. If the child made the common phoneme classification, he was told he was correct; if he failed to do so, the experimenter repeated the syllables and pointed to the two that went together. During the final phase, feedback was given only for the triads the child had received during the initial phase. Thus for each group of subjects, four triads occurred four times each and were reinforced each time. These were triads from the stop set for the stop group and triads from the fricative set for the fricative group. Four triads occurred twice each and were not reinforced. These were triads from the fricative set for the stop group and triads from the stop set for the fricative group.

The reading test consisted of one list of 36 regular words, one list of 36 exception words, and one list of 36 nonsense words. For a given regular word, such as *cut,* there was a corresponding exception word, *put,* and a corresponding nonsense word, *lut.* (The stimuli are given in Baron, 1979.) Either pronunciation of the nonsense word—by analogy with the regular word or by analogy with the exception word—was counted as correct. The stimuli were printed in large letters on index cards. Stimuli within a list were arranged in order of increasing difficulty,

TABLE IX

Triads Used in Experiment Three

Training triads (stop group)			Training traids (fricative group)		
1. *pi*	*l̄oo*	*pi*	1. *fi*	*l̄oo*	*fi*
2. *rō*	*bā*	*bā*	2. *rō*	*shā*	*shā*
3. *lō*	*be*	*bā*	3. *lō*	*she*	*shā*
4. *ti*	*pi*	*la*	4. *si*	*fi*	*la*
5. *n̄oo*	*pā*	*pi*	5. *n̄oo*	*fā*	*fi*
6. *vā*	*ra*	*bā*	6. *chā*	*ra*	*shā*
7. *tā*	*pi*	*pō*	7. *sā*	*fi*	*fō*
8. *bā*	*kā*	*ve*	8. *shā*	*tā*	*che*
9. *bō*	*bā*	*ve*	9. *shō*	*shā*	*che*
10. *pi*	*tā*	*mi*	10. *fi*	*sā*	*mi*
11. *ve*	*bā*	*bō*	11. *che*	*shā*	*shō*
12. *kā*	*ve*	*bā*	12. *tā*	*che*	*shā*
13. *pi*	*mi*	*tā*	13. *fi*	*mi*	*sā*
14. *tā*	*pō*	*pi*	14. *sā*	*fō*	*fi*

Test triads (both groups)					
1. *pi*	*mi*	*tā*	9. *shā*	*che*	*tā*
2. *tā*	*shā*	*che*	10. *ve*	*bō*	*bā*
3. *tā*	*pō*	*pi*	11. *shā*	*shō*	*che*
4. *shā*	*che*	*shō*	12. *kā*	*bā*	*ve*
5. *kā*	*bā*	*ve*	13. *sā*	*fi*	*mi*
6. *fō*	*sā*	*fi*	14. *pō*	*tā*	*pi*
7. *ve*	*bō*	*bā*	15. *fi*	*fō*	*sā*
8. *sā*	*fi*	*mi*	16. *tā*	*pi*	*mi*

as judged by the authors and experimenters. The lists were administered to all subjects in the order regular, exception, nonsense. Cards were presented one at a time and the child was asked to say what each word said. Before the first nonsense word was presented, the child was told that the remaining items were not real words. If a child had great trouble with a particular list, the experimenter handed him the pile of cards and asked him to find any words that he knew.

2. Results and Discussion

In scoring the classification test, trials on which a child repeated a syllable incorrectly both times it occurred were omitted, since the child may have misheard or misremembered the syllable. The data of one child who performed randomly on the training trials were not included, on the grounds that the child probably failed to understand the task. For each subject, percentage correct (i.e., common phoneme) responses on correctly repeated test trials was calculated. On the reinforced trials, the children averaged 69% correct (SD = 17%). A group of 17 undergraduates who, as part of another experiment, had classified the same triads under instructions like those of Experiment Two, averaged 90% common phoneme classifications (SD = 9%). Even though the children had been reinforced for making common phoneme classifications and the adults had been given free classification instructions, the adults made significantly more common phoneme classifications and significantly fewer similarity classifications than the children [$t(36)$ = 4.63 and 2.94, respectively; $p < .005$ for both, one tailed]. This result suggests that children are less *able* than adults to make common phoneme classifications. The difference in free classification performance between children and adults seen in Experiment Two seems to be due, at least in part, to children's lesser ability to discern whether two syllables have a phoneme in common.

Children's errors in the present experiment provided a further indication that they were sensitive to the overall similarity of syllables. Of all errors, 63% were similarity classifications and 37% were anomalous classifications. Similarity errors clearly prevailed [$t(20)$ = 4.49, $p < .005$, one tailed]. When children failed to do what they were told, i.e., make common phoneme classifications, they tended to make similarity classifications instead.

When we compare the performance of the two groups of subjects, the fricative group and the stop group, no differences are apparent. Specifically, on the reinforced triads in which two syllables shared a consonant, the former group did no better than the latter [70% correct for the fricative group, 71% for the stop group; $t(19)$ = $-.20$]. Thus, there is no evidence that children find it easier to identify common phonemes when those phonemes are fricatives than when they are stops.

The children did seem to improve on the reinforced triads from the initial phase to the final phase of the test. They went from 67 to 73% correct [$t(20)$ = 1.67, p = .06, one tailed]. However, their learning seemed to be specific to the triads on which they had been trained. During the final phase, performance on new triads was significantly worse than performance on old triads [65% correct as compared to 73%; $t(20)$ = 1.89, $p < .05$, one tailed; note that each triad was old for half the subjects and new for half]. The children did not do significantly better on the first transfer trial than they had on the very first trial of the test [66 versus 65%, $t(20)$ = .64]. Thus, the brief training given children in this experiment had only specific effects; it did not give them a strategy they could apply to new triads.

Proportion of common phoneme classifications on all trials correlated highly with total number of words read correctly [r = .81, $t(12)$ = 4.85,

$p < .005$, one tailed; only those 14 subjects who read at least one word from each list were included in this and subsequent analyses of reading ability]. A correlation between performance on the classification test and reading ability was expected on the basis of previous results. We can now ask whether performance on the classification test relates more closely to ability to read by rules than to ability to use specific associations. That is, does performance on the classification test correlate more highly with the ability to read nonsense words than with the ability to read exception words? Does performance on the classification test correlate more highly with the tendency to make sound-preserving errors than with the tendency to make meaning-preserving errors?

Proportion of common phoneme responses on the classification test correlated .86 with number of nonsense words read correctly and .76 with number of exception words read correctly. (Performance on nonsense words and exception words correlated .92.) The former correlation is higher than the latter, but not significantly so $[t(11) = .96]$. Thus, with this measure of rule use—performance on nonsense words relative to exception words—there is no firm evidence that the classification test correlates with rule use. However, in another study that involved a larger number of subjects, this comparison did reach significance (Baron & Treiman, 1980a). In that study, number of common phoneme classifications in a similar task did correlate more highly with ability to read nonsense words than with ability to read exception words.

With the second measure of rule use—tendency to make sound-preserving errors rather than meaning-preserving errors—the results are more encouraging. To carry out the analysis, we had to drop four subjects who made no errors of either type, leaving ten subjects. We defined a sound-preserving error as an error in which a real word is pronounced according to a rule or analogy that does not apply and that produces a nonword pronunciation. (For example, *foo* for *few* is a sound-preserving error because of the analogy with *dew; foi* is not a sound-preserving error because *ew* is never pronounced as *oi*. Analogies are defined as in Baron, 1979.) A subject's ratio of sound-preserving errors to all errors in which a real word was read as a nonword was considered as his tendency to make sound-preserving errors. A meaning-preserving error is one in which a real word is read as a semantically related word. (See Baron, 1979, for examples of such errors with these stimuli.) The tendency, to make meaning-preserving errors is the ratio of such errors to all errors in which a word is misread as another real word. The correlation of common phoneme responses with tendency to make sound-preserving errors was .60 $[t(8) = 2.12, p < .05$, one tailed]; the correlation with tendency to make meaning-preserving errors was $-.51$ $[t(8) = 1.68, p$

< .1, one tailed]. The former correlation coefficient is significantly higher than the latter [$t(7)$ = 2.32, p < .05, one tailed]. With this measure of rule use, then, performance on the constrained classification test appears to correlate with use of rules in reading.

To summarize the results of Experiment Three, we have shown that children lack the *ability* to tell that two syllables have a phoneme in common. Even when they are told that the common phoneme classification is the correct one, they make this classification less frequently than do adults. Children seem to be no more able to make common phoneme classifications with fricative consonants than with stop consonants. Finally, we have provided evidence that ability to make common phoneme classifications relates to ability to read by rules as distinct from word-specific associations.

IV. CONCLUSIONS

We have been considering children's ability to make use of the discrete segments of a spoken word in various tasks and in learning to read. These segments could correspond to syllables, phonemes, or other units. What is crucial is that the child represents the word not as an indivisible whole but in terms of potentially separate parts. The ability to use segmental representations of this kind seems to improve with age. This developmental trend could be explained in two general ways. One possibility is that people represent speech in terms of segments from the very earliest age. But even though the young child has such a representation, he does not *know* he has it; he cannot use it in many tasks for which it would be helpful. Development consists in a gradual coming-to-consciousness of what one already knows (see Rozin, 1975). The segmental representation which had formerly been implicit becomes explicit, and the child gains the ability to use it in a wide variety of tasks. A second possible explanation, one that we have proposed here, is that young children do not represent speech in terms of segments, either consciously or unconsciously. Rather, they represent the sound of a word or syllable "integrally," as an indivisible whole. This possibility is consistent with children's ability to hear and speak, and with their ability to judge that certain pairs of words sound different and that others are more alike. The fact that a child can do these things implies that he has *some* internal representation of speech—it does not tell what kind of representation. The possibility that young children represent spoken words wholistically is consistent with their apparent difficulties in hearing or repeating novel words (particularly those that are unlike any familiar words), and with their difficulties in telling *how* words sound alike or different. According to this view, what changes with development is the way one represents spoken words. The wholistic representation of the child becomes the piece-wise representation of the adult.

Our experiments have not decided between these two views of the development of segmental analysis, but the results of Experiments Two and Three are at least consistent with the second view. We have shown that in classification tests children perform differently than adults—that they perform in a way that suggests they represent syllables as wholes. Converging evidence from other sorts of tests is required. For example, in memory tests do children confuse syllables that are similar overall or syllables that share a phoneme? Experiments to answer this question are currently underway (Treiman & Breaux, forthcoming).

We have also asked whether the difficulty of phonemic analysis varies with the class of phoneme. If there were such variation, and if the acoustically most distinct phonemes were the easiest to analyze, the difficulty of phonemic analysis could stem from the fact that phonemes do not in general correspond to separate, invariant units of sound. In the counting task of Experiment One, children did count phonemes more accurately with fricative–vowel–fricative syllables than with stop–vowel–stop syllables. However, no differences were found between two-phoneme syllables containing stops and those containing fricatives. In Experiment Three, which also used two-phoneme syllables, children learned to make common phoneme classifications equally well whether the shared phonemes were fricatives or stops. We looked at differences between vowels and consonants in the free classification task of Experiment Two. Children did make more common phoneme classifications with vowels than with consonants, but this effect did not reach significance.

This mixed bag of results underlines the need to distinguish between *having* a representation of a syllable as composed of separate phonemes and *doing* something with that representation. Many segmental analysis tests require both these things. They require one to form a segmental representation, and they also require one to count the segments, compare the representations of different words, or perform other manipulations. It may be no easier to form a segmental representation when the segments are of one type as opposed to another. If it were, we should have found clear differences among classes of phonemes in all of our tasks. But type of phoneme may affect how easy it is to use that representation in certain situations. For example, suppose one wishes to translate the segments in one's internal representation into a form that can be spoken aloud. One will have an easier time when the segments are fricatives rather than stops, since fricatives can be pronounced in isolation while stops cannot. Thus in cases where verbalization is useful (perhaps in the phoneme-counting task of Experiment One, particularly with the longer syllables), an advantage of fricatives will be apparent.

The distinction between having a segmental representation and doing something with it is important when we consider how best to measure segmental analysis ability. Many commonly used tasks, such as rhyme judgment and phoneme counting, require one to form segmental representations of speech, but they also require other abilities. In rhyme judgment, one must compare the representations of two different words and determine if they meet a certain criterion; in phoneme counting, one must count the number of phonemes in the representation. If we want to measure the ability to represent spoken words segmentally, uncontaminated by these other abilities, new procedures will be required. One possibility is to use traditional tasks, but to develop control tests that measure everything necessary for success *except* the ability of interest— the ability to form segmental representations. Recall that we took this approach in Experiment One, when we used ability to count nonspeech sounds as a control test. This sort of solution does not guarantee adequate measurement, however. With very young children, few may be able to do the control test. In this case, we will get little information about whether they can form segmental representations. And even if children of a given age *can* represent speech segmentally with effort, the effort required to perform the other aspects of the task may be so great as to prevent them from doing so. It may also be necessary, we think, to develop tests that require a segmental representation of speech, but few other abilities. Such a test might be one in which children repeat nonsense words, especially those composed of sequences of phonemes illegal in English (e.g., *nree, tlee*). To repeat such words accurately, a segmental representation would seem to be required. One would have to control for purely motor factors, however.

Finally, we have been concerned with the relation between segmental analysis and reading. There is clearly a correlation between performance on segmental analysis tests and performance on reading tests, as we have shown again. Our contribution has been to show that segmental analysis correlates most highly with one aspect of reading ability—use of spelling–sound rules. This aspect of reading is reflected in the ability to read novel words and in the tendency to make phonetically plausible errors in reading. The correlation between segmental analysis and reading may be totally accounted for by the correlation between segmental analysis and use of rules in reading. To state these results in another way, Phoenician children seem to be better than Chinese children at phonemic analysis tasks. We have found similar results in a comparison of Phoenician and Chinese adults (Baron *et al.*, 1980). In that study, Phoenicians made more common phoneme responses in a free classification test, were more rapid and accurate in a task that required them to judge whether pairs of words shared a segment, and were more able to repeat and to spell illegal nonsense words such as *tlee*. The study with children and the study with adults concur in suggesting that people who rely on spelling–sound rules (i.e., Phoenicians) tend to perform well on segmental analysis tests.

How can we account for the relationship between ability to represent speech segmentally and use of spelling–sound rules? As we have said, causal links could run in either direction or in both. A prereader who represents speech segmentally (even if his representations do not correspond exactly to the representations of English orthography—see Read, 1975), may have less difficulty in learning that letters stand for segments than a child who does not represent speech segmentally. And whether or not a child has a segmental representation of speech to begin with, as he learns to read English he would presumably come to represent spoken words to himself in the same way that English spelling represents them. Our best guess is that both of these things occur; that cause and effect run in both directions. But clear experimental evidence is lacking.

A demonstration that segmental analysis ability plays a causal role in the learning of spelling–sound rules could be important for educators. While training in phonemic analysis is often included in successful reading programs (e.g., Williams, 1980), we do not know whether this training by itself plays a role in the programs' success. Experiments must be done to provide conclusive evidence on this point. The most direct approach is to train prereaders in segmental analysis skills and to determine whether such training improves their ability to learn spelling–sound rules. It is important to show that effects of phonemic analysis training are specific to the learning of spelling–sound rules, for otherwise general motivational effects could account for the results. We are currently carrying out studies using this design, and are finding that phonemic analysis instruction does improve prereaders' ability to benefit from spelling–sound rules (Treiman & Baron, forthcoming). The demonstration of a causal link from segmental analysis to ability to learn spelling–sound rules is just a first step, however. Many questions remain before the educational implications of such a link can be understood. How substantial are the benefits of segmental analysis training? Which children (if not all) benefit from such training? How general are the effects, beyond the specific words used in training? What types of training are most useful, those that are directed at the formation of segmental representations or those directed at the manipulation of those representations? And if the latter, what sort of manipulation? Are different types of manipulation required for "analytic" and "synthetic" phonics instruction? Training and transfer studies may help to answer these questions.

ACKNOWLEDGMENTS

We thank the many children and teachers who helped us. Experiment One was carried out by R. T., with advice from A. M. Liberman, as part of her senior thesis at Yale University. June Hodge ran the subjects for Experiment Three. Financial support was provided by a grant from the Spencer Foundation through the University of Pennsylvania, National Science Foundation Grant BMS74-23158, and National Institute of Health Grant MH-29453. Vurpillot (1976) is quoted with the permission of the author and publisher.

REFERENCES

Baron, J. Mechanisms for pronouncing printed words: Use and acquisition. In D. LaBerge & S. J. Samuels (Eds.), *Basis processes in reading: Perception and comprehension.* Hillsdale, New Jersey: Erlbaum, 1977.

Baron, J. Intelligence and general strategies. In G. Underwood (Ed.), *Strategies in information processing.* New York: Academic Press, 1978.

Baron, J. Orthographic and word-specific knowledge in children's reading of words. *Child Development,* 1979, **50,** 60–72.

Baron, J., & Strawson, C. Use of orthographic and word-specific knowledge in reading words aloud. *Journal of Experimental Psychology: Human Perception and Performance,* 1976, **2,** 386–393.

Baron, J., & Treiman, R. Use of orthography in reading and learning to read. In J. F. Kavanagh & R. L. Venezky (Eds.), *Orthography, reading, and dyslexia.* Baltimore, Maryland: University Park Press, 1980. (a)

Baron, J., & Treiman, R. Some problems in the study of differences in cognitive processes. *Memory and Cognition,* 1980, **4,** 313–321. (b)

Baron, J., Treiman, R., Wilf, J., & Kellman, P. Reading and spelling by rules. In U. Frith (Ed.), *Cognitive processes in spelling.* New York: Academic Press, 1980.

Boder, E. Developmental dyslexia: A diagnostic approach based on three atypical reading-spelling patterns. *Developmental Medicine and Child Neurology,* 1973, **15,** 663–687.

Bruce, D. J. The analysis of word sounds by young children. *British Journal of Educational Psychology,* 1964, **34,** 158–169.

Calfee, R. C., Chapman, R. S., & Venezky, R. How a child needs to think to learn to read. In L. W. Gregg (Ed.), *Cognition in learning and memory.* New York: Wiley, 1972.

Calfee, R. C., Lindamood, P., & Lindamood, C. Acoustic-phonetic skills and reading—kindergarten through twelfth grade. *Journal of Educational Psychology,* 1973, **64,** 293–298.

Elkonin, D. B. USSR. In J. Dowining (Ed.), *Comparative reading.* New York: Macmillan, 1973.

Firth, I. *Components of reading disability.* Ph.D. dissertation, University of New South Wales, 1972.

Fowler, C. A., Liberman, I. Y., & Shankweiler, D. On interpreting the error pattern in beginning reading. *Language and Speech,* 1977 **20**, 162–173.

Fox, B., & Routh, D. K. Analyzing spoken language into words, syllables and phonemes: A developmental study. *Journal of Psycholinguistic Research,* 1975, **4**, 331–342.

Garner, W. R. *The processing of information and structure.* Hillsdale, New Jersey: Erlbaum, 1974.

Garner, W. R. Interaction of stimulus dimensions in concept and choice processes. *Cognitive Psychology,* 1976, **8**, 98–123.

Gibson, E. J. *Principles of perceptual learning and development.* New York: Appleton, 1969.

Gibson, E. J., & Levin, H. *The psychology of reading.* Cambridge, Massachusetts: MIT Press, 1975.

Gleitman, L. R., & Rozin, P. The structure and acquisition of reading I: Relations between orthographies and the structure of language. In A. S. Reber & D. L. Scarborough (Eds.), *Toward a psychology of reading.* Hillsdale, New Jersey: Erlbaum, 1977.

Jastak, J., Bijou, S. W., & Jastak, S. R. *Wide range achievement test.* Wilmington, Delaware: Guidance Associates, 1965.

Liberman, A. M., Cooper, F. S., Shankweiler, D., & Studdert-Kennedy, M. Perception of the speech code. *Psychological Review,* 1967, **74**, 431–436.

Liberman, I. Y., Shankweiler, D., Fischer, F. W., & Carter, B. Explicit syllable and phoneme segmentation in the young child. *Journal of Experimental Child Psychology,* 1974, **18**, 201–212.

Liberman, I. Y., Shankweiler, D., Liberman, A. M., Fowler, C., & Fischer, F. W. Phonemic segmentation and recoding in the beginning reader. In A. S. Reber & D. L. Scarborough (Eds.), *Toward a psychology of reading.* Hillsdale, New Jersey: Erlbaum, 1977.

Lockhead, G. R. Processing integral stimuli: A note. *Psychological Review,* 1972, **79**, 410–419.

Lukatela, G., & Turvey, M. T. Some experiments on the Roman and Cyrillic alphabets of Serbo Croatian. In J. F. Kavanagh & R. L. Venezky (Eds.), *Orthography, reading, and dyslexia.* Baltimore, Maryland: University Park Press, 1980.

Luria, A. R. Differences between disturbance of speech and writing in Russian and in French. *International Journal of Slavic Linguistics and Poetics,* 1960, **3**, 12–22.

McNeil, J. D., & Stone, J. Note on teaching children to hear separate sounds in spoken words. *Journal of Educational Psychology,* 1965, **56**, 13–15.

Mattingly, I. G. Reading, the linguistic process, and linguistic awareness. In J. F. Kavanagh & I. G. Mattingly (Eds.), *Language by ear and by eye: The relationships between speech and reading.* Cambridge, Massachusetts: MIT Press, 1972.

Read, C. *Children's categorization of speech sounds in English.* Urbana, Illinois: National Council of Teachers of English, 1975.

Rosner, J., & Simon, D. The Auditory analysis test: An initial report. *Journal of Learning Disabilities,* 1971, **4**, 384–392.

Rozin, P. The evolution of intelligence and access to the cognitive unconscious. In J. Sprague & A. N. Epstein (Eds.), *Progress in psychobiology and physiological psychology* (Vol. 6). New York: Academic Press, 1975.

Rozin, P., Bressman, B., & Taft, M. Do children understand the basic relationship between speech and writing? The mow-motorcycle test. *Journal of Reading Behavior,* 1974, **6**, 327–334.

Saffran, E. M., & Marin, O. S. M. Reading without phonology: Evidence from aphasia. *Quarterly Journal of Experimental Psychology,* 1977, **29**, 515–525.

Savin, H. B. What the child knows about speech when he starts to learn to read. In J. F. Kavanagh & I. G. Mattingly (Eds.), *Language by ear and by eye: The relationships between speech and reading.* Cambridge, Massachusetts: MIT Press, 1972.

Shand, M. A. Syllabic vs. segmental perception: On the inability to ignore "irrelevant" stimulus parameters. *Perception and Psychophysics,* 1976, **20,** 430–432.

Shankweiler, D., & Liberman, I. Y. Misreading: A search for causes. In J. F. Kavanagh & I. G. Mattingly (Eds.), *Language by ear and by eye: The relationships between speech and reading.* Cambridge, Massachusetts: MIT Press, 1972.

Shepard, R. N. Attention and the metric structure of the stimulus. *Journal of Mathematical Psychology,* 1964, **1,** 54–87.

Shepp, B. E. From perceived similarity to dimensional structure: A new hypothesis about perceptual development. In E. Rosch & B. B. Lloyd (Eds.), *Cognition and categorization.* Hillsdale, New Jersey: Erlbaum, 1978.

Singh, S., & Woods, D. R. Perceptual structure of 12 American English vowels. *Journal of the Acoustical Society of America,* 1971, **49,** 1861–1866.

Singh, S., Woods, D. R., & Becker, G. M. Perceptual structure of 22 prevocalic English consonants. *Journal of the Acoustical Society of America,* 1972, **52,** 1698–1713.

Smith, L. B., & Kemler, D. G. Developmental trends in free classification: Evidence for a new conceptualization of perceptual development. *Journal of Experimental Child Psychology,* 1977, **24,** 279–298.

Vurpillot, E. *The visual world of the child.* New York: International Universities Press, 1976.

Ward, T. B. Separable and integral responding by children and adults to the dimensions of length and density. *Child Development,* 1980, **51,** 676–684.

Williams, J. Teaching decoding with an emphasis on phoneme analysis and phoneme blending. *Journal of Educational Psychology,* 1980, **72,** 1–15.

Wood, C. C., & Day, R. S. Failure of selective attention to phonetic segments in consonant-vowel syllables. *Perception and Psychophysics,* 1975, **17,** 346–350.

A COGNITIVE–DEVELOPMENTAL THEORY OF READING ACQUISITION[1]

GEORGE MARSH,* MORTON FRIEDMAN,†
VERONICA WELCH,† AND PETER DESBERG*

Departments of Psychology
California State University, Dominguez Hills
Carson, California
and
†University of California, Los Angeles
Los Angeles, California

I. INTRODUCTION

The purpose of the present article is to present a descriptive cognitive–developmental theory of reading acquisition along with some sup-

[1] Experiment I was completed while the first author was on a NIMH postdoctoral fellowship at the University of California at Los Angeles. A preliminary report of the first experiment was presented at the NATO Conference on Cognition and Instruction in Amsterdam, The Netherlands, June 1977. A preliminary report of the second experiment was reported at the NATO Conference on Intelligence and Learning, York, England, July 1979. The authors would like to thank the students at the University Elementary School and the Los Angeles and Torrance City Schools who participated in the two experiments.

199

portive evidence. The authors believe that cognitive–developmental theory offers the best potential description and explanation for the cognitive achievements of learning to read and write. A basic assumption of cognitive–developmental theory is that any cognitive achievement is the result of the interaction of a complex organism with a complex environment. A second basic assumption is that any cognitive process goes through a number of stages which change qualitatively with development.

The authors agree with Waller (1978) that most previous attempts to apply cognitive–developmental theory to reading have been unsatisfactory. They have consisted primarily of correlational studies between performance on traditional Piagetian tasks and standardized reading tests. This current level of research is not due to any deficiency on the part of cognitive–developmental theory which has been applied successfully to the study of the development of language, memory, and moral development as well as various areas of problem solving. In our view the major deficiency in the previous literature is due to the limited conception of reading which underlies standardized achievement tests. This conception is generally associative in nature and looks upon reading as the cumulative acquisition of correct responses where the child quantitatively increases in speed, accuracy, and "automaticity." The present article will demonstrate that children may respond correctly on a reading task by using a number of qualitatively different strategies which change with development.

The major alternative to a cognitive developmental approach to reading acquisition is the human information processing (HIP) approach. The HIP approach also treats reading as a complex task, and has stimulated some interesting research on the reading process. However, in our opinion, it has not yet developed to the point of useful application to instruction. (See Marsh, 1978, for a critique of the HIP approach.)

Cognitive–developmental theory sets as its primary goal the description and explanation of developmental change, and uses naturalistic observation and controlled observation as well as artificial laboratory experiments as a data base. Cognitive–developmental theory also has developed a number of useful pedagogical principles which will directly aid in instruction (Case, 1978). These principles will be discussed in a later section of this article. The core concepts in a cognitive–developmental approach are knowledge, strategies, and meta-knowledge (Flavell, 1977). Knowledge consists of the information and cognitive structures which are present at any given stage of development. These structures change with development as a result of interaction with the environment. Knowledge refers to the child's cognitive competence. Strategies are processes which a child uses to cope with environmental inputs. They are a joint product of the child's knowledge and the environmental task demands. The present approach does not limit the concept of strategies to conscious, planful processes although they may be accessible to consciousness later in development as meta-knowledge increases. Meta-knowledge refers to the person's abilities to reflect upon and verbally describe the knowledge and strategies which they have and are using. Meta-knowledge typically develops much later than both knowledge and strategies. Performance on any cognitive task is often characterized by a gap between knowledge and the strategies used to implement that knowledge.

The emphasis in this article will be the development of strategies in reading unknown words. This emphasis on reading novel words is motivated by two considerations. This generative ability is, in our opinion, the most challenging aspect of reading acquisition and the one which is most likely to engage high-level cognitive processing strategies. It is, therefore, one in which we would expect to find qualitative developmental differences. The ability to read aloud unknown and novel words gives an indication of children's knowledge of orthographic structure and its relation to the language system they already possess. It also provides insight into the ways in which children read known words.

II. STAGES IN THE DEVELOPMENT OF READING ACQUISITION

The proposed sequence of stages in the development of reading is shown in Table I. Many children are either preoperational or in the transitional stage to concrete operations when they begin reading instruction. A major characteristic of young children in these stages is that they are unable to deal with more than a few items of information at one time and that they approach intellectual tasks with strategies that are reasonable but oversimplified (Case 1978, p. 439). These two factors account for the response patterns of young children on traditional Piagetian tasks such as conservation.

A. Stage One—Linguistic Guessing

In learning to read, the young child in the first stage approaches the task with a strategy of simple rote association. The rote association is between an unsynthesized visual stimulus and an unanalyzed oral response. The child typically centers on one aspect of the visual stimulus such as the first letter and associates that with the oral response. Children in the first stage find it very difficult to decenter from the unanalyzed oral response to perform such tasks as phonemic segmentation (Golin-

TABLE I

Proposed Stages of Reading Acquisition

Task	Strategy	Example
	Stage One—Linguistic Substitution	
Known word	Rote	See *boy;* read *boy*
Unknown word in	—	See *cime;*
isolation		read *don't know*
Unknown word	Linguistic	See *the cime went*
in context	guess	*to the store;*
		read *the boy* etc.
	Stage Two—Discrimination Net Substitution	
Known word	Rote	See *boy;* read *boy*
Unknown word in	Guess based on	See *cime;* read *cats*
isolation	visual similarity	
Unknown word in	Guess based on	See *the cime* etc.;
context	linguistic and	read *the child* etc.
	visual cues	
	Stage Three—Sequential Decoding	
Known word	Rote or	See *boy;* read *boy*
	decode	
Unknown word in	Decode	See *cime;*
isolation or context	left to right	Read *kĭmĕ*
	Stage Four—Hierarchical Decoding	
Known word	Rote	See *boy;*
	decode	read *boy*
Unknown word	Decode using	See *cime;*
in isolation	higher order	read: *sīm*
or context	rules	
	Analogy	See *faugh;*
	(alternative strategy)	read: *faff* by
		analogy to *laugh*

koff, 1978). Their natural strategy is congruent with the "whole word" approach to teaching reading, in which an unanalyzed word is the required response. Rozin, Poritsky, and Sotsky (1971) found that young children who were having great difficulty with regular reading instruction could easily learn to associate Chinese ideographs with English words. A rote learning strategy is diagnosed by an inability to respond to novel or unknown words. The child in the first stage does have a reasonable strategy when faced with reading an unknown word in sentence context. The child simply assimilates the unknown word into this existing natural language scheme by substituting a syntactically and semantically appropriate word into the sentence frame for the unknown word. This strategy has been studied in oral reading errors which occur in the classroom during initial reading.

Biemiller (1970) reports two additional stages. The next stage appears to be a transitional stage fron Stage One to Stage Two in which the child either refuses to respond or says he does not know when encountering an unknown word. Here the child is trying to coordinate two items of information at once—the context and some of the graphemic information—and is unable to accomplish this dual coordination. In Stage Two the child's response is consistent with both the partial graphemic cues and the sentence context.

What are the mechanisms responsible for the change from Stage One to Two? According to cognitive developmental theory, a strategy change is a result of accommodation to the task environment brought about by conflict between the existing strategy and task requirements.

The "linguistic guessing" strategy of Stage One which depends primarily on sentence context is inadequate for several reasons. First, the strategy sometimes produces a semantically or syntactically anomolous sentence. According to Weber (1970), good readers are more sensitive to this conflict as indexed by their tendency to make a second response. Second, the child encounters words in isolation in which case the linguistic guessing strategy may be of little use. Third, some teachers and other adults correct the child's "error" even when the sentence makes sense.

B. Stage Two—Discrimination Net Guessing

All of these environmental task demands encourage the child to pay some attention to the printed stimulus when encountering a new word. In the second stage the child typically responds to an unknown isolated word on the basis of its shared graphemic features with a known word. The number of graphemic features a young child can process is limited initially to the first letter, and it is only later that additional features such as word length, final letter, etc. are added. The child at this stage appears to be operating according to a "discrimination net" mechanism in which graphemic cues are processed only to the extent necessary to discriminate one printed word from another. Such a "discrimination net" strategy is typically found in learning tasks in which children and adults are required to learn novel material by rote. At Stage Two the child almost always limits his response to previously learned printed words.

C. Stage Three—Sequential Decoding

Stage Three is characterized by the use of combinational rules which allow the reader to "decode" novel words. What factors are involved in the child's switching from strategies of Stage One and Two to strategies of Stage Three? The major environmental factor is probably the increase in the number of items in the print vocabulary. So long as the number is limited, a rote learning or discrimination net strategy is optimal. In many basal reading programs only a few words are taught and these are chosen to be minimally similar to each other on the basis of first letter, length etc. However, as the print vocabulary grows the memory load increases and a rote learning strategy has diminishing returns. Also as the reading vocabulary increases, partial graphemic cues are no longer sufficient to discriminate one word from another, making the discrimination net strategy of limited use.

A second possible factor is the increase in cognitive processing capacity as the child moves into the stage of concrete operations. Older children may be able to pay attention to a word's sound as well as its meaning, and to process the order of a series of letters and to coordinate this series with a series of sounds. These increased cognitive abilities may allow them to induce or to successfully be taught the alphabetic principle. In Stage Three the term "decoding" is quite appropriate because the child in this stage can only deal with invariant relations in the form of a simple code between letters and sounds.

The shift from Stage Two to Stage Three is described in a naturalistic observational study by Cohen (1974–75), and a controlled observational study by Barr (1974–75). Both investigators studied children's initial reading acquisition in the first year of instruction. Both studies reported that good readers begin to produce substitution errors with a high graphemic similarity to the correct word. More and most importantly they produce nonword errors, and errors not in their print vocabulary. Both of these latter errors are reliable signs of the use of the decoding strategy of Stage Three. Both studies showed that method of instruction (basal vs phonics) made a difference. However, the instructional effects were overlaid on children's natural strategies. In Barr's study, all children, regardless of instructional method, started out using a rote strategy as indexed by their substitution errors in reading unknown words. However, all the children in the phonics groups switched to a decoding strategy by the end of the first grade. In addition, several subjects in the basal reading program switched to a decoding strategy by the end of the first year. We know little about the exact factors in instruction which produce the shift from Stage Two to Stage Three. The term "phonics" covers a multitude of techniques for either explicitly or implicitly facilitating the child's understanding of the relationship between printed and spoken language. The only thing that can be said for sure is that these techniques will interact with the child's natural strategies. Calfee, Chapman, and Venezky (1972) reported that children who are learning to read fall into a bimodal distribution on most phonics reading tasks. They can either not do them at all or do them easily. Such an all or none bimodal distribution is typical of qualitative differences in children at different stages. Even in the absence of any explicit "phonics" training, children's increasing cognitive–developmental capacity may allow them to induce orthographic structure and its relation to sound. This was shown by some of Barr's subjects in the basal group and by other studies in which extensive exposure is given (e.g. Staats, Brewer, & Gross, 1970). On the other hand, it appears that the environmental pressure to decode novel words which is a typical instructional demand of phonics programs facilitates transition from Stage Two to Stage Three.

There are several limitations to the naturalistic observational studies described previously. One limitation is that they depend completely on error analyses and do not tell us anything about what strategy children are using when they read a word correctly. In many circumstances a substitution strategy used by a child in Stage One or Two who encounters a new word will produce a correct response. Second, these naturalistic studies have typically been confined to the first year of reading instruction and therefore only provide information concerning early stages of reading acquisition. As stated previously, a child in Stage Three treats the alphabetic principle as a simple invariant code where each letter represents a single sound. It is at this stage that simple phonemic alphabets such as *ITA* or the natural language equivalents produced by a restricted vocabulary are most congruent with the child's natural processing strategies. Children in Stage Three can decode new words if they are regular, and invariant word patterns such as the consonant–vowel–consonant (CVC) pattern where the vowel has a checked (short) pronunciation. The child at Stage Three is not able to deal with regularly spelled words which require conditional and other higher order rules in which the sound associated with a given letter is dependent on other graphemic elements within the word such as the long vowel, silent *e* pattern. Venezky and his colleagues (1974) have investigated the development of orthographic knowledge by presenting subjects of different ages with novel or pseudowords conforming to orthographic rules of higher order complexity. This pseudoword technique provides information beyond that provided by naturalistic observation.

D. Stage Four—Hierarchical Decoding

Children in Stage Three typically use a simple sequential decoding strategy based on one-to-one correspondence. This strategy is successful on invariant patterns such as CVCs but produces errors on more complex patterns. An example is shown in Table I in which three errors are produced by the child in Stage Three when reading *cime*. The *C* is pronounced /K/ instead of /S/ as required by the following rule: The letter *C* is pronounced /S/ when followed by vowels *i, e,* and *y* and /K/ when followed by *a, o,* and *u,* for example, *cute* vs *city.* Second, the child in Stage Three will pronounce the vowel as short rather than long and the final *e* may be pronounced. It is not until Stage Four that the child has the ability to deal with conditional rule patterns and other complex rules of orthographic structure. These word patterns require a hierarchical rule system which involves conjunctive, disjunctive, and class inclusion rules. Marsh (1969) has provided a detailed description of the conceptual components involved in these higher order rules. The ability to use higher order rules probably depends upon an increase in cognitive processing capacity which is typically not present until the middle years of childhood.

III. MORPHOPHONEMIC AND ANALOGY STRATEGIES

It is clear from the previous discussion that English orthographic structure does not map to sound as a simple code but instead as a complex cipher. In addition many English spellings are morphophonemically based. A simple example is inflections such as plurals, past tenses etc. which have an invariant spelling that is unrelated to their sound but related to their meaning. Marsh (1970) suggested that these inflections be taught on a morphological basis rather than a grapheme–phoneme correspondence basis since even young children know the morphophonemic rules underlying their alternation. Chomsky and Halle (1968) have argued that the English orthographic system generally represents morphophonemic relationships rather than surface phonology because the mature reader is a proficient language user and therefore already knows the morphophonemic rules underlying such sound changes as the vowel shift (*sane–sanity*), palatization (*reduce–reduction*), etc. Carol Chomsky

(1970) has suggested that these morphophonemic patterns are based on low frequency Latinate words and it is doubtful that they could be in young children's vocabulary. Smith and Baker (1976) and Baker and Smith (1976) have investigated adult performance on English stress assignment rules for polysyllabic words which depend on a complex interaction of phonemic, morphophonemic and syntactic factors. They found that the Chomsky and Halle theory did not completely predict adult's performance on nonwords constructed to assess knowledge of these rules.

Developmental studies of children's knowledge of complex morphophonemic rules are sparse. Moskowitz (1973) studied children's knowledge of the vowel shift rule using orally presented nonword pairs with final silent *e* pattern and the *-ity* suffix (i.e., *sane–sanity*). She found that children in the third grade and above were able to learn these patterns. On the basis of her subject's comments (e.g. "Oh! you want me to make the long vowel short") Moskowitz concluded that the children learned these patterns based on their knowledge that free and checked vowels are often spelled with the same letter (e.g., *mat, mate*) rather than on their knowledge of lexically related pairs (e.g., *sane–sanity*). The vowel shift rule using the suffix *-ity* can also be based on grapheme–phonemic correspondence rules (i.e., a vowel is checked when followed by a consonant and another vowel).

Myerson (1980) studied the development of knowledge of five English sound patterns. Those patterns which are marked in the orthography such as the vowel shift and palatization are acquired much earlier than stress patterns which are not marked in the orthography. However the interpretation of this finding is confounded by the greater complexity of stress assignment rules.

A number of investigators have pointed out that an unknown word may be read by analogy to a known word rather than by use of combinatorial rules. Baron (1977) provides evidence for the use of the analogy strategy by adults but the evidence is based primarily on the subject's meta-knowledge of their strategies as reflected in their post hoc verbalizations. Baker and Smith (1976) using a conflict technique where reading by rule and reading by analogy would produce different pronunciations found evidence for both rule and analogy processes in adults' placement of stress on polysyllabic words. The cognitive–developmental approach presented here would predict that older children and adults would have a number of different strategies available in reading and the use of various strategies would depend on specific task factors. As the reader begins to encounter material with uncontrolled vocabulary, he will find more lexically based spellings and irregularly spelled words. There is evidence to suggest that as reading proficiency increases, there is also a shift from word recognition based on access to phonemic form to word recognition based on access to meaning (see Barron, 1978, for a review of this literature). In addition, the reader may internalize visual word forms (Ehri, 1979). All these factors would suggest a possible shift in strategies.

Therefore, a question to be addressed by the present article is the course of development of lexically based and analogy strategies and whether or not they replace or supplement rule-based strategies. In a preliminary study the present authors (Marsh, Desberg, & Cooper, 1977) used a conflict technique to study the development of the analogy strategy. In a production task there was a marked developmental shift in strategies between the fifth grade and adolescent (eleventh grade) and adult (college) samples. However, in a judgment task in which the subjects were asked to choose between the two alternative pronunciations, the fifth grade subjects' choice performance was not significantly different than that of the older subjects. This pattern of results is consistent with the concept of a production deficiency discussed previously. Fifth grade children were capable of using the analogy strategy and it is the predominant strategy used in a judgment task. However, a rule strategy is their predominant strategy in a free production task.

The next section of this article describes two empirical studies of the development of strategies typical of Stages One through Four along with an assessment of strategies based on knowledge of lexical relations and analogies. The study included both normal and reading disabled children and normal adults. The major purpose of the study was to provide an empirical foundation for the proposed developmental sequence described in the introduction to this article and to assess the age-grade level at which various strategies typically emerge.

IV. EMPIRICAL EVIDENCE CONCERNING STRATEGIES

A. Experiment I

1. Method

a. Subjects. The subjects were 20 second grade children from a university laboratory elementary school; 60 fifth grade children, 40 from a large urban public school system and 20 from the laboratory school; and 40 college students, 20 from UCLA and 20 from California State University, Dominguez Hills. There were no significant differences in patterns of responding as a function of school population so the results were combined in the data analysis. All these subjects were reading at grade level. The reading disabled subjects were 15 children from a special school for learning disabled children. These reading disabled subjects ranged in age from 11 to 15. Their mean expected reading grade level based on mental age was approximately eighth grade. Their mean actual reading level on the California Achievement Test was approximately fourth grade.

b. Materials. The materials consisted of two short paragraphs adapted from the Gray Oral Reading Test. A number of nonwords were inserted into noun positions in the story sentences. Four of the nonwords were simple CVC patterns (e.g., *han*) and four were long vowel silent *e* patterns (e.g., *hane*). Three words contained the *-ity* suffix which tested for knowledge of the vowel shift rule (e.g., *hane, hanity*). In addition to these words, there were three parallel nonwords which assessed the subject's knowledge of the conditional c-rule (e.g., /c→s/ when followed by *i, e,* or *y*) as well as previously discussed vowel patterns (e.g., *cim, cime, cimity*).

There were also four words which assessed the subject's use of analogy strategies. These words would be pronounced one way by subjects using a decoding strategy and a different way by subjects using an analogy strategy (e.g., the word *faugh* is pronounced *faw* by a decoding strategy and *faff* by analogy to the word *laugh*). The nonword *som* was excluded from the data analysis since it was often pronounced as the real word *some* and it was not clear if this was due to use of analogy or substitution strategies.

c. Procedure. Each subject was individually asked to read the stories aloud. They were told that there were some unusual words in the stories but that they should try to read all the words as best they could. If subjects stated that they did not know the word they were encouraged to try to read it anyway. Very few responses in our data were omission or "don't know" responses. Following the reading of the story the subjects were asked to read the same nonwords in isolation. The subjects were asked why they pronounced the word the way they did and if they know a word which looked like or was spelled like the nonword. The two stories were counterbalanced across subjects.

2. Results

The primary data analysis was done on the pronunciation of the words in the story context. Subjects generally persevered and gave a consistent response in both the story and isolation conditions. The subjects' strategy was assessed by their pronunciation rather than their verbal explanations of the strategies used since we were interested primarily in knowledge rather than meta-knowledge.

The percentage of subjects using each strategy is shown in Table II. An overall developmental difference is indicated by the main effect for grade level which was significant [$F(1, 23) = 29.42$, $p < .001$]. Post hoc Newman–Keuls comparisons of each grade level with every other grade level showed that all groups differed significantly from each other in performance on the strategies except the second graders and the reading disabled subjects. In performance on different types of nonwords there was significant overall interaction between grade level and word type [$F(12, 492) = 2.68$, $p < .001$].

  a. Stage I. The number of real words substituted for the nonwords differed as a function of age-grade level. All groups differed significantly from each other on this measure on post hoc (Newman–Keuls) testing ($p < .01$).

  b. Stage II. In performance on the short vowel (CVC) patterns there was a significant difference between the learning disabled children and the normal readers of all grade levels ($p < .01$). The normal readers in second grade, fifth grade, and college did not differ significantly from each other on these patterns. Newman–Keuls comparisons showed that the learning disabled children and the second graders were significantly inferior to the fifth grade subjects and college subjects on the performance of the long vowel–silent *e* pattern (CVCe) and the conditional c-rule ($p < .01$). The college students were also significantly superior to the fifth grade subjects in performance on these patterns ($p < .01$).

  c. Analogy Strategy. There was a similar significant difference between second grade and learning disabled children on the one hand and the fifth grade children and college students on the vowel shift pattern and the analogy words ($p < .01$). The college students were also significantly superior to fifth grade subjects on the vowel shift pattern ($p < .01$).

  d. Comparison within Grade Levels. Both the learning disabled children and the normal second grade readers showed significantly inferior performance on the long vowel and vowel shift patterns compared with the short vowel rule ($p < .01$). The performance of all children on the c-rule and analogy words was significantly inferior to the performance on all the vowel patterns ($p < .01$). The college subjects did not differ significantly on the three vowel rules but did significantly worse on the c-rule and analogy words ($p < .01$).

3. Discussion

  a. Stage One and Two. None of the subjects in this study showed a majority of Stage One and Two substitution responses. However, 25% of the learning disabled children's responses were substitution responses

TABLE II

Mean Percentage of Strategy Responses in Experiment I

	Substitution real word (%)	Decoding			Analogy (%)	
		Sequential (%)	Hierarchical (%)			Analogy
Rule		Short vowel	Long vowel	c-rule	Vowel shift	
Pattern		CVC	CVCe	c(iey)	CVCe: CVC-ity	faugh: (laugh)
Example		han	hane	cim	cime: cimity	
Group						
Second grade (N = 20)	10	82	48	6	43	14
Disabled (N = 15)	24	58	40	25	36	20
Fifth grade (N = 60)	5	88	65	40	59	34
College (N = 35)	0	96	83	70	84	38

which was over twice the percentage found in normal second grade subjects. In the naturalistic observational studies reported previously, Stage One and Two are characteristic of the first year of reading instruction when the instruction is started at 5 or 6 years of age. Most of the substitution responses obtained in this study had graphemic features in common with the nonword which is characteristic of Stage Two as opposed to Stage One. There was a clear decrease with age and reading proficiency in the percentage of Stage One and Two responses. The reading disabled children were still relying on the substitution strategy to a considerable degree.

b. Stage Three. The normal second grade readers are predominantly in Stage Three as indexed by their high performance on the novel CVC word patterns as compared to more complex patterns. There is no significant developmental increase in normal readers from second grade through the adult sample in performance on these CVC patterns. In contrast the reading disabled children are inferior to all normal readers on Stage Three word patterns. They are transitional between Stages Two and Three in that they often gave substitution responses even to the simple CVC word patterns.

c. Stage Four. There was a clear developmental increase in Stage Four responses between the second and the fifth grade as indexed by performance on the conditional rules (i.e., the long vowel rule CVCe and the c-rule). There is also a considerable decalage between performance on the long vowel (CVCe) patterns and the conditional c-rule. This may be a function of the number of exemplars of the two rules in the reading vocabulary of the school age child. The long vowel CVCe pattern is quite common while the pattern in which the letter c is pronounced as /s/ is quite rare (cf. Venezky, 1974). A second factor may be the greater cognitive complexity of the c-rule as compared to the long vowel rule. The pronunciation of the vowel as long or short is determined by the simple presence or absence of the final e. In contrast the pronunciation of the initial c is based on a complex disjunctive rule (i.e., c is pronounced /s/ when followed by either of the graphemes, i, e, or y, and /k/ when followed by either a, o, or u). It is clear from this study that the shift from Stage Three to Stage Four occurs between the second and fifth grades. The learning disabled children resemble the normal second grade children in their ability to perform on the long vowel rule and are slightly superior to second graders on the c-rule. The pattern of responding on the vowel shift rule with the suffix -*ity* appears similar to the performance on the long vowel (CVCe) patterns. As discussed in the introduction, this performance could be a result of either the use of a grapheme–phoneme correspondence rule or knowledge of the morphophonemic pattern. Our results suggest that Moskowitz (1973) is correct and that Stage Four is sufficient for performance on this pattern. We did not find any performance differences in children on patterns which had a morphophonemic basis (e.g., *hane–hanity* to *sane–sanity*) compared with patterns which did not have obvious analogies (e.g., *taze–tazity*) and in general those who produced the vowel shift did not produce the analogous words in the post hoc probe.

d. Analogy Strategy. In this study, in contrast to our previous study (Marsh *et al.*, 1977), the subjects did not produce a preponderance of analogy responses. There was no significant increase in analogy responses between fifth grade children and adults. The percentage of analogy responses of fifth grade subjects was similar to the percentage in the Marsh *et al.* (1977) study but the adults in this study produced only 38% analogy responses as compared to over 70% in the previous study. The pattern of results between the previous study and the present study suggests that the analogy strategy is an optional strategy for adults and its use is strongly determined by task factors. In the previous study all the words had analogies while in the present study only some of the words had obvious analogies. As stated previously, the analogy strategy appears to be available by Stage Four but its use appears to depend on a number of task factors such as production vs judgment task, and content.

B. Experiment II

One of the predictions of the cognitive developmental approach is that there will be a qualitative shift in the stimulus factors which are most important at each stage. In Stage Two the most important factor will be the visual familiarity of the words the child reads, since each word is entered in episodic fashion into lexical memory based on its visual appearance. In Stages Three and Four the important factor will be the phonemic regularity of the word patterns. Evidence for such a qualitative shift in stimulus factors has been reported by Pick (1978) who finds that younger children make word similarity judgments in a matching to sample task based on the words' visual similarity, while older children choose on the basis of phonemic similarity. Similarly Barron (1980) has reported that poor readers' judgments in a lexical decision task are primarily affected by visual factors while good readers' judgments are affected primarily by phonemic factors.

This study was designed to investigate the relative role of visual familiarity and phonemic regularity in reading children of different ages and ability levels. An additional question of interest is the availability of the analogy strategy in Stage Three. According to Sternberg (1977), second grade children are capable of analogical reasoning and Baron (1979) has reported that second grade children and older learning disabled children were capable of producing analogy responses after a brief training session in which they were given some examples. Both of these studies suggest that the analogy strategy may be available in Stage Three but there is a production deficiency as found previously in fifth grade subjects. In the present study all the children were told the analogical basis for constructing the nonwords. A third purpose of this study was to compare the effects of using real words and nonwords on the strategies employed. A fourth purpose was to compare the strategies used in reading and spelling. The development of strategies in spelling will be discussed elsewhere. (Marsh, Friedman, Desberg, & Welch, 1980).

1. Method

a. Subjects. The subjects were 20 second and 21 fourth grade children reading at grade level and 24 reading disabled children from classes for "educationally handicapped (EH)" in the fourth grade who were reading 2 years below grade level.

b. Procedure. Subjects were asked to read or spell two 20-word lists. The first list contained 20 high-frequency real words one-half of which were regularly spelled and the other half of which were irregularly spelled. The second list contained a transformation of each of the words in the first list into nonsense words. This was accomplished by changing one of the letters in the words. Subjects received the two lists as either a reading or spelling task in one of four counterbalanced orders.

In a previous study (Marsh *et al.,* 1977) a production deficiency was found in fifth grade subjects' use of the analogy strategy in reading. In order to minimize the gap between competence and performance in the use of the analogy strategy all subjects were told that the nonwords were real words with one letter or sound changed.

2. Results

The major result for the purpose of the present chapter is the interaction between the word type and groups [$F(1, 61) = 3.17$, $p < .05$]. The reading disabled EH children performed better on the visually familiar real words than on the unfamiliar nonwords. There was no difference in performance on real versus nonwords in normal second and fourth grade readers. Phonemic regularity was a significant factor in both reading and spelling at all grade levels [$F(1, 61) = 436$, $p < .001$]. In addition, the fourth grade normal readers were significantly superior to the fourth grade EH and second grade children who did not differ significantly from each other. The reading disabled children and second graders showed significantly more Stage Two substitution errors than the normal fourth grade subjects. All the groups showed a greater use of analogy responses than in Experiment I and groups did not differ significantly on this factor.

3. Discussion

Most of the subjects in this study were in Stages Three and Four. The learning disabled subjects showed better performance on visually familiar real words as found in Barron's (1980) study but phonemic regularity was the major factor in performance of normal readers. The lack of an overall significant difference between real words and nonwords which conform to English orthography indicates that results using nonwords can be generalized to unknown real words when subjects are beyond Stage Two. Another methodological conclusion is that substitution strategies can be diagnosed by using words in isolation as well as words in context as in Experiment I. The third finding of the present study is that Stage Three children have the competence to use the analogy strategy, but it is typically not used spontaneously. However, it can fairly easily be elicited in reading either by instructions as in the present study or by training as in Baron's (1979) study. Such production deficiencies which are typical of the development of children's cognitive strategies (Flavell, 1977) are also apparent in the use of the analogy strategy in reading.

V. SUMMARY

A. Research Implications

The major theme of this article has been that reading acquisition is a cognitive developmental process. We have described four stages of reading acquisition. The shift from Stage Two to Stage Three occurs at approximately 7 years of age in our studies and is therefore congruent with the shift from the preoperational stage to the stage of concrete operations in traditional Piagetian terms. Since the major purpose of this article was to describe the knowledge and strategies used in reading new words by children at different age-grade levels we did not independently assess the child's cognitive stage by using traditional Piagetian tasks. We are presently engaged in research which will explore the relationship between reading strategies and general cognitive–developmental stages. As Piaget and others have shown, the fact that a child gets an item correct or incorrect on a test sheds little light on the child's knowledge and strategies. For example, a child who reads an unknown word correctly can be doing so by using any of the four strategies described in this article. It is only by devising more analytical tasks that a child's knowledge and strategies can be revealed. The tasks described in this article are designed to provide an indication of the stages at which the child is functioning by indexing the strategies which are used when a child encounters an unknown word.

The early stages of reading acquisition have previously been described through naturalistic observation (e.g., Biemiller, 1970; Cohen, 1974–75; Weber, 1970). Naturalistic observation is essential during the initial stages of research in order to assure that the theory has ecological validity. Naturalistic observation, however, is a very inefficient and time-consuming technique. It has severe limitations in that it is unable to diagnose what strategies the children are using when they are responding correctly. Also, it cannot easily be used to describe the later stages of reading acquisition. The pseudoword technique employed by Venezky (1974) and his colleagues has considerably more analytical power in precisely describing the child's ability to deal with unknown words of various levels of cognitive complexity. However most previous research using pseudowords did not differentiate between the use of the combinational rule and the use of analogy strategies.

We feel that the conflict technique employed by Marsh et al. (1977) has been the most useful technique in identifying the analogy strategy, which seems to be available in the early stages of reading acquisition but is usually not employed spontaneously until later in development and then only in certain situations.

B. Instructional Implications

One of the great advantages of the cognitive–developmental approach is that it has been successfully applied as a theory of instruction. In our opinion, the best articulation of a cognitive–developmental theory as a guide to instruction has been presented by Case (1978), whose instructional approach has been successfully applied to training on school tasks such as mathematics as well as traditional Piagetian tasks. According to Case (1978, p. 442) several steps are essential in using the cognitive–developmental approach in instruction. The first step is to do a task analysis of material to be taught. A task analysis of reading consists of a description of the relationship between printed language and oral language. A detailed description of this relationship has been provided by Venezky (1970) in terms of its combinatorial rule structure. Chomsky and Halle (1968) have provided an alternative description of the English phonotactic system which they claim has relevance to the orthographic system. Our research as well as that of others (Moskowitz, 1973) suggests although mature readers may operate according to Chomsky and Halle's system (Smith & Baker, 1976) it has little psychological reality for the child beginning to learn to read.

The second and critically important step in instruction is to analyze children's spontaneously generated strategies by presenting exemplars of the task materials to children at different cognitive–developmental levels. A powerful application of this technique is to invent a revision of the task so if children are approaching it one way they will generate one set of responses and if they are approaching it a different way they will generate a different set (e.g., Sieglar, 1977). The task of reading unknown words has been used in this article to diagnose four different strategies which change with development.

The third major step, according to Case (1978), is to design instruction so that the limits of the spontaneously generated strategy will be apparent. This is the well-known conflict technique in which the child's natural strategy is shown to him to be inadequate. For example, in Stage One the linguistic guessing strategy might be shown to be inadequate for reading words in isolation. The discrimination net strategy of Stage Two might be shown to be inadequate in discriminating highly similar words (e.g., *bit, bet, bat, but*) and in correctly responding to unknown words. The sequential decoding strategy of Stage Three can be shown to be inadequate to pronounce words involving higher order rules. We have assumed that most children naturally discover the inadequacy of various early strategies by exposure to larger samples of printed language. However Barr's (1974–75) research indicates that specific instructional treatments can also accelerate the changes in children's natural strategies.

The fourth step described by Case is to provide ways of minimizing the load on working memory. This can be accomplished by breaking the instruction down into smaller steps so as to minimize the memory load at any one time. An example of this instructional strategy is the cumulative approach in teaching the child to "blend" letter sounds in a sequential decoding strategy. In this approach two letter–sound units are blended initially (e.g., *a–t*) and additional sounds are added cumulatively (e.g., *c–at*). A similar approach might be useful in teaching higher order rules. For example in teaching long vowel rules it would be possible to deal with one vowel and introduce additional rules one at a time. In the case of the c-rule, an initial complex disjunctive concept could be made simple initially by restricting the number of word exemplars. A second approach is to increase the familiarity of the task. Phonemic segmentation and blending might initially be taught using compound words, then syllables, and finally phonemes as in the program designed by Gleitman and Rozin (1977). Another way to simplify the task is to increase the salience of the aspects of the task to which the child must attend. An example is in Experiment II in which young children who were verbally instructed about the relationship of unknown words to known words successfully applied the analogy strategy (cf. Baron, 1979).

As Case (1978) points out, these instructional strategies may be difficult and costly to implement on a large scale basis since they require individual diagnosis and instruction. Most children successfully pass through the stages of reading acquisition if they are exposed to almost any form of reading instruction. Exposure to larger and larger samples of printed language along with some feedback appears to be sufficient for normal development to occur. However, there is a small group of children for whom typical instruction appears to be inadequate. These children are variously labeled as dyslexic, reading disabled, educationally handicapped etc. In our first study a group of adolescents from a special school for the learning disabled apparently had not completely made the transition from Stage Two to Stage Three as indexed by their use of the substitution strategy and relatively low performance on Stage Three tasks.

In our second study there were a group of children in special classrooms in a regular school system who were functioning in a fashion similar to children who are 2 years younger. These children and most children who have difficulty in learning to read show what Boder (1971) calls the dysphonetic pattern. They are unable to read and spell unknown regularly spelled words. In our terminology they are unable to make the transition from Stage Two to Stage Three and Four. A major question for future research is the relationship between cognitive maturity and reading acquisition. It is possible for a child to learn to read during the late preoperational period but the knowledge and strategies used will differ qualitatively from the knowledge and strategies of the older child. The preoperational child is probably limited to Stage One and Two strategies. These strategies will become more and more inadequate as the child attempts to expand his reading vocabulary by rote, episodic memory. We believe that concrete operations may be a necessary condition for entry into Stage Three and Four in which the child is able to deal in generative fashion with the orthographic system. However, the existence of older children who are presumably cognitively mature and yet are still apparently in Stage One and Two suggests that concrete operations is not a sufficient condition for entry into Stage Three and Four. Children do not automatically learn to read as they grow to adulthood as they automatically learn to conserve. Specific experiences with printed language are apparently also a necessary condition. It is in the case of reading disabled children in which the cognitive–developmental approach will hopefully have the greatest instructional pay-off. One of the suggestions growing out of the present research is that the analogy strategies may be an important alternative in learning to read for the reading disabled child. Older children and adults apparently naturally increase the use of the analogy strategies although it is rarely, if ever, included in formal reading instruction. The present studies along with that of Baron (1979) suggest that younger children and reading disabled children are capable of using this strategy when cued by instruction or brief training. It is not yet known if this cuing effect will automatically allow young reading disabled children to transfer the strategy to new situations and to use it productively. As Baron (1977) has implied, this strategy involved "using the rules without knowing them" and therefore may be a powerful alternative strategy for children who are having trouble making the transition from Stages One and Two to Stages Three and Four.

It is clear that much remains to be done to validate the cognitive–developmental approach both as a descriptive theory and an explanation for reading acquisition. The instructional suggestions presented here are only suggestive and have not as yet been implemented or empirically validated. However, we hope that this article will encourage those who are interested in cognitive development and reading to consider the application of the cognitive–developmental approach to reading instruction.

REFERENCES

Baker, R. G., & Smith, P. T. A psycholinguistic study of English stress assignment rules. *Language and Speech*, 1976, **19**, 9–27.
Baron, J. What we might know about orthographic rules. In S. Dornic & P. M. Rabbit (Eds.), *Attention and Performance* (Vol. 6). Hillsdale, New Jersey: Erlbaum, 1977.
Baron, J. Mechanisms for pronouncing printed words: Use and acquisition. In D. LaBerge & S. Samuels (Eds.), *Basic processes in reading: Perception and comprehension.* Hillsdale, New Jersey: Erlbaum, 1978.
Baron, J. Orthographic and word specific mechanisms in children's reading of words. *Child Development* 1979, **50**, 60–72.
Barr, R. The effect of instruction on pupil reading strategies. *Reading Research Quarterly*, 1974–75, **10**, 555–582.
Barron, R. W. Access to meanings of printed words: Some implications for reading and learning to read. In F. Murray (Ed.), *Development of the reading process.* Newark, Delaware: IRA, 1978.

Barron, R. W. Visual-orthographic and phonological strategies in reading and spelling. In U. Frith (Ed.), *Cognitive processes in spelling*. New York: Academic Press, 1980.

Biemiller, A. J. The development of the use of graphic and contextual information as children learn to read. *Reading Research Quarterly*, 1970, **6**, 75–96.

Boder, E. Developmental dyslexia; prevailing diagnostic concepts and a new diagnostic approach. In H. Mykebust (Ed.), *Progress in learning disabilities* (Vol. II). New York: Grune & Stratton, 1971.

Calfee, R. C., Chapman R., & Venezky, R. How a child needs to think to learn to read. In L. W. Gregg (Ed.), *Cognition in Learning and Memory*. New York: Wiley, 1979.

Case, R. A developmentally based theory and technology of instruction. *Review of Educational Research*, 1978, **48**, 439–463.

Chomsky, C. Reading, writing and phonology. *Harvard Educational Review*, 1970, **40**, 187–309.

Chomsky, N., & Halle, M. *The sound pattern of English*. New York: Harper, 1968.

Cohen, A. S. Oral reading errors of first grade readers taught by a code emphasis approach. *Reading Research Quarterly*, **10**, 1974–75.

Ehri, L. E. Linguistic insight: Threshold of reading acquisition. In T. G. Waller & G. E. Mackinnon (Eds.), *Reading research: Advances in theory and research* (Vol. I). New York: Academic Press, 1979.

Flavell, J. H. *Cognitive development*. New York: Prentice-Hall, 1977.

Gleitman, L. R., & Rozin, P. The structure and acquisition of reading I. Relations between orthographies and the structure of language. In A. S. Reber & D. L. Scarborough (Eds.), *Toward a psychology of reading*. New York: Erlbaum, 1977.

Golinkoff, R. M. Phonemic awareness skills and reading achievement. In F. Murray & J. J. Pikulski (Eds.), *The Acquisition of reading*. Baltimore, Maryland: University Park Press, 1978.

Marsh, G. *Conceptual skills in beginning reading*. (Tech. Rep. No. 18). Southwest Regional Laboratory, Los Alamitos, California, July 1969.

Marsh, G. *The role of morphophonemic rules in beginning reading*. Paper presented at American Educational Research Association meeting, Minneapolis, March 1970.

Marsh, G. The HIP approach to reading. In F. Murray (Ed.), *Efficient processing in reading*. Newark, Delaware: International Reading Association, 1978.

Marsh, G., Desberg, P., & Cooper, J. Developmental changes in strategies of reading. *Journal of Reading Behavior*, 1977, **9**, 391–394.

Marsh, G., Friedman, M. P., Desberg, P., & Welch, V. Development of strategies in learning to spell. In U. Frith (Ed.), *Cognitive processes in spelling*. New York: Academic Press, 1980.

Moskowitz, B. A. On the status of vowel shift in English. In T. E. Moore (Ed.), *Cognition and the acquisition of language*. New York: Academic Press, 1973.

Myerson, R. F. Children's knowledge of selected aspects of sound pattern of English. In R. Wales & P. Smith (Eds.), *Child's acquisition of language*, in press.

Pick, A. D. Perception in the acquisition of reading. In F. Murray & J. J. Pikulski (Eds.), *The acquisition of reading*. Baltimore, Maryland: University Park Press, 1978.

Rozin, P., Poritsky, S., & Sotsky, R. American children with reading problems can easily learn to read English represented by Chinese characters. *Science*, 1971, **171**, 1264–1267.

Sieglar, R. S. *Cognition, instruction, development and individual differences*. Presented at NATO Conference on Cognition and Instruction, Amsterdam, June 1977.

Smith, P. T., & Baker, R. G. The influence of English spelling patterns on pronunciation. *Journal of Verbal Learning and Verbal Behavior*, 1976, **15**, 267–285.

Staats, A. W., Brewer, B. A., & Gross, M. C. Learning and cognitive development: Representative samples, cumulative-hierarchical learning, and experimental-longitudinal methods. *Monographs, Society for Research in Child Development,* 1970, **35,** 1–85.

Sternberg, R. J. *Componential investigations of human intelligence.* Presented at NATO Conference on Cognition and Instruction, Amsterdam, June 1977.

Venezky, R. L. *The structure of English orthography.* The Hague: Mouton, 1970.

Venezky, R. L. Language and cognition in reading. In B. Spilsky (Ed.), *Current trends in educational linguistics.* The Hague: Mouton, 1974.

Waller, T. G. Think first; read later: Piagetian prerequisites for reading. In F. Murray (Ed.), *Development of reading process.* Newark, Delaware: International Reading Association, 1978.

Weber, R. M. First graders' use of grammatical context in reading. In H. Levin & J. P. Williams (Eds.), *Basic studies on reading.* New York: Basic Books, 1970.

IDENTIFYING AND REMEDIATING FAILURES IN READING COMPREHENSION: TOWARD AN INSTRUCTIONAL APPROACH FOR POOR COMPREHENDERS[1]

ELLEN BOUCHARD RYAN

Department of Psychology
University of Notre Dame
Notre Dame, Indiana

[1] Work on this article was partially supported by NSF grant BNS76-09559, of which E. Ryan is principal investigator. Appreciation is hereby expressed for the comments made on an earlier version by John Cavanaugh, Linnea Ehri, George Ledger, and Bernice Wong.

I. INTRODUCTION

Reading, the extraction of meaning from written text, is an active constructive process in which "expectancies about syntax and semantics within contexts lead to hypotheses which can be confirmed (or rejected) with only a small portion of the cues available in the text" (Ryan & Semmel, 1969, p. 82). Since the speech of 6-year-old children reflects acquisition of the basic syntactic and semantic structure of their language, children learning to read might be expected to experience no difficulty in applying knowledge of sentence structure to the reading task. However, empirical evidence and theoretical reasoning suggest the contrary.

Vygotsky (1934/1962) argued that the abstract nature of the reading task required deliberate attention to sentence structure beyond the spontaneous use of structure typical in normal speaking and listening. This distinction between deliberate control over language structure and spontaneous linguistic skills has proven useful in characterizing cognitive advances during the early school years in abilities to deal with language stimuli (cf. Mattingly, 1972; Ryan, 1980). For example, between the ages of 4 and 8 years children become much better able to focus on the grammatical structure of word strings to improve recall or to provide judgments of acceptability. A special aspect of the abstractness of the reading task, highlighted by Olson (1977), is the need to interpret the meaning of sentences without the aid of naturalistic context. As Olson has pointed out, reading and writing provide the primary opportunities for dealing with sentence meaning per se rather than with a sentence merely as a cue to the speaker's intended meaning. Thus, the lag of deliberate control behind spontaneous knowledge as well as the lack of immediately relevant context during reading interfere with the beginning reader's ability to apply his syntactic and semantic knowledge to text. The large amount of attention devoted to decoding by novices further detracts from the limited potential for utilization of phrase and sentence structure.

Whereas many children gradually acquire the effective sentence and passage processing skills necessary for good comprehension, the poor reader appears to remain relatively deficient in the use of active, organizing strategies. In addition to a brief review of the current evidence for this deficiency, the present article offers methodological suggestions for improved diagnosis of successful and unsuccessful strategies and for teaching comprehension skills to poor readers. The discussion of strategy assessment and training derives mainly from an attempt to apply analyses and procedures recently developed within the areas of developmental memory research and of cognitive behavior modification. Before addressing individual differences in reading skills, we first describe the cognitive framework from which we view the reading process.

II. COGNITIVE PROCESSES IN READING

A. A Cognitive Framework

Our analysis of the cognitive processes involved in reading is based on Flavell's (1977) description of the four categories of memory phenomena: basic processes, knowledge base, strategies, and metamemory. *Basic processes,* what Atkinson and Shiffrin (1968) called structural features, are the relatively unmodifiable fundamental operations and capacities of the cognitive system. With regard to memory, Campione and Brown (1979) have identified three key quantitative properties of the immediate, short-term, and long-term stages of memory, i.e., capacity (amount of space), durability (the relative permanence of information), and efficiency (temporal aspects of the selection and manipulation of information). *Knowledge base* refers to an individual's organized knowledge about the world. Of course, prior knowledge plays a critical part in the perceptual aspects of reading, such as letter–word recognition and the identification of word meanings. Of even more importance for reading comprehension is the constructive interaction between the incoming message and the reader's general knowledge of the world (cf. Baker & Stein, 1981; Royer & Cunningham, 1978).

Strategies (called control processes by Atkinson and Shiffrin, 1968; and plans by Miller, Galanter, & Pribram, 1960) refer to any organized sequence of voluntary purposeful actions taken to enhance a desired outcome. Particular strategies differ in generality and in hierarchical complexity, but they all operate for an individual somewhat like a computer program (or subroutine). In introducing his book on information strategies, Underwood (1978) indicates that specific definitions of strategies vary substantially but that the notion of choice is consistently a key feature. Choice need not be reflective nor conscious, but alternatives must be available. Memory strategies that have received substantial attention from developmental researchers include rehearsal, semantic organization, imagery, and elaboration. Additional strategies relevant to reading include use of contextual cues in word recognition, constructive processing of sentences, selective attention to main points, use of titles and subtitles, and self-testing.

Metacognition refers to knowledge about cognition and includes sensitivity to the need for a strategy, awareness of one's basic process capabilities and available strategies, and understanding of means–goal relationships. Also encompassed by the term metacognition is on-line awareness of current internal states, such as comprehension, test readiness, and motivational level. Metacognitive aspects of reading would include immediate on-task knowledge of comprehension and memory levels as well as knowledge of reading strategies and their appropriate application.

A fifth aspect of the cognitive system, not explicitly included by Flavell (1977), is *executive functioning*. Essentially, executive functioning (Belmont & Butterfield, 1977) refers to the selection, adaptation, and monitoring of strategies on the basis of metacognitive knowledge. Examples of executive functioning include the plan to use a plan (Miller *et al.*, 1960), reviewing one's work, checking a proposed problem solution against reality constraints, and rereading a section of text which has not been adequately understood. Using a computer analogy, executive functioning involves the writing, updating, selection, and coordination of subprograms in order to achieve the specified goal.

B. Application to Reading

In order to illustrate the application of our cognitive framework to the reading process, let us consider *eye movements,* a particular critical aspect of reading. The basic process of moving eyes across text is an unmodifiable prerequisite for reading. Equally universal and unchangeable is the fact that information is received by the reader only when the eye is focused on the text, not when the eye is moving (Huey, 1968). On the other hand, what the eye "sees" when focused and the extent to which the reader exercises voluntary active control over the eye movements do vary substantially among and within readers.

The less active, less strategic a reader behaves in a given situation the less control he is exerting over the reading process. On the passive end of the continuum would be a reader who looked at each word in each line of text for exactly the same time period, regardless of word length or familiarity, text comprehension, or reading purpose. Slightly more strategic is the reader who spends more time on words that cannot be readily identified, tries to sound out the words using decoding skills, and tries to use the sentence context. More in control yet is the reader who systematically uses sentence and passage context to guide the timing and location of eye fixation. A reader functioning executively would be monitoring his comprehension, checking that his current comprehension level matched the needs of the particular reading task (e.g., locate one place name vs study for an important multiple-choice examination), and revising eye movement patterns accordingly. Before reading a text in preparation for an essay test on the main ideas, such an individual would consider alternative study methods (e.g., rereading, underlining, note taking, and outlining), select one method, monitor its effectiveness, revise the selected strategy if necessary, and study until self-testing revealed adequate learning. Clearly, the looking ahead, rereading, and self-testing of executive reading require eye movement patterns dramatically different from those of the passive reader.

Even though adults tend to process information much more actively while reading than children, we adults do not always perform as well as we might. We have all, for example, read two (or 20!) pages of text before realizing that our eyes had moved systematically from left to right across each line while our attention was directed elsewhere (e.g., useless daydreaming or solving an unrelated but pressing problem). Recognition of our attention lapse and ability to locate the section of text where our attention first wandered are examples of the comprehension monitoring aspect of metacognition. A reader's reaction to this attention "lapse" can vary from executively primitive to executively mature. Failure to realize the comprehension problem or automatic continuation of sequential eye movements despite a vague sense of comprehension difficulties would be seriously inadequate reactions. On the other hand, merely returning automatically to the section where comprehension had begun to suffer may not be the most effective approach. An executive reader could ask himself whether there was sufficient time to backtrack, whether the gap was likely to matter in terms of overall comprehension goals for the task, whether it would be profitable to set the book aside and direct undivided attention to the distracting problem, or whether he should engage in more active reading behaviors (e.g., underlining, notetaking, skimming) in order to avoid another lapse of attention.

The remainder of this article will focus on individual differences among readers in strategy usage, metacognition, and executive functioning.

III. OVERVIEW OF STRATEGY DEFICIENCIES OF POOR READERS

In this section, we will provide a brief survey of good–poor reader investigations which, taken altogether, establish a variety of aspects in which good readers process text in a more active, strategic fashion. Since an excellent, comprehensive review of good–poor reader comparisons has been published rather recently (Golinkoff, 1976) and since limitations related to widely varying criteria for subject selection have been well discussed (Golinkoff, 1976; Valtin, 1978), we will focus only on the main findings. In the subsequent section, we will present some methodological improvements which would allow for more clearly defensible specific conclusions regarding strategy deficiencies.

A. Processing of Sentences

Investigating the hypothesis that poor readers have less control over syntax even in oral contexts, Vogel (1974, 1975) assessed the oral syntactic abilities of 20 dyslexic second-grade children and 20 age-matched normal controls. A multivariate analysis revealed that the dyslexic children were deficient in oral syntax; specifically, they were found to be substantially inferior to their normal counterparts on seven of the nine tests of oral syntax, including oral cloze, sentence repetition, spontaneous speech, and knowledge of morphology. A related finding of differences on an oral test of sentence memory was reported by Firth (1972) who conducted an extensive investigation of 8-year-old good and poor readers in Australia.

Having equated a group of fourth-grade good readers with a group of poor–average readers on ability to associate simple familiar words, Weinstein and Rabinovitch (1971) compared the two groups on recall for lists of nonsense words and grammatical markers (i.e., function words and suffixes), half of which were in sentence order and half randomly ordered. Whereas the good readers learned the structured list much better than the random list, the poor–average readers learned the two types of list with equal difficulty. Since the good and poor–average readers did not differ in their recall of unstructured lists, it is clear that the contrast between the two groups on the structured lists derives from the better readers' ability to utilize the syntactic cues even though the strings were meaningless. In a somewhat related experiment, Guthrie and Tyler (1976) examined the recall for meaningful, anomalous, and random word strings of 18 good and 18 poor readers, matched on reading comprehension but of different ages. In both spoken and written conditions and for both groups, meaningful sentences were easier than anomalous which were in turn easier than random. Performance of the two groups was similar for spoken sentences, but the poor readers did not perform as well on the written sentences. The lack of differential sensitivity to structural elements in this study contrasts with the Weinstein and Rabinovitch finding and may be due to the unusual kind of matching (i.e., on reading comprehension). After considering several alternative explanations for the poor readers' weaker performance, the authors present a reasonable case that the poor readers were not decoding adequately during the silent reading task. Analysis of intrusion errors supported this explanation since the majority of the errors reflected inadequate decoding (e.g., correct first letter only) rather than poor short-term memory (phonological or semantic confusion). Guthrie and Tyler concluded that deficiency in reading comprehension was at least partly attributable to a failure to identify completely a sufficient proportion of words during the course of reading. It should be noted that such a failure presumably involved a strategy deficiency, not a lack of basic ability, since the poor (older) readers were equated with the good readers on reading comprehension. It may be that poor monitoring of comprehension level was responsible to some extent for the poor reader's performance.

In terms of oral reading, good–poor reader comparisons also have yielded evidence of differential use of sentence cues. Among first graders, Weber (1970a,b) obtained a differential pattern of error correction. The better readers corrected 85% of the errors which made the sentence ungrammatical but only 27% of the grammatically acceptable errors. The poorer readers, on the other hand, corrected the two types of errors at an approximately equal rate (42 vs 32%). An analysis of juncture, pitch, and stress variables for the oral reading behavior of 7-year-old children by Clay and Imlach (1971) yielded the information that only the top quarter of the children were processing cues at the intersentence and phrase levels. Among fifth graders, Steiner, Wiener, and Cromer (1971) observed a striking contrast between good and poor readers (matched on IQ, age, and sex) on a task in which the children were required to read a story aloud as they cranked a machine on which were presented the words from a passage one at a time. The large majority of good readers grouped their words into meaningful syntactic units even when reading the isolated words. They imposed grammatical organization either by anticipating subsequent words or by remaining silent until a phrase had been identified. The poor readers' performance contrasted strongly in that they appeared to be responding to these words as unrelated items in a list, in a manner quite similar to most of the first graders in the Clay and Imlach study.

Isakson and Miller (1976) asked two groups of fourth-grade children (equivalent on word recognition skills but differing on reading comprehension) to read aloud sentences, some of which had verbs which violated syntactic and/or semantic constraints. Readers attending to sentence structure and meaning would be expected to experience difficulty with sentences containing inappropriate verbs. On the other hand, individuals reading text word by word would be expected to be insensitive to the acceptability of the sentence verb. Indeed, the good comprehenders predictably exhibited an increasing number of errors across semantic and syntactic/semantic violations, while the poor comprehenders were not disrupted in their oral reading by the substitution of inappropriate words within sentences. Following up this finding of differential attention to sentence cues, Isakson and Miller (1978) had good and poor compre- henders from each grade between second and sixth read aloud sentences appropriate to their grade level. Even though the groups had been matched on recognition of words in isolation, the good comprehenders at each grade level made significantly fewer errors in the sentence task than the corresponding group of poor readers. For the good compre- henders, it seems clear that on-line comprehension of the sentence being read facilitated word identification.

In a thorough investigation of eye movements during oral and silent reading conducted over half a century ago, Buswell (cited by Golinkoff, 1976) compared good and poor readers from second grade through college in terms of eye–voice span, i.e., the number of words or letter spaces that separate the point focused by the eye from the word being pro- nounced in oral reading. Among his findings were the fact that eye–voice span increases with reading ability (within and across grades) and that the eye–voice span shrinks at sentence boundaries for good compre- henders. In terms of regressions (eye movements back to previous words or word parts), such "checking" movements occurred most frequently for poor readers within the same word whereas they were most likely to occur after a long forward movement for the good reader. The average eye–voice span across the grades for poor readers was 8.7 letter spaces, just a little more than the length of one word. The more recent research with eye–voice span described by Levin and Kaplan (1970) is consistent with Buswell's earlier work in suggesting that good readers utilize a scan- for-meaning strategy while poor readers tend to decode one word at a time.

The use of contextual cues for word recognition has been investigated in other studies with the cloze procedure (in which subjects are asked to fill in blanks within a sentence or passage). For example, fourth-grade good readers were found by Samuels, Begy, and Chen (1975) to be superior to poor readers in ability to generate the word missing from a context and also in their awareness of when their answer was incorrect. In a similar study, Cromer and Weiner (1966) found that poor readers in the fifth grade made many fewer meaningful and grammatical choices than their good reader peers. The finding that the responses were less consensual further supports the notion that poor readers' responses are less constrained by the context. On a multiple-choice cloze task (Guthrie, 1973), 10-year-old poor readers displayed less sentence comprehension and less use of syntactic cues during silent reading than both a same-age normal group and a younger normal group matched on reading level. Neville and Pugh (1976–77) demonstrated differential utilization of contextual information by showing that fifth-grade good readers, but not poor readers, produced fewer appropriate cloze responses when the amount of context available during responding was reduced.

Examining both oral reading and cloze task performance, Willows and Ryan (1981) have assessed the extent to which syntactic and semantic information guides the reading performance of skilled and less-skilled readers in the fourth, fifth, and sixth grades. Since the emphasis was upon qualitative rather than quantitative differences in skilled and less-skilled readers' errors, all reading passages were selected from first- and second-grade books. The two tasks (reading of geometrically transformed text and cloze performance) were selected in order to reduce availability of graphemic information and to encourage reliance on textual cues. Both the skilled and less skilled readers made considerable use of contextual information in the two tasks. However, the skilled readers made proportionally greater use of both syntactic and semantic information, even when only the prior context was considered. Furthermore, no change occurred across grade levels, indicating a stable difference between the two types of readers in their sensitivity to contextual cues.

In a related investigation, the sentence processing skills of equally intelligent good and poor readers in the first grade were compared (Ryan & Ledger, 1979). Similar to the intermediate grade study, poor readers displayed relatively less effective utilization of sentence cues in the quality of oral reading errors as well as in a cloze (oral) task. Nonsignificant advantages for the good readers also appeared on the three other nonreading measures of syntactic skill. One of these oral indices, corrections of ungrammatical sentences, related strongly for good readers with almost all measures of intelligence, syntactic skill, and reading performance. In the light of stable good–poor reader differences in sentence processing skills across the intermediate grades (Willows & Ryan, 1981) and early group differences in the application of sentence skills in nonreading contexts (Ryan & Ledger, 1979; Vogel, 1974, 1975), the longitudinal examination of children's utilization of sentence cues in listening and reading tasks from kindergarten through the intermediate grades would seem highly advisable.

As discussed by Willows and Ryan (1981), it is critical that a fair comparison of comprehension skills among good and poor readers control for probable differences in decoding ability. This control can be accomplished by using simple texts (e.g., Willows & Ryan), by matching groups on decoding skills (e.g., Guthrie, 1973; Isakson & Miller, 1976, 1978), or by using the auditory modality (e.g., Vogel, 1974, 1975). The following paragraph deals with another alternative, the use of pictograph or logograph sequences.

In 1970, Denner employed a pseudoreading task with logographs (abstract symbols each of which represents a word) to assess syntactic competence independently of decoding in prereaders as well as good and poor readers. Four groups of children were included: first-grade average readers, first-grade problem readers, fifth-grade problem readers, and Head Start preschoolers. All the children were able to learn the logographs with ease, but the problem readers and preschoolers were less likely to integrate a meaningful sequence of logographs. For example, having learned individual actions for logographs such as *jump, over,* and *box,* the younger children and poor readers responded less often with one synthesized action to the logograph sequence for *jump over box.* The fifth-grade problem readers were significantly poorer in synthesizing the sequence spontaneously than the average first-grade readers, yet significantly better than the younger poor readers and the preschoolers. Given that the instructions for enacting the logograph sequence were deliberately vague to allow for spontaneous decisions, it is possible that many children were actually synthesizing the sequence in their minds but responded with separate enactions because of what they thought was expected of them. Keeton (1977) investigated this possibility by requesting subsequent oral recall of each particular logograph sequence from her first-grade subjects. In contrast to integrators (who demonstrated each sequence with a single enaction), the nonintegrators tended to recall only the number of words equal to their digit span capacity and did not retain much of the syntactic/semantic structure of the sequences. Thus, it would seem that the enactions provide a reasonable cue as to the manner in which the sequence has been encoded. Denner's study suggests that the logograph enaction technique can provide a sensitive, nonreading measure of sentence processing style.

Wong (1978) examined the ability to infer spontaneously the implied consequences of individual sentences among second- and sixth-grade good and learning-disabled readers. In this task (developed by Paris, Lindauer, & Cox, 1977), recall of each sentence in a list was prompted by a retrieval cue derived from explicit words in the original sentence or from information implied by it. Good and poor readers performed equally well under the explicit condition, but the implied cues served much more effectively as memory aids for the good readers. Poor readers showed significantly better recall with the implicit cues after being instructed to elaborate on each sentence during learning. These findings support the interpretation that poor readers tend to be inactive learners who can benefit substantially from prompts to engage in more active learning behaviors.

Several successful training projects suggest methods by which active utilization of contextual cues among poor readers can be enhanced. By emphasizing meaning relationships between key structural elements within and between sentences, Ruddell's (1976) program led to enhanced sentence and paragraph meaning comprehension among first- and second-grade children. Comprehension also has been facilitated by practice with cloze exercises (Kennedy & Weener, 1973; Samuels, Dahl, & Archwamety, 1974), and with a sentence anagram task requiring children to construct a sentence by rearranging a randomly ordered set of words (Weaver, 1979).

We have considered a variety of studies illustrating the poor reader's tendency to process words occurring in sentences more as separate words than as parts of meaningful sentences. In Section III,B we will examine the poor reader's relative performance on reading comprehension tasks.

B. Comprehension of Printed Passages

With comprehension level as dependent variable, Oakan, Wiener, and Cromer (1971) manipulated the conditions under which good and poor readers from the fifth grade processed information. For poor readers, reading comprehension was assessed normally (called by the researchers "poor visual input") and also after recognition training on the words included in the passage ("good visual input"). For good readers, on the other hand, reading comprehension assessed normally was called "good visual input" while the "poor visual input" condition consisted of written transcripts of a poor reader's rendition of the original passage. Both groups (equated on intelligence) were also tested for comprehension after listening to a good reader's rendition of a passage and to a poor reader's rendition. Although the authors' inclusion of all these conditions in a factorial analysis of variance seems inappropriate, comparisons of means yield three important findings: (1) the poor readers did not suffer from a general comprehension deficit as both groups performed equally well with the good auditory input; (2) poor readers' comprehension of the visual input did not benefit from word identification training and was still only equivalent to their comprehension of poor auditory input; (3) for the good readers, comprehension of the ordinary visual input was far superior to listening comprehension or to comprehension of the poor visual input. These results support the authors' argument that the comprehension difficulties of poor readers cannot be due solely to identification problems but may be largely attributable to the manner in which input is organized. The good readers impose organization whereas poor readers seem to require that organization be provided to them. Underlining this conclusion are investigations by Rickards and Hatcher (1978) and by Levin (1973). In the former, poor comprehenders' recall of subordinate material was elevated to the level of good comprehenders by interspersing meaningful learning questions throughout the text. The questions apparently served as semantic cues reminding the poor readers to relate new details to the main ideas of the passage. In the latter study, poor comprehenders instructed to employ a visual imagery organizational strategy exhibited improved performance on subsequent comprehension questions.

Using prose recall as a measure of comprehension, Smiley, Oakley, Worthen, Campione, and Brown (1977) compared listening and reading performance of good and poor seventh-grade readers. Using a procedure adapted from Johnson (1970), Brown and Smiley (1977) had divided two stories into idea units and gathered adult norms concerning the relative importance of each unit to the theme of the entire story. Under both listening and reading conditions with these stories, good readers recalled more than poor readers and the likelihood of their remembering a particular unit was more clearly related to that unit's structural importance. The poor seventh-grade readers performed similarly to normal first graders on the listening task in terms of level of recall as well as pattern of sensitivity to the relative importance of the ideas, and their performance was substantially less mature than that of a group of normal third graders. Since Brown and Smiley (1977) had found in an earlier study that third graders' ratings of structural importance were much less in agreement with adult ratings than those of seventh graders, it would seem reasonable to expect that the poor readers in seventh grade have even less of a notion of the relative importance of phrase units within a passage. Like a number of previously mentioned studies, this research clearly indicates that poor reading comprehension is a characteristic which can override age and grade across the span of elementary grades. Furthermore, the deficit for these seventh grade youngsters appears to be a general comprehension deficit, in contrast to other studies (e.g., Oakan et al., 1971) where the deficit is specific to reading. It might well be that reading and listening comprehension may come with increasing age to involve more and more the same processes. Or, it might be that a specific reading deficit is observed primarily when the groups are equated for intelligence.

The failure of poor readers in the Smiley et al. study to identify and respond to the relative importance of information suggests a metacognitive problem which probably contributes to comprehension difficulties and other studying problems. The topic of metacognition and reading is addressed briefly in the following section.

C. Metacognition and Strategy Flexibility

In her review, Golinkoff (1976) suggested that the better comprehension and more flexible strategy deployment exhibited by good readers might be due to an awareness of what good reading comprehension is and when it has occurred. Schallert, Kleiman, and Rubin (1977) have argued that efficient use of the sampling options available in reading (e.g., setting own pace, rereading when necessary, previewing material to organize further readings) requires that readers constantly monitor their own comprehension and evaluate what they are reading. Evidence is accruing that these processes of monitoring and evaluating are very difficult for youngsters at the age of initial reading instruction (Flavell, 1977). It has been demonstrated that younger children have difficulty assessing the communicative adequacy of messages and that they report having understood messages with obvious ambiguities or missing bits of information. Observing that young children were unaware of blatant deficiencies in game directions until instructed to carry them out, Markman (1977) has concluded that young children do not spontaneously engage in much active, constructive processing while listening to directions. The lack of differential correction of ungrammatical errors (Weber, 1970a,b) and the insensitivity of prose recall to the relative importance of ideas (Smiley *et al.*, 1977) indicate that poor readers may indeed lag behind their successful peers in the spontaneous monitoring and evaluating required for good comprehension.

With respect to flexible reactions to different purposes for reading, good and poor readers appear to differ substantially. Anderson (1937, cited by Golinkoff, 1976) observed that only the good readers among a group of college students made appropriate, consistent modifications in eye movement patterns in response to instructions to read for gist, for moderate knowledge, or for detailed understanding even though the eye movements of both groups were influenced similarly by variations in text difficulty. A recent ingenious adaptation of the cloze procedure (DiVesta, Hayward, & Orlando, 1979) yielded evidence that poor readers in sixth, seventh, and eighth grades have not fully learned to control reading for comprehension. Two comparable versions of a cloze task were prepared by placing the key paragraph (with information critical to completion of the blanks) either before or after the cloze paragraph. The greater the overall comprehension level of the readers the smaller the gap between accuracy based on previous vs subsequent context. The poor readers suffered relatively more than good readers from the requirement to monitor their comprehension and to search the subsequent text for needed information.

A number of issues related to cognitive and metacognitive aspects of reading have been addressed by Forrest and Waller (1979). Good, average, and poor readers in third and sixth grades read passages under four instructional conditions (read for fun, to make up a title, to skim, and to study). Analyses of the comprehension scores indicated that the tendency to adjust one's reading strategy to fit the purpose does vary across reading and grade levels. Third-grade good readers, but not poor readers, showed a comprehension decrease for skim instructions. Only the sixth-grade good readers exhibited higher retention in both study and title conditions than in the skim condition.

As a measure of metacognition, the children were asked to rate their confidence for each comprehension item. Prediction accuracy improved across grade and reading level. It may be that poor monitoring of comprehension in young/poor readers leads to a lack of awareness that a different reading strategy is appropriate. Responses to a lengthy interview revealed little knowledge on the part of the younger/poorer readers regarding how to monitor their own comprehension. The older/better readers reported that they would prepare for a test by rereading and self-testing while the less sophisticated readers would be ready for the test after the first reading. Whereas the latter group would need to await the teacher's feedback about test performance, the former group could identify cues to the degree of their success on the test such as question difficulty, time spent answering questions, and the number of certain answers.

Further research on metacognition and reading would definitely help to clarify the causes underlying good–poor reader differences. Awareness of the automatic and strategic processes of reading (cf. Myers & Paris, 1978) can be expected to be less advanced among poor readers. Also, remediation of poor reading may necessitate remediation in the monitoring of ongoing comprehension and in the appropriate strategic adjustments to comprehension failures.

D. Summary—Good–Poor Reader Differences

A substantial body of evidence exists that poor readers fail to take maximum advantage of grammatical and contextual meaning cues in their reading. Furthermore, comprehension and recall studies seem to indicate that poor readers fail to impose organization upon a text and that they are less sensitive to the relative importance of information units within a passage. Not only does comprehension suffer, but also word identification within context cannot benefit from prediction, the prior elimination of unlikely alternatives. According to Smith (1975), older children with low reading ability tend to read as if they neither expect nor care that the material might make sense, but seem determined to get all the words right. He also claims that identification suffers as a problem reader generates anxiety all of which leads to a reluctance to predict. Thus, the poor reader tends to engage in laborious word-for-word reading, and his difficulty becomes a self-fulfilling prophecy.

The few published projects in which poor readers have been taught to predict, to test hypotheses, or to image sentence meaning offer much promise for remediation and suggest that deficiencies are at the level of strategy, not of basic capacity. Additional research on the relation between poor readers' disinclination to use strategies and possible metacognitive deficiencies would be invaluable. Along these lines, Resnick and Beck (1976) have recommended that reading instruction seek to establish a metacognitive system whereby children would be able to monitor and organize their own comprehension processes.

Even though some evidence regarding strategy deficiencies among poor readers is available, improved methodological procedures could yield more definitive results concerning the nature and extent of these. Several procedural recommendations are discussed in the next section.

IV. METHODOLOGICAL SUGGESTIONS FOR IMPROVED DIAGNOSIS OF STRATEGY DEFICIENCIES IN POOR READERS

On the basis of the foregoing review of good–poor reader comparisons, the claim (cf. Golinkoff, 1976; Meichenbaum, 1976) that poor comprehenders suffer from strategy deficiencies seems reasonably well supported. However, investigations to date have tended to focus on demonstrations of performance differences, rather than fine-grained process analyses. Before any form of remediation can be prescribed for poor readers, detailed analyses of the target strategies (processing activities engaged in by successful readers) and of the inappropriate activities engaged in by the unsuccessful readers are required.

A. Cognitive Functional Analysis

Given the great variation in types of poor readers as well as the lack of process information typically contained in group-comparison studies,

Meichenbaum (1976) recommends the implementation of in-depth studies with individual poor readers as a fruitful avenue for future research, and he carefully outlines how one would proceed using a cognitive–functional approach. The goal is to ascertain for an individual subject the nature of his cognitive strategies and the manner in which they either contribute to or interfere with adequate performance. For any given task, the researcher develops a preliminary characterization of required strategies by logically analyzing task demands and by observing and/or interviewing others doing the task. However, the sequence of psychological processes involved for a given individual can be fully appreciated only after the task demands have been systematically manipulated. The presence or absence of a particular cognitive strategy can be inferred from changes in performance associated with specific task modifications. For an analysis of reading strategies, alterations in the following aspects of the task might be included; instructions, degree of tutorial assistance, difficulty of material (in terms of vocabulary, syntax, imposed organization), modality (listening vs reading), required response (e.g., recognition vs recall), time constraints, and task setting (e.g., at school vs at home; with parent, teacher, or stranger). Such systematic probing of both the child's capabilities and his deficits leads to a detailed diagnosis of processing problems. In addition, individualized remediation techniques naturally follow from the diagnostic testing.

This in-depth analysis of individual poor readers' abilities poses some difficulties. First, although group norms may be available for the original tasks employed, such norms on all of the modified tasks cannot be feasibly obtained. Thus, in many cases, comparisons of a subject's performance on a simplified version of a given task can be made only with average readers' performance on the unmodified task. Second, the heterogeneity of poor readers and the individualization of procedures may preclude any valuable generalizations. It appears, then, that this probing analysis of strategies and capabilities will contribute best to our general knowledge of poor readers when conducted with several poor readers at a time in conjunction with group studies utilizing similar tasks with good and poor readers. In support of this proposal is one of the major conclusions made by Valtin (1978) after a critique of current and past research on dyslexia, namely, that an exploratory approach based on individual cases ought to be employed to supplement the traditional experimental group research.

B. Separate Measurement of Strategies

For group studies where individually tailored diagnostic sessions are not appropriate, how can the investigator penetrate the surface of performance differences to characterize the differential processing activities of achieving and nonachieving readers? For memory research, Belmont and Butterfield (1977) insist that separate simultaneous measures of strategy usage should be incorporated into all experiments to complement the behavioral measures. Within the memory literature, several such strategy indicators have been employed, such as lip movements, evidencing rehearsal during a rote memory task (Flavell, Beach, & Chinsky, 1966), timing patterns of self-administered stimulus sequences as evidence of particular types of rehearsal strategies (Belmont & Butterfield, 1977; Borkowski, Cavanaugh, & Reichhart, 1978), and clustering measures of free recall as indices of subjective organization (Moely, 1977). Although the emphasis among reading researchers has been on inferring strategy differences from group behavioral differences associated with various task modifications, some more direct measures of reading processes have been employed: photographic records of eye movements; reading aloud fixation times (cf. Mackworth, 1977); analyses of oral reading intonation, errors, and corrections; assessment of eye–voice span; and degrees of subvocalization as a function of difficulty of materials and instructions (cf. Hardyck & Petrinovich, 1970). However, rarely are these strategy measures obtained along with an overall performance measure in the manner recommended by Belmont and Butterfield.

For example, the previously discussed research by Oakan et al. (1971) would have been substantially more enlightening about text organizational strategies if this task modification study had included more direct processing measurements, such as eye movement records. In related research, Steiner et al. noted anecdotally that the good readers displayed drastically different strategies from the poor readers in a word-by-word condition where subjects paced themselves by turning a crank controlling the presentation of words. If the self-pacing had been timed, the oral reading tape-recorded, and comprehension scores obtained, this interesting remark could have been transformed into extremely useful statistical evidence regarding the extent to which good and poor readers differ in reading strategies and the manner in which particular strategies contribute to comprehension. In a computerized experiment, one could also have subjects control the presentation of words on a screen by pressing a button. This procedure would allow for smoother and faster presentation of sequences than the hand crank and would offer the advantage of automatic time measurements. In fact, subjects could be offered choices such as presentation by word, phrase, four-word unit, or sentence by the computer and comprehension compared under conditions where presentation format and timing are either subject-controlled or experimenter-controlled.

The research on adult prose learning (Ausubel, 1963; Rothkopf, 1971) ought to have natural links to strategy analyses of successful and unsuccessful reading in that the focus has been on "mathemagenic" activities (behaviors giving birth to learning). However, the prose learning literature depends almost exclusively upon inferences about these mathemagenic activities from retention differences associated with manipulations of the acquisition situation (e.g., special instructions, the types and placement of questions). In fact, as Faw and Waller (1976) have argued, many of the findings of enhanced learning could be accounted for in terms of increased time on task, rather than qualitatively different processing activities. Separate measures of the type and intensity of processing would greatly enhance the detail and scope of generalizations possible in prose learning studies. Furthermore, process measures (e.g., time on sections, eye movement records, and underlining data) would allow for individual difference analyses within experimental conditions. If some learners modify their processing activities in response to shifts in task instructions or questions and others do not, comparisons of mean retention levels can obscure possibly large learning effects for those who do implement a different strategy. It would seem, then, that the sensitivity of good and poor readers to the kinds of task modifications employed within the prose learning paradigm should be investigated, but with an emphasis upon individual difference analyses derived from separate indices of processing activity. A major step in this direction is the recent article by Doctorow, Wittrock, and Marks (1978), which includes an analysis of differences between better and poorer readers in overall performance as well as a sentence-generation measure of processing.

In studies of selective attention in reading (e.g., Forrest & Barron, 1977; Pelham & Ross, 1977), memory data for intentional vs incidental information would be more clearly interpretable if the relative amount of time spent reading the two types of information were assessed via eye movement records or self-presentation timing patterns. Selective attention research as well as investigations of children's awareness of relative importance of idea units to a passage (e.g., Brown & Smiley, 1977; Smiley et al., 1977) might include time and instructions for subjects to underline or to take notes on their reading material. These realistic natural additions to the usual "read-and-remember" instructions would then yield valuable data concerning what the subject thought was important while he was reading. For example, the spontaneous and instructed use of underlining and note taking were examined by Brown and Smiley (1978) in a developmental investigation of prose recall. Compared with children who only used a strategy under instructions, spontaneous strategy users showed greater sensitivity to the relative importance of idea units in the actual underlining and notes as well as in subsequent recall. Further examination would be required to determine whether a subgroup could be identified of nonspontaneous strategy users who possessed the required knowledge of differential importance of ideas but lacked experience with the appropriate application of this knowledge for underlining or notes. Extrapolating these findings to poor readers, one might expect that instructions to underline or take notes while studying a passage would be most effective after specific training on the identification of the main ideas in a text.

Whereas most reading studies report overall performance data without process measures, some analysis of reading processes lack necessary performance indicators. For example, the important eye movement studies conducted by Buswell (1920, cited by Golinkoff, 1976) would clearly have been much more revealing about appropriate and inappropriate strategies if comprehension scores of the passages read had been available to complement the eye movement data. In particular, an apparently sophisticated processing strategy (e.g., fewer regressions of the eyes or faster silent reading) can be identified as such only if the goal behavior (e.g., reading comprehension) is successful. For example, Mackworth (1977) found that the poorest readers apparently read faster silently than orally, but eye fixation data revealed they had not read the whole passage.

The past research (again reported earlier) concerning the integration of logograph sequences also suffers from an inadequate link between process measures and goal behavior. Enactions of logograph sequences (Denner, 1970; Keeton, 1977) have been interpreted as a measure of comprehension strategy to the extent that an integrated action derives from an understanding of the sequence as a meaningful sentence and correspondingly, a word-by-word enaction derives from viewing the sequence as a list of words. However, since these studies have not specified the goal for the children (e.g., comprehension or recall), the distinction between integrators and nonintegrators may be more reflective of cognitive styles than of strategies (i.e., deliberate goal-oriented activities).

Applying the advice to combine strategy measurement with assessments of target behaviors, we have adapted the original logograph enaction task and developed a Pictograph Sequence Memory Task (Ledger & Ryan, 1981; Ryan & Ledger, 1979). Initially, children are taught names and enactions for each of approximately 40 easily identifiable pictographs. Then they are given a series of pictograph sequence memory trials in which they first "read" a sequence of pictograph cards (e.g., "Put red block into large green truck") and recall the sequence after a 10-second delay. They are instructed to do anything they want during the delay to help them remember the pictographs. Toys necessary for enaction of the sequences are available to the child. In this case, any enactions observed during task performance can be interpreted as strategic in that the activity involves some depth of processing, and also the enactions can be categorized as integrative (sentence meaning) or nonintegrative (word-for-word meaning). In contrast to the previous logograph tasks, enaction here is not the required target behavior but rather an optional goal-directed, memory enhancing activity. Children who use integrated enactions with the toys do in fact recall much more of the sequence than children who do not. Furthermore, with practice on the task, some children, who originally appeared to do nothing to help themselves remember, have been observed to evolve the ideal integrated enaction strategy from more primitive enactions. The initial attempt to prepare actively for future retrieval involved using the toys as word markers. For example, "red block" might be represented by a *red* truck and a green *block*. The obvious disadvantage of this procedure (i.e., the ambiguity among "red block," "green truck," and "block truck") seems to have led some of these children to the integrated strategy. With regard to whether the sequence has been processed as a list of pictograph names or as a meaningful sequence, syntactic and semantic analyses of the recalled sequence provide additional information. Another strategy indicator, which has not been employed as yet, would be based on intonation analyses (cf. Clay & Imlach, 1971) of the original "reading" of the pictograph sequence and of its subsequent recall. With a procedure such as the Pictograph Sequence Memory Task, the information processing strategies of the successful recallers can be quite carefully distinguished from those of the unsuccessful recallers.

In situations where unobtrusive strategy measures cannot be included, attempts should be made to assess the same or similar processes within the good and poor readers in a separate, related task. Verbal report elicited from children about their use of strategies during a task is preferable to no information at all, but the relationship between strategy use and verbalization of strategies is not sufficiently direct to allow strong inferences from one to the other (Cavanaugh & Borkowski, 1979). Although ability to verbalize appropriate strategies usually lags behind ability to use them, there are also occasions when rules can be verbalized but are not applied. In reading, phonics rules are perhaps the prime example of rules of thumb that some children can readily repeat without being able to apply.

As a consequence of adopting the general principle of separate strategy measurement, reading researchers would have to become creative and go beyond traditional techniques. In seeking new strategy indicators, one must keep in mind the necessity that strategy assessment not interfere with the target behavior being investigated. For example, eye movement research has been criticized because the rigid positioning of the head and elaborate apparatus typically required for some photographic systems may seriously affect readers' strategies and flexibility (Wanat, 1976). Technological advances which allow for the monitoring of eye movements without artificial constraints on the reader provide definite advantages (Hawley, Stern, & Chen 1974; Mackworth, 1977; Pugh, 1978).

Two major recommendations, then, are that reading researchers attempt to include separate strategy measurements as much as possible in the group comparison studies and also that strategies not be assessed outside the context of specific goals, whose level of attainment is also evaluated. Linking the strategy indices to performance measures allows for individual difference analyses within the groups of good and poor readers. For any given task, there may be several qualitatively different successful strategies and/or several distinct unsuccessful strategies. In particular, an important achievement which could result from such research programs would be the subcategorization of poor readers according to strategies employed as well as the adequacy, modifiability, and flexibility of their strategy use.

C. Distinguishing between Competence and Strategy

If good readers are found to perform a given task better than poor readers, a difference in strategy usage is only one of the possible reasons. Separate strategy measures can substantiate less strategy usage for the poor readers, but such data cannot distinguish between an easily modifiable disinclination to use the strategy and competence limitations that resist modification. Comparison of spontaneous performance in uninstructed conditions with performance under instructions to use the target strategy provided an excellent opportunity for isolating strategy deficiencies. If good and poor readers do not differ under strategy instructions, then the poor readers' weaker performance without instructions may be explained in terms of less spontaneous strategy usage. Precisely such a pattern of results for memorization processes among good and poor readers has been observed by Torgesen (1977). If group differences persist, but are diminished under instructions, then spontaneous strategy use is implicated but cannot be taken as the complete explanation for the original poor reader disadvantage. Further work would be necessary to determine whether the appropriate strategy was sufficiently well instructed; whether good readers might be more proficient in use of the strategy; whether the task has been analyzed appropriately; or whether the two groups differ in some aspect of basic competence. If group differences are unchanged across instructed and uninstructed conditions, no firm evidence for a strategy deficiency is available.

D. Methodological Summary

In order to clarify the sources of poor readers' difficulties, three methodological suggestions for future research have been presented: cognitive functional analysis, especially detailed task analysis; separate strategy measures to complement performance data; and experimental designs which compare good and poor readers under conditions with and without strategy instructions. Incorporation of these recommended procedures into good–poor readers studies would lead to more precise identification of strategy deficits exhibited by poor readers.

V. REMEDIATION OF POOR READING COMPREHENSION

In previous sections, we have reviewed evidence that poor comprehenders are less strategic than good comprehenders and discussed methodological innovations which might lead to more specific characterizations of poor readers' strategies and how they contrast with those of good readers. This section is intended to outline approaches for training reading comprehension skills and for enhancing generalization of trained skills.

A. Instructional Approach

The instructional approach being developed by memory researchers (cf. Belmont & Butterfield, 1977; Borkowski & Cavanaugh, 1979; Campione & Brown, 1979) has much to contribute to the area of reading research. With relatively brief training sequences (from one to three sessions in length), young and mentally retarded children have been successfully taught in a variety of situations to enhance their memory performance by implementing a target strategy. Examples of strategies taught effectively include rehearsing a serial list while awaiting a recall test (Kennedy & Miller, 1976); cumulative rehearsal while pacing oneself through a self-presentation list of items to be recalled (Belmont & Butterfield, 1977); cumulative rehearsal within clusters while pacing oneself through a list of clusterable items (Cavanaugh & Borkowski, 1979); elaboration of possible relations between each stimulus and response for paired-associate learning (cf. Borkowski & Cavanaugh, 1979); studying a list of items until ready for a test of recall (Campione & Brown, 1977; Brown, Campione, & Barclay, 1979).

From a theoretical point of view, training in the use of strategies tests our understanding of the presumed control processes involved in successful execution of a task and also allows one to distinguish between remediable strategy deficiencies and possible nonremediable capacity deficits. From a practical point of view, the success of the recent memory training studies leads to optimism concerning possible contributions for the teaching of reading strategies.

In their description of the instructional approach, Belmont and Butterfield (1977) emphasize three major points—task analysis, direct strategy measurement, and high standards of evaluation. As discussed earlier, systematic analyses of task and subject attributes are necessary for diagnosis of deficiencies which need remediating. For successful training, task analyses are also required for the maintenance and transfer tasks. Just as strategy measurement is critically important for identification of strategy problems, separate assessment of strategy utilization is necessary for valid inferences about processing changes induced by the training. Finally, particular attention should be given to standards of evaluation, or, in other words, the goals of the training project. Belmont and Butterfield recommend setting very high goals in terms of size of instructional effect as well as its durability and transfer to other similar situations. For example, the goal attained by them in several studies has been recall performance by trained retarded adolescents equivalent to the level of normal adults. High evaluation standards among proponents of the instructional approach are also exemplified by the two-way tactic successfully employed in two studies (Belmont & Butterfield, 1971; Brown, Campione, Bray, & Wilcox, 1973). The successful group is prevented from engaging in the strategy presumed to be responsible for the original performance difference while the unsuccessful group is induced to adopt that strategy. If the relative levels of performance of the two groups switches completely, then the trained strategy has definitely been identified as the source of the original difference. In keeping with the high standards of evaluation, an important characteristic of the instructional approach is the interpretation of training failures—these failures are assumed to be due to "instructional deficits" rather than "learner deficits."

In order for instructional training to be successful in terms of maintenance as well as generalization, Borkowski and Cavanaugh (1979) recommend that training be conducted in depth (involving active semantic processing); that it be prolonged (at least over several days); that feedback be included regarding purpose and value of strategies acquired; and that generalization tasks conducive to use of the trained strategy be selected.

A study recently completed in our laboratory (Ledger & Ryan, 1981) represents a first effort to apply the principles of the instructional approach to the problem of improving reading comprehension. For this project, the Pictograph Sequence Memory Task described earlier was employed. Sixty prereading kindergarten children were divided into three groups equated for recall performance on an initial memory test with eight pictograph sequences: Training (N = 24), Practice Control (N = 24), and No-practice Control (N = 12). Children in the training group were instructed and guided in the use of a semantic integration enaction strategy during three sessions held on separate days. The trained strategy involved reading the pictograph sequence as a sentence, inserting *the*'s where appropriate, and enacting the sentence meaning with the available toys. The major hypothesis was that children given sufficient training in the integration of pictograph sentences, provided with awareness of the usefulness of the integration strategy, and given the opportunity for active manipulation of stimulus materials would be better able to recall the content of pictograph sentences than control groups given (a) either practice with pictograph sentence recall or (b) only the pretest and later generalization and maintenance tests. Separate measurement of strategy involved observation and analysis of enactions carried out with toys of sentences such as "Put big red car on blue block," as well as counts of *the*'s inserted into the recalled sequences. Recall was scored in terms of the number of words in the appropriate order and number of correct sequences.

The training of semantic integration was successful in that the trained group performed better (for recall scores and strategy indicators) than either control group on two Pictograph Sentence Memory Tasks, the posttest administered 1 day after training and the maintenance test administered approximately 2 weeks after training. In fact, the training group's recall scores on the maintenance test were twice as great as for the practice control group and almost four times as great as the group's pretraining scores. Further evidence that enactions were responsible for the enhanced recall is provided by the significant correlations obtained within the training group between enactions and recall scores. Thus, within the group receiving instruction, the children improving most in their level of recall were those who learned to use enactions best. In addition, the trained children performed significantly better than practice control children on an oral sentence integration generalization test, which required delayed recall of long, integratable sequences of words presented without intonation at the rate of one word per 2 seconds. For this task, the content words as well as the corresponding toys available for enactions were different from the pictograph tests.

The Pictograph Sequence Memory Task allows for testing and teaching sentence comprehension skills outside the context of reading. With kindergarteners who have not yet learned to read, the task might prove to be quite useful in predicting which children will become word callers, and a child's response to brief semantic integration training might reveal how easily his tendency to process pictograph sequences (and presumably printed sentences) in a word-by-word fashion could be remediated. One could also speculate that the active, enactive aspects of our semantic integration strategy may be important components for initial reading comprehension instruction especially for children with the predisposition to deal with text passively. For poor readers, the Pictograph Sequence Memory Task would provide an opportunity to assess sentence comprehension strategies in a pseudoreading situation which eliminates word recognition problems and reduces, by its novelty, motivational difficulties. This kind of task also holds substantial promise as a context for teaching the (typically passive) poor reader some *active* semantic integration, comprehension strategies. One key advantage of the Pictograph Sequence Memory Task is that separate measurements of strategy use enable the researcher or teacher to specify the reason for poor performance in many cases (e.g., failure to be active, inconsistent use of the strategy, use of a partial form of the strategy, or failure to benefit from use of the strategy).

B. Self-Instructional Training

Self-instructional training, as developed within the area of cognitive behavior modification, is another type of training procedure which promises to be very useful in the training of reading strategies and skills. Meichenbaum and Asarnow (1978) have reviewed the literature concerning the self-instructional training of children in self-control (the ability to think before acting) and in various academic skills. These individually tailored *think-aloud* training programs are based on a cognitive–functional analysis of children's task performance to identify the psychological processes engaged in by successful performers and those in which the subject is failing. The training sequence proceeds from modeling the experimenter's instructions, to overt rehearsal, and finally to covert rehearsal. The goal is to lead the child systematically to the point where his self-statements guide and control his successful performance on the target task. According to Meichenbaum and Asarnow (1978, pp. 6–7), the general outline for self-instructional training programs has been

> to teach a variety of performance-relevant skills: (1) problem identification and definition or self-interrogation skills ("What is it I have to do?"); (2) focusing attention and response guidance which is usually the answer to the self-inquiry ("Now, carefully stop and repeat the instructions"); (3) self-reinforcement involving standard setting and self-evaluation ("Good, I'm doing fine"); and (4) coping skills and error-correction options ("That's okay . . . Even if I make an error I can go slowly"). Such cognitive training is conducted across tasks, settings and people (trainer, teacher, parent) in order to ensure that children do not develop task-specific response sets, but instead that they develop generalized strategems.

In terms of evidence for efficacy, Meichenbaum and Asarnow conclude that self-instructional training programs tend to achieve durable instructional effects but that generalization to classroom behavior and/or classroom tasks has been very difficult to obtain. As generalization has become more clearly the goal set by researchers, recent training efforts have been increasingly successful in achieving some degree of generalization.

Self-instructional training has been applied specifically to reading in a study by Bommarito and Meichenbaum (cited by Meichenbaum & Asarnow, 1978). This training program was designed to enhance the reading comprehension of each of a group of junior high poor comprehenders (reading comprehension at least 1 year below their academic grade and below their vocabulary level). The children participated in six 45-minute individual sessions. Following Gagne (1964), the reading comprehension task was analyzed into a hierarchical set of objectives. For the training, then, each step in the hierarchy was translated into self-statements and cognitive strategies that could be modeled by the experimenter and rehearsed by the child (initially overtly and eventually covertly). The major focus of the training was critical thinking and the learning of heuristic rules to be applied to any reading matter. The self-instructional format was not regimented or rote, but rather individually tailored and responsive to each child. Thus, the child helped by analyzing his own strategies, by suggesting rules for particular exercises, and by giving feedback on how well the rules or strategies seemed to be working for him. Of particular importance is the fact that the experimenter modeled coping self-statements dealing with frustration and failure as well as problem-solving self-statements.

By the final training session, the poor reader's internal dialogue was similar to the following passage:

> Well, I've learned three big things to keep in mind before I read a story and while I read it. One is to ask myself what the main idea of the story is. What is the story

about? A second is to learn important details of the story as I go along. The order of the main events or their sequence is an especially important detail. A third is to know how the characters feel and why. So, get the main idea. Watch sequences. And learn how the characters feel and why.

While I'm reading I should pause now and then. I should think of what I'm doing. And I should listen to what I'm saying to myself. Am I saying the right things?

Remember, don't worry about mistakes. Just try again. Keep cool, calm, and relaxed. Be proud of yourself when you succeed. Have a blast! (Meichenbaum & Asarnow, 1978, pp. 15 and 16)

The self-instructional training program was successful in that the trained group was significantly different from a practice placebo group as well as an assessment control group. The average change for the self-instructionally trained group was 11.5 months on the Nelson test of reading comprehension and 13 months on the GAP test of cloze exercises. The superiority of the trained group was maintained after a 1-month interval. Clearly, such a training program would be most helpful for children with the ability to detect main ideas and sequences but with a tendency not to exercise that ability while reading.

An important aspect of self-instructional training is the analysis of apparently single acts into component behaviors or strategies and the sequenced training of each of the components. Even at the end of the self-instructional training in the above study, the poor readers were consciously attending to five components of reading comprehension (get the main idea, watch sequences, learn how the characters feel and why, monitor self-statements, cope effectively). This deautomatization process, according to Meichenbaum (1977), is critical to the elimination of bad habits and the eventual reformation of automatic good habits. Thus, the requirement to focus attention on single acts is not in contradiction with but rather a necessary prerequisite for the automaticity in reading subskills regarded by LaBerge and Samuels (1974) as critical for good comprehension.

Meichenbaum and Asarnow have also discussed why self-instructions are effective in allowing students to engage in a kind of thinking they could not, or would not, otherwise do. Verbalizations can facilitate behavior in cognitive tasks in the following ways: (1) task and stimulus array information may be organized and the subject assisted in generation of alternative solutions; (2) feedback may be more easily evaluated given verbal mediators to distinguish relevant from irrelevant dimensions; (3) memory load of a task is reduced with active rehearsal of hypotheses and plans; (4) a positive task-orientation, help in monitoring problem-solving behaviors, and ways of coping with failure and distractors are provided.

C. Integration of Self-Instructional Training with the Instructional Approach

One could consider the Instructional Approach, once taken beyond the context of memory, as a broad framework within which self-instructional training fits as a particularly promising form of training. In terms of the Borkowski and Cavanaugh training program criteria, self-instructional training is usually prolonged in that the process of teaching children to verbalize complex sets of instructions and then internalize them takes a long period of time. Also, this process gradually shifts active participation and mental involvement toward the child. The in-depth processing is ensured by the heuristic, rather than rote, nature of the instructions as well as by the interaction between experimenter and subject regarding the most suitable self-instructions. With regard to feedback, not only is information about value and purpose of the strategies a critical part of self-instructions but also included is self-reinforcement for successful behaviors and coping statements for failures and getting off the track. In terms of Belmont and Butterfield's criteria, the cognitive functional analysis required for self-instructional training is at least as sophisticated as the task analyses conducted by memory researchers. In fact, self-instructional training has tackled much more complex activities, such as reading comprehension, than the memory researchers, and consequently is better able to deal with sequence-automatization problems. With regard to separate strategy measures, *overt* self-instruction can provide a rich natural source of information about the implementation and awareness of strategies. The problems of evaluation in terms of appropriate maintenance and generalization tasks are similar for self-instructional training in memory research.

The cognitive behavior modification tradition of individualized therapy does contrast with the verbal learning tradition of standardized instructions for all subjects within a given condition. However, the Bommarito and Meichenbaum study (cited by Meichenbaum & Asarnow, 1978) as well as a serial recall project by Asarnow and Meichenbaum (1979) illustrate well how self-instructional training can be conducted and evaluated for groups of children. These two studies adhere to the valuable principle proposed by Kendall (1977) that one should avoid struggling to write universally applicable self-verbalization instructions but rather seek to incorporate the preferred self-instructional content into each child's ongoing self-talk. In the future, more detailed guidelines for modifying individual self-talk within the context of group studies need to be developed.

D. Generalization of Training

The major topic of current concern among researchers evaluating strategy training (Borkowski & Cavanaugh, 1979; Campione & Brown, 1977; Meichenbaum & Asarnow, 1978; Stokes & Baer, 1977) is generalization. Since a key characteristic of those in need of training is a resistance to generalization, it has become abundantly clear that instructional schemes will have to focus more and more on ways to facilitate transfer of training. Campione and Brown (1979) have outlined the following requirements for generalization on the part of a subject: (1) realization that some strategy is needed; (2) evaluation of a task's requirements and selection of a potentially useful routine from a pool of available strategies; (3) execution of the task with the selected strategy and monitoring of its efficiency; and (4) assimilation of feedback from internal monitoring and external sources, if available, for future decisions in similar situations. As Borkowski and Cavanaugh suggest, the generalization task should be very carefully selected so that it differs in surface appearance from the training and maintenance tasks while providing a clear opportunity for utilization of the acquired strategy, or some slightly modified version. Recommending that training should be designed with the generalization goal clearly in mind, Brown and Campione (1979) suggest the training of target processes and behaviors across multiple settings as well as inclusion within the training package of direct instructions regarding generalization.

Procedural innovations with the potential for greatly improving generalization include (1) shifting training from specific to widely applicable, basic strategies; and (2) direct training of executive functioning (selection, monitoring, and modification of strategies in task appropriate ways). Presumably, the methodology eventually developed for the first approach will involve initial training of a general strategy which then generates specific strategies in specific situations. In contrast, the second approach would necessitate training several specific strategies and then training the appropriate selection and modification of these particular strategies for various situations. In both cases, the goal is flexible learning, the ability to think for oneself.

In terms of the first approach, Brown and Campione (1979) have argued for a shift from the training of specific strategies to the direct training of more general strategies and executive skills, such as checking, planning, questioning, self-testing, and monitoring of problem-solving attempts. A powerful argument presented for this training scheme is that truly general skills can be applied across a great variety of problem situations without the fine-grained task discriminations required for appropriate generalization of specific strategies. Self-instructional training efforts have been most successful in obtaining generalization to the classroom with training of very general self-questioning skills (e.g., "What is my problem?"; "How should I solve it?"; "Am I doing OK?"). An initial success with direct training of general strategies has been reported by Brown, Campione, and Barclay (1979), who taught two groups of retarded adolescents (MA = 6 and MA = 8) a stop-test-and-study routine to prepare for a recall test on an ordered list of picture names. The task of studying until ready for a recall test requires knowledge about which are the difficult items, the ability to study difficult items differentially, and repeated self-testing to determine whether the list has been learned. The general routine of studying and self-testing was acquired, and the older trained subjects maintained their superiority a year later. Furthermore, they successfully transferred the acquired routine to a prose memory task in which the gist of a passage was to be recalled. Compared to control groups, the trained students studied longer, engaged in more observable self-checking behavior, and retained more idea units from the passage. Like more mature learners, their recall of idea units was more closely related to thematic importance than that of their untrained peers. This change in type of strategy selected for training clearly illustrates the radical change in instructional schemes that can follow from placing emphasis on generalization in design of training programs.

Attacking the problem of generalization from the other direction, some memory researchers (Belmont & Butterfield, 1977; Borkowski & Cavanaugh, 1979) have suggested training executive control directly. This approach involves training several specific strategies and then training the appropriate selection (and revision) of these for a variety of similar tasks. In a study illustrative of this method of training for generalization (Belmont & Borkowski, 1978), retarded junior high students trained on two examples of a memory technique performed better on maintenance and generalization tasks than those who had been trained on only one example. The key details of the most sophisticated form of this kind of generalization instruction have been presented by Borkowski and Cavanaugh (1979):

> First, we need to identify several strategies each of which are operative in different learning situations. Second, we need to train children on several strategies, making sure that they know when and how to apply them. Third, we need to train the instructional package so that common elements between training and generalization contexts are evident, and distractors minimal. Fourth, we need to develop child-generated search routines, probably through the use of self-instructional procedures, that encourage the child to analyze a task, scan his or her available strategic repertoire, and match the demands of the task with an appropriate strategy and retrieval

plan. Fifth, we need to instruct children in such a way that we utilize whatever skills they possess, in order to bring each child to an awareness of the advantage of executive monitoring and decision-making in solving problems. Finally, we may need to reinforce, in a very explicit way, successful executive functioning in order for it to come under the control of natural environmental contingencies, such as a child's good feelings about solving a difficult problem. (p. 54)

An alternative tactic for achieving generalization with instruction on specific strategies might be called the planned sequence approach. The training of several strategies would seem to have substantial payoff when they fit together into a sequence designed to lead the student systematically from an easily trained specific strategy to a more general, complex strategy. A gradual change in tasks toward increased similarity with the generalization testing contexts facilitates a student's decisions regarding applicability of trained strategies (Borkowski & Cavanaugh, 1979); and a sequence of instruction from concrete situations and strategies to more abstract situations and strategies would also seem to induce substantial generalization (Kendall, 1977). For example, consider the following proposal for enhancing reading comprehension of intermediate-grade poor readers. Without planning the training program around generalization as the goal, we might have chosen to employ only an adapted form of our successful training procedure for semantic integration of pictograph sequences (Ledger & Ryan, 1981) and then tested for generalization to reading comprehension. However, the recent recommendations that we train for generalization would lead to the adoption of the following training sequence: semantic integration of pictograph sequences, with enactions; semantic integration of printed sentences (composed of familiar vocabulary), with enactions; semantic integration of printed sentences, with visual imagery. Generalization to a passage with easily imaged content should be substantially facilitated by the smaller discrepancy between the final training task and the generalization task, while the impact of the training should be facilitated by the concrete and active nature of the initial task. Following Kendall's suggestion to move from concrete to abstract labeling of the strategy, the first instruction would be of the following form: "You should make the toys do what the words say. This will help you understand and remember the words"; and the final instructions: "You should imagine a picture of what each sentence says. This will help you understand and remember the sentences. It will also help you remember and put together stories that you read in school or at home." Clearly, the value of the graded sequence per se could be evaluated only if one control group received all training sessions on the imagery task and another group received the equivalent amount of training on the pictograph task.

What is meant by generalization differs rather dramatically between the memory and cognitive behavior modification researchers. Traditionally, the generalization task in a memory experiment has been quite similar to the training task whereas the generalization goals of cognitive behavior modification have gone beyond the laboratory to the classroom—the goal is observable change in classroom behavior and/or in academic tasks. In attempting to integrate the two traditions, one would profit from seeking training and generalization tasks that meet as well as possible the stringent criterion set up by the memory researchers for a good generalization task (i.e., different surface appearance but conducive to use of the trained strategy) and the requirement of cognitive behavior modifiers and teachers that improvement in the classroom be achieved. Perhaps the inclusion of tasks testing both near and far generalization (Borkowski & Cavanaugh, 1979) should become established practice.

VI. CONCLUSIONS

This article has focused on the search for remediable strategic deficiencies that might underly poor reading performance. The brief overview of good–poor reader comparisons illustrated the abundance of information regarding performance differences between unsuccessful readers and their more successful counterparts. Taken altogether, these studies also suggest strongly that poor readers generally fail to utilize word recognition and comprehension strategies as effectively. For example, poor readers exhibited less attention to sentence contexts in oral reading errors and intonation patterns, cloze procedure tasks, and silent reading comprehension. Furthermore, there are many hints of metacognitive problems among poor readers even though data are currently available only for less sensitivity to the relative importance of ideas, less adaptation to differing task goals, and less awareness of ways to study and to monitor comprehension.

In order to identify specific deficiencies, however, future research must measure strategic activities as directly as possible and link process and performance measures in interpretations of strategy use and effectiveness. Task analyses need to become more and more fine-grained and individualized to provide the base for clear specification of appropriate and inappropriate strategies being applied. Optimally, studies would compare task performance and spontaneous use of strategies in uninstructed conditions with the corresponding performance and strategy indicators for conditions in which the subject is instructed to use a particular strategy.

With regard to remediation of poor reading strategies, researchers in the developmental memory and cognitive behavior modification areas have much to offer. In addition to careful diagnosis of the strategies leading to successful and unsuccessful task performance, recommendations for instructional training include emphasis on active semantic processing; sufficient training; feedback regarding purpose and value of strategies acquired; high standards of evaluation; gradual transfer of control from experimenter to learner; and appropriate generalization tasks. Our recent research with the Pictograph Sequence Memory Task illustrates how the instructional approach can be applied to the teaching of comprehension strategies. It should be noted that much of this training literature has been focused on simple strategies with young children who tend not to be strategic at all and that the problem of diagnosing and dealing with competing strategies increases dramatically as the strategies to be trained become more complicated and the trainee more mature. For the more complex situations typical of reading, self-instructional training procedures can be especially valuable (e.g., Meichenbaum & Asarnow, 1978). The emphasis in the self-instructional training literature on deautomatization and rebuilding of complicated skills and the generalization goal of improved classroom performance are important additions to the instructional approach.

Training poor readers to use effective strategies not only provides practical benefits, but also allows for an excellent test of specific versions of the strategy deficiency hypothesis. Even with direct strategy measurement, comparisons of good and poor readers cannot unequivocally establish that failure to use a particular strategy well is the cause of the observed performance differences. Furthermore, observation of poor readers when instructed to use a given strategy is required for distinguishing between the two critical aspects of strategy strength, as defined by Baron (1978): inclination to use the strategy and proficiency in its implementation. These instructional approaches will be most helpful for the child who exhibits proficient and effective use of a strategy under instruction while failing to use the strategy spontaneously. For children using the strategy ineffectively, instruction in the specific components of the strategy and their integration would be required. Children with serious decoding problems would benefit from direct reading instruction as well as training in the selection and proficient use of specific comprehension strategies.

The increasing trend toward training for generalization is likely to yield important practical benefits in terms of the remediation of poor reading performance. As researchers focus on generalization, they are led more and more to look beyond individual specific strategies to executive functions (e.g., planning, strategy selection and revision, monitoring, and checking) and to an individual's metacognitive knowledge (awareness) about his own cognitive processing. Using the training principles of both the instructional and self-instructional approaches a sequence of strategy training steps presumably could be mapped out and implemented to take a child from a low level of reading comprehension and a well-diagnosed ineffective pattern of strategy use to a substantially improved reading comprehension level achieved through the more effective application of relevant comprehension strategies. For the effect of such instruction to be durable and generalizable, the training sequence would not only show the child how to seek sentence meaning but also would guide him in the continuous monitoring of strategy use, provide multiple opportunities to use the strategy in the original form as well as to adapt it, and convince the child of the strategy's payoff and generality.

Given that a poor reader probably initially tends to approach the reading task passively, this nonstrategic style is amplified during the first few years of schooling through decreasing expectations that reading makes sense and increasing expectations of failure. Successful strategic behavior must be based on a good understanding of the problem or goal and knowledge of the relationship between that goal and particular strategies (Paris, 1978). Whereas the skilled reader defines reading as the extraction of meaning from text, it appears that many poor readers use a working definition closer to "say all the words correctly." Furthermore, poor readers are probably less aware of the payoff of various reading strategies in word recognition, comprehension, or recall. Generalized improvement in reading performance is more probable if the training procedures are designed in light of the need for improved executive functions and increased self-awareness. In particular, poor readers would benefit from a better understanding of the need for appropriate goal definition and of the value of possible strategies.

In closing, we suggest that Ann Brown's (1980, p. 456) list of deliberate planful processing activities which give rise to reading comprehension might well serve as appropriate targets for future training studies.

(1) clarifying the purposes of reading, that is, understanding the task demands, both explicit and implicit, (2) identifying the aspects of a message that are important, (3) allocating attention so that concentration can be focused on the major content area rather than unessential detail, (4) monitoring ongoing activities to determine whether comprehension is occurring, (5) engaging in review and self-interrogation to determine whether goals are being achieved, (6) taking corrective action when

failures in comprehension are detected, and (7) recovering from disruption and distractions—and many more deliberate, planful activities which render reading an efficient information gathering activity.

REFERENCES

Asarnow, J., & Meichenbaum, D. Verbal rehearsal and serial recall: The mediational training of kindergarten children. *Child Development,* 1979, **50,** 1173–1177.

Atkinson, R. C., & Shiffrin, R. M. Human memory: A proposed system and its control processes. In K. W. Spence & J. T. Spence (Eds.), *The psychology of learning and motivation: Advances in research and theory* (Vol. 2). New York: Academic Press, 1968.

Ausubel, D. P. *The psychology of meaningful verbal learning.* New York: Grune & Stratton, 1963.

Baker, L., & Stein, N. The development of prose comprehension skills. In C. Santa & B. Hayes (Eds.), *Children's prose comprehension: Research and practice.* Newark, Delaware: International Reading Association, 1981, in press.

Baron, J. Intelligence and general strategies. In G. Underwood (Ed.), *Strategies in information processing.* New York: Academic Press, 1978. Pp. 403–450.

Belmont, J. M., & Butterfield, E. C. Learning strategies as determinants of memory deficiencies. *Cognitive Psychology,* 1971, **2,** 411–420.

Belmont, J. M., & Butterfield, E. C. The instructional approach to developmental cognitive research. In R. V. Kail, Jr. & J. Hagen (Eds.), *Perspectives on the development of memory and cognition.* Hillsdale, New Jersey: Erlbaum, 1977. Pp. 437–481.

Borkowski, J. G., & Cavanaugh, J. C. Maintenance and generalization of skills and strategies by the retarded. In N. R. Ellis (Ed.), *Handbook of mental deficiency: Psychological theory and research.* Hillsdale, New Jersey: Erlbaum, 1979.

Borkowski, J. G., Cavanaugh, J. C., & Reichhart, G. J. Maintenance of children's rehearsal strategies: Effects of amount of training and strategy form. *Journal of Experimental Child Psychology,* 1978, **26,** 288–298.

Brown, A. L. Metacognitive development and reading. In R. J. Spiro, B. Bruce, and W. F. Brewer (Eds.), *Theoretical issues in reading comprehension.* Hillsdale, New Jersey: Erlbaum, 1980.

Brown, A. L., & Campione, J. C. Permissible inferences from the outcome of training studies in cognitive development research. In W. S. Hall & M. Cole (Eds.), *Quarterly Newsletter of the Institute for Comparative Human Development,* 1978.

Brown, A. L., Campione, J. C., & Barclay, C. R. Training self-checking routines for estimating test readiness: Generalization from list learning to prose recall. *Child Development,* 1979, **50,** 501–512.

Brown, A. L., Campione, J. C., Bray, N. W., and Wilcox, B. L. Keeping track of changing variables: Effects of rehearsal training and rehearsal prevention in normal and retarded adolescents. *Journal of Experimental Psychology,* 1973, **101,** 123–131.

Brown, A. L., & Smiley, S. S. Rating the importance of structural units of prose passages: A problem of metacognitive development. *Child Development,* 1977, **48,** 1–9.

Brown, A. L., & Smiley, S. S. The development of strategies for studying texts. *Child Development,* 1978, **49,** 1076–1088.

Campione, J. C., & Brown, A. L. Memory and metamemory development in educable retarded children. In R. V. Kail, Jr. & J. W. Hagen (Eds.), *Perspectives on the development of memory and cognition.* Hillsdale, New Jersey: Erlbaum, 1977. Pp. 367–405.

Campione, J. C., & Brown, A. L. Toward a theory of intelligence: Contributions from research with retarded children. In R. J. Sternberg & D. K. Detterman (Eds.), *Human intelligence*. Norwood, New Jersey: Ablex, 1979.

Cavanaugh, J. C., & Borkowski, J. G. The metamemory-memory 'connection': Effects of strategy training and transfer. *Journal of General Psychology*, 1979, **101**, 161–174.

Clay, M. M., & Imlach, R. Juncture, pitch and stress as reading behavior variables. *Journal of Verbal Learning and Verbal Behavior*, 1971, **10**, 133–139.

Cromer, W., & Wiener, M. Idiosyncratic response patterns among good and poor readers. *Journal of Consulting Psychology*, 1966, **30**, 1–10.

Denner, B. Representational and syntactic competence of problem readers. *Child Development*, 1970, **41**, 881–882.

DiVesta, F. J., Hayward, K. G., & Orlando, V. G. Developmental trends in monitoring text for comprehension. *Child Development*, 1979, **50** (1), 97–105.

Doctorow, M., Wittrock, M. C., & Marks, C. Generative processes in reading comprehension. *Journal of Educational Psychology*, 1978, **70** (2), 109–118.

Faw, H. T., & Waller, T. G. Mathemagenic behaviours and efficiency in learning from prose materials: Review, critique, and recommendations. *Review of Educational Research*, 1976, **46**, 691–720.

Firth, I. *Components of reading disability*. Unpublished Ph.D. dissertation, University of New South Wales, Australia, 1972.

Flavell, J. M. *Cognitive development*, New York: Prentice-Hall, 1977.

Flavell, J. H., Beach, D. R., & Chinsky, J. M. Spontaneous verbal rehearsal in a memory task as a function of age. *Child Development*, 1966, **37**, 283–299.

Forrest, D. L., & Barron, R. W. *Metacognitive aspects of development of reading skill*. New Orleans: Society for Research on Child Development, 1977.

Forrest, D. L., & Waller, T. G. *Cognitive and metacognitive aspects of reading*. Paper presented at the biennial meeting of the Society for Research on Child Development, San Francisco, 1979.

Gagne, R. Problem solving. In A. Melton (Ed.), *Categories of Human Learning*. New York: Academic Press, 1964.

Golinkoff, R. A comparison of reading comprehension processes in good and poor comprehenders. *Reading Research Quarterly*, 1976, **11**, 623–659.

Guthrie, J. T. Reading comprehension and syntactic responses in good and poor readers. *Journal of Educational Psychology*, 1973, **65** (3), 294–299.

Guthrie, J. T., & Tyler, S. J. Psycholinguistic processing in reading and listening among good and poor readers. *Journal of Reading Behavior*, 1976, **8** (4), 415–426.

Hardyck, C. D., & Petrinovich, L. F. Subvocal speech and comprehension level as a function of the difficulty level of reading material. *Journal of Verbal Learning and Verbal Behavior*, 1970, **9**, 647–652.

Hawley, T. T., Stern, J. A., & Chen, S. C. Computer analysis of eye movements during reading. *Reading World*, 1974, **13**, 307–317.

Huey, E. B. *The psychology and pedagogy of reading*. Cambridge, Massachusetts: MIT Press, 1968.

Isakson, R. L., & Miller, J. W. Sensitivity to syntactic and semantic cues in good and poor comprehenders. *Journal of Educational Psychology*, 1976, **68** (6), 787–792.

Isakson, R. L., & Miller, J. W. *Comprehension and decoding skills of good and poor readers*. Paper presented at the meeting of the American Education Research Association. Toronto, March, 1978.

Johnson, R. E. Recall of prose as a function of the structural importance of the linguistic unit. *Journal of Verbal Learning and Verbal Behavior*, 1970, **9**, 12–20.

Keeton, A. Children's cognitive integration and memory processes for comprehending written sentences. *Journal of Experimental Child Psychology*, 1977, **23** (3), 459–471.

Kendall, P. C. The efficacious use of verbal self-instructional procedures with children. *Cognitive Therapy and Research*, 1977, **1**, 331–341.

Kennedy, B. A., & Miller, D. J. Persistent use of verbal rehearsal as a function of information about its value. *Child Development*, 1976, **47**, 566–569.

Kennedy, D. K., & Weener, P. Visual and auditory training with the cloze procedure to improve reading and listening comprehension. *Reading Research Quarterly*, 1973, **8**, 524–541.

LaBerge, D., & Samuels, S. J. Toward a theory of automatic information processing in reading. *Cognitive Psychology*, 1974, **6**, 293–323.

Ledger, G. W., & Ryan, E. B. The effects of semantic integration training on recall for pictograph sentences. *Journal of Experimental Child Psychology*, 1981, in press.

Levin, H., & Kaplan, E. Grammatical structure in reading. In H. Levin & J. Williams (Eds.), *Basic studies on reading*. New York: Basic Books, 1970. Pp. 119–133.

Levin, J. R. Inducing comprehension in poor readers: A test of a recent model. *Journal of Educational Psychology*, 1973, **65**, 10–24.

Mackworth, N. H. The line of sight approach. In S. F. Wanat (Ed.), *Language and reading comprehension*. Newark, Delaware: International Reading Association, 1977. Pp. 1–22.

Markman, E. M. Realizing that you don't understand: A preliminary investigation. *Child Development*, 1977, **48**, 986–992.

Mattingly, I. G. Reading, the linguistic process, and linguistic awareness. In J. F. Kavanaugh & I. G. Mattingly (Eds.), *Language by ear and by eye*. Cambridge, Massachusetts: MIT Press, 1972. Pp. 133–147.

Meichenbaum, D. Cognitive factors as determinants of learning disabilities: A cognitive functional approach. In R. Knights & D. Bakker (Eds.), *The neuropsychology of learning disorders: Theoretical approaches*. Baltimore, Maryland: University Park Press, 1976.

Meichenbaum, D. *Cognitive-behavior modification: An integrative approach*. New York: Plenum, 1977.

Meichenbaum, D., & Asarnow, J. Cognitive-behavior modification and metacognitive development: Implications for the classroom. In P. Kendall & S. Hollon (Eds.), *Cognitive-behavioral interventions: Theory, research and procedures*. New York: Academic Press, 1978.

Miller, G. A., Galanter, E., & Pribram, K. *Plans and the structure of behavior*. New York: Holt, 1960.

Moely, B. E. Organizational factors in the development of memory. In R. V. Kail & J. W. Hagen (Eds.), *Perspectives on the development of memory and cognition*. Hillsdale, New Jersey: Erlbaum, 1977. Pp. 203–235.

Myers, M., & Paris, S. G. Children's metacognitive knowledge about reading. *Journal of Educational Psychology*, 1978, **70**, 680–688.

Neville, M. H., & Pugh, A. K. Context in reading and listening: Variations in approach to cloze tasks. *Reading Research Quarterly*, 1976, **12** (1), 13–31.

Oakan, R., Wiener, M., & Cromer, W. Identification, organization and reading comprehension for good and poor readers. *Journal of Educational Psychology*, 1971, **62**, 71–78.

Olson, D. R. From utterance to text: The bias of language in speech and writing. *Harvard Educational Review*, 1977, **47**, 257–281.

Paris, S. G. Coordination of means and goals in the development of mnemonic skills. In

P. Ornstein (Ed.), *Memory development in children.* Hillsdale, New Jersey: Erlbaum, 1978. Pp. 259–273.

Paris, S. G., Lindauer, B. F., & Cox, G. L. The development of inferential comprehension. *Child Development,* 1977, **48,** 1728–1733.

Pelham, W. E., & Ross, A. D. Selective attention in children with reading problems: A developmental study of incidental learning. *Journal of Abnormal Child Psychology,* 1977, **5,** 1–8.

Pugh, A. K. *Silent reading: An introduction to its study and teaching.* London: Heinemann Educational Books, 1978.

Resnick, L. B., & Beck, I. I. Designing instruction in reading: Interaction of theory and practice. In J. T. Guthrie (Ed.), *Aspects of reading acquisition.* Baltimore, Maryland: Johns Hopkins University Press, 1976. Pp. 180–204.

Rickards, J. P. , & Hatcher, C. W. Interspersed meaningful learning questions as semantic cues for poor comprehenders. *Reading Research Quarterly,* 1978, **13,** 538–553.

Rothkopf, E. Z. Experiments on mathemagenic behavior and the technology of written instruction. In E. Z. Rothkopf & P. E. Johnson (Eds.), *Verbal learning research and the technology of written instruction.* New York: Teachers College, 1971. Pp. 284–303.

Royer, J. M., & Cunningham, D. J. *On the theory and measurement of reading comprehension.* (Tech. Rep. No. 91). Urbana: Center for the Study of Reading, University of Illinois, 1978.

Ruddell, R. B. Language acquisition and the reading process. In H. Singer & R. B. Ruddell (Eds.), *Theoretical models and processes of reading* (2nd Ed.). Newark, Delaware: International Reading Association, 1976. Pp. 22–38.

Ryan, E. B. Metalinguistic development and reading. In L. W. Waterhouse, K. M. Fischer, & E. B. Ryan, *Language awareness and reading.* Newark, Delaware: International Reading Association, 1980.

Ryan, E. B., & Ledger, G. W. *Differences in syntactic skills between good and poor readers in the first grade.* Paper presented to the Midwestern Psychological Association, Chicago, 1979.

Ryan, E. B., McNamara, S. R., & Kenney, M. Linguistic awareness and reading performance in beginning readers. *Journal of Reading Behavior,* 1977, **9,** 399–400.

Ryan, E. B., & Semmel, M. I. Reading as a constructive language process. *Reading Research Quarterly,* 1969, **5,** 59–83.

Samuels, S. J., Begy, G., & Chen, C. C. Comparison of word recognition speed and strategies of less skilled and more highly skilled readers. *Reading Research Quarterly,* 1975, **11,** 72–86.

Samuels, S. J., Dahl, P., & Archwamety, T. Effect of hypothesis-test training on reading skill. *Journal of Educational Psychology,* 1974, **66,** 835–844.

Schallert, D. L., Kleinman, G. M., & Rubin, A. D. *Analysis of differences between oral and written language.* (Tech. Rep. No. 29). Urbana: Center for the Study of Reading, University of Illinois, 1977.

Smiley, S. S., Oakley, D. D., Worthen, D., Campione, J. C., & Brown, A. L. Recall of thematically relevant material by adolescent good and poor readers as a function of written vs. oral presentation. *Journal of Educational Psychology,* 1977, **69,** 381–388.

Smith, F. The role of prediction in reading. In S. S. Smiley & J. C. Towner (Eds.), *Language and reading.* Bellingham, Washington: Western Washington University Press, 1975. Pp. 29–35.

Steiner, R., Wiener, M., & Cromer, W. Comprehension training and identification for poor and good readers. *Journal of Educational Psychology,* 1971, **62,** 506–513.

Stokes, T. F., & Baer, D. M. An implicit technology of generalization. *Journal of Applied Behavioral Analysis*, 1977, **10**, 349–367.

Torgesen, J. K. Memorization processes in reading-disabled children. *Journal of Educational Psychology*, 1977, **69**, 571–578.

Underwood, G. Concepts in information processing, In G. Underwood (Ed.), *Strategies of information processing*. New York: Academic Press, 1978. Pp. 1–22.

Valtin, R. Dyslexia: Deficit in reading or deficit in research? *Reading Research Quarterly*, 1978, **14**, 203–225.

Vogel, S. A. Syntactic abilities in normal and dyslexic children. *Journal of Learning Disabilities*, 1974, **7**, 103–109.

Vogel, S. A. *Syntactic abilities in normal and dyslexic children*. Baltimore, Maryland: University Park Press, 1975.

Vygotsky, L. S. *Thought and language*. Cambridge, Massachusetts: MIT Press, 1962.

Wanat, S. Relation between language and visual processing. In H. Singer & R. Ruddell (Eds.), *Theoretical models and processes of reading*. 2nd Edition. Newark, Delaware: International Reading Association, 1976. Pp. 108–136.

Weaver, P. A. Improving reading comprehension: Effects of sentence organization instruction. *Reading Research Quarterly*, 1979, **15**, 129–146.

Weber, R. M. A linguistic analysis of first grade reading errors. *Reading Research Quarterly*, 1970, **5**, 427–457. (a)

Weber, R. M. First-graders' use of grammatical context in reading. In H. Levin & J. Williams (Eds.), *Basic studies on reading*. New York: Basic Books, 1970. (b)

Weinstein, R., & Rabinovich, M. S. Sentence structure and retention in good and poor readers. *Journal of Educational Psychology*, 1971, **62**, 25–30.

Willows, D. M., & Ryan, E. B. Differential utilization of syntactic and semantic information by skilled and less skilled readers in the intermediate grades. *Journal of Educational Psychology*, 1981, in press.

Wong, B. *Comprehension and retention of implied consequences in good and learning-disabled readers*. Paper presented to the Psychonomic Society, San Antonio, 1978.

INDEX